Praise for *What Every Adoptive Parent Needs to Know*

"*What Every Adoptive Parent Needs to Know* offers deep insights into what adoptive families of hurt children deal with on a day-to-day basis. It is not a sanitized overview but rather an intense examination of parent-child interactions in adoption. Cremer-Vogel and the Richards have shared personal aspects of adoption that are not covered in most pre-adoptive trainings. They offer readers the 'guts' of adopting children who have been wounded early in life. Prospective adoptive parents should not read this book if they fear truth; conversely, they must read this if they want to know the reality of what they may face."

Gregory C. Keck, PhD, Founder and Director of the Attachment and Bonding Center of Ohio and coauthor of *Adopting the Hurt Child* and *Parenting the Hurt Child*

"This is just the book that we have been searching for! *What Every Adoptive Parent Needs to Know* combines a poignant story of adoption and attachment disturbance with professional insights and guidance by Kate Cremer-Vogel, an engaged, empathic, and effective therapist. By integrating current research with keen clinical observations, Cremer-Vogel and the Richards have produced a new standard for understanding and compassionately parenting adopted children. This will become our textbook for staff and parents alike. Thank you!"

Elizabeth Kohlstaedt, PhD, Clinical Director, Intermountain (Children's Home)

"Kate Cremer-Vogel and Dan and Cassie Richards capture the bewildering world of parenting children with attachment difficulties in *What Every Adoptive Parent Needs to Know*. The Richards open their lives in the book and Cremer-Vogel is expert at connecting the dots between behavior and theory, helping parents and professionals view adoption dynamics in a new way. Using the Richards' adoption story as a map through the maze of attachment issues, the reader will leave with many suggestions on how to stay on the right path to healing."

Regina M. Kupecky, LSW, coauthor of *Adopting the Hurt Child* and *Parenting the Hurt Child*

What Every
Adoptive
Parent
Needs to Know

Healing Your Child's
Wounded Heart

Kate Cremer-Vogel MS, LCPC

Cassie and Dan Richards

Mountain Ridge Publishing

BOZEMAN 2008

Library of Congress Control Number: 2008922320

What Every Adoptive Parent Needs to Know

ISBN 978-0-615-18845-4
For information, write:
Mountain Ridge Publishing
P.O. Box 11746
Bozeman, MT 59719
www.mountainridgepublishing.com

The information contained in this book is based on the personal and professional experiences of the authors. It is not intended as a substitute for consulting with a health care professional. Mountain Ridge Publishing and the authors are not responsible for any adverse effects or consequences resulting directly or indirectly from the use of any of the information or suggestions discussed in this book. All matters pertaining to your family's health should be supervised by a health care professional.

To Park Yung Do and Suh Mee Jung
For all you have taught us about ourselves
Mom and Dad

To Dan and Cassie Richards
And to all adoptive parents
For your courage and loving commitment
Kate Cremer-Vogel

Contents

Acknowledgments

Dan and Cassie Richards' commitment to healing themselves and their children is remarkable. I am indebted to them both for their willingness to embark upon this project. Over the past five years of working together writing this book, I have seen their lives blossom and change. Dan and Cassie's relationships with their children have improved dramatically—through their concerted efforts, their children are truly healing from the wounds of their abandonments. I admire the Richards greatly and commend them on their success.

Without having met Dan Hughes, this book would not have been written. Dan was responsible for teaching me that through a personal, empathic relationship with a child, we can heal a child's wounded heart and mind. After over 300 hours of training with Dan, I assimilated this principle and its methods, and learned how to teach them to my clients. It was through Dan's use of the empathic approach with me and his other trainees that we were able to learn how to be empathic with others in a way that can facilitate such dramatic change. Thank you, Dan for how you've changed my life and enabled me to help others so meaningfully.

I am indebted as well to the many other attachment-oriented trainers I have had including Glen Cooper, Kent Hoffman, and Bert Powell of the Marycliff Institute in Spokane, WA, and Robert Marvin, who developed the Circle of Security™ Project; Alann Schore, Dan Siegel, Bruce Perry, Bessel van der Kolk, Regina Kupecky, Violet Oaklander, and those at the Gestalt Institute of Central Ohio.

The support of my colleagues throughout my career as a therapist, and especially those with whom I've worked in the field of enhancing attachment in families, has been invaluable to my work and continued learning. I thank them all for their ongoing support.

The dozens of parents, families, and children with whom I've worked have all taught me something about the capacity for humans to endure as well as to change. I am grateful to them all for their willingness to open to new ideas and accept a helping hand.

I thank our editors for their work on the project and our publishing coaches for their creativity, energy, and expertise, which were clearly a turning point for the project, launching it into a professional realm we could not have imagined before they came on board.

And, finally, a special thanks to my husband, Curt, who continues to lend me his optimism, enthusiasm, and humor in our day-to-day life together. I would not have been able to accomplish the immense task of writing this book without his loving support.

Kate Cremer-Vogel

We are deeply grateful to Dan Hughes for the pioneering work he has done in the field of healing attachment problems and trauma in children. He has revolutionized the approach to this therapy, taking it from its discredited and misguided beginnings to a new gentle and more positive empathic direction. We are thankful that he was able to inspire Kate to continue his work with such passion.

We are especially grateful to the forces of the universe that put Kate on Cassie's path. Her patience, intelligence, and insights taught us to view ourselves and those close to us in a new, empathic, and more compassionate light. We were able to reverse 30 years of dysfunction and guide our family to authentic connection.

We would add to our gratitude list Harriet and John Tamminga for involving us in their efforts to facilitate the adoption of foreign-born children in our state. Their work has given a second chance to many children abandoned abroad.

We are grateful to two very special Korean women who surrendered their babies so that these treasures could become ours. The joy these children have brought us greatly outweighs the difficult moments described herein.

We wish to express appreciation to the many individuals who were our pilot readers in the early stages of this project as well as our present publishing coaches. Their many suggestions were helpful in transforming this project from a naïve dream into a professional reality.

Dan and Cassie Richards

Authors' Note

Although it is the case that in some families, fathers assume the role of primary caregiver, it is more common for the mother to take this position. In the book's informational material we will generically refer to the primary parent as "she," and then for clarity, when referring to the child, we will use "he."

With the exception of using the actual name of the therapist/commentator, Kate Cremer-Vogel, we have changed all identifying references to provide anonymity for the family. The names in the Richards' story are pseudonyms and the places are fictional.

Introduction

Early in 2002, Cassie Richards introduced herself to me after I gave a presentation about attachment disorder to a group of therapists and parents. I was immediately impressed by her enthusiasm and quest for knowledge. Cassie's sincere anguish about the struggles she and her husband had experienced raising two adopted children three decades ago affected me deeply. That conversation ignited our mutual determination to write a book for adoptive parents that would guide them through the process of raising their children. Our goal was to create a work that would demonstrate, explain, and offer solutions to the real-life problems most adoptive families encounter. The challenges the Richards faced were both universal and specific, so although some aspects of their experience may not match those in your situation, there are issues central to raising the adoptive child that will likely be yours as well.

Parents who have adopted or who are contemplating adoption are to be commended for their optimism, generosity, and courage. Understandably, at the outset, adoptive parents focus on the prospect of joy in creating a family, their desire to make a difference, and the vision of hugs and happy faces. Though these are part of the adoptive experience, unless parents understand and can successfully handle challenges specific to adoption, the positive payoffs may become elusive. One of the most important things adoptive parents need to be aware of is the effect abandonment and neglect can have on a child. It is crucial that parents understand that it is not *whether* the adopted child has experienced abandonment, rather it's *how* the child's abandonment by his birth mother has affected him.

All adoptees experience primal disruption at the time of separation from their birth mothers. For some, this emotional insult will be absorbed and the adoptee will experience a good adjustment into his "forever family." Many adoptees, however, remain marked by their original abandonment, which is all too often coupled with a lack of adequate nurturing early in life. We've compassionately come to refer to the adoptee's trauma as a deep wounding of the child's heart—a wounding that makes the child challenging to raise in predictable ways.

The essential message of this book is this: if parents are well trained and guided with precise knowledge, *they can heal their child's wounded heart.* Through a research-derived method we call *therapeutic parenting,* parents can assist their once-abandoned or traumatized child in closing his developmental gaps, healing his body and his brain. What trained parents find surprising is that this approach not only allows them to begin right away to heal a newly adopted child, but it also enables them to significantly improve their relationships with their older adopted children, even if they have already left the nest. In fact, the Richards achieved success even though they did not begin using the therapeutic parenting approach until their children were in their late 20s. A child's need to feel deeply understood by his parents does not vanish—it can lie dormant for years and yet be quickly awakened by a compassionate parent trained in the skillful use of empathy.

Due to the Richards' discovery and use of the therapeutic parenting approach in their present-day interactions with their adopted, now-adult children, attachment disruption has given way to true bonding and identity depression has begun to heal. It is via this true story of a family that persevered through years of difficulties and finally succeeded in their quest for individual and relational wellness that we wish to inspire adoptive parents, parents-to-be, and the professionals with whom they work. The Richards' determination and commitment never to give up instills hope as their story unfolds. Dan and Cassie have generously allowed me to draw on their life story in order to present information, provide guidance, and furnish an introduction to the therapeutic parenting approach that led to their success.

Part I of the book includes a detailed narrative written by Dan and Cassie Richards that illustrates the real life of a family that struggles with problems common in adoption. Although this is a story about two Korean adoptees, the same issues faced by the Richards may arise in raising same-race adoptees, whether they've been adopted from the USA or abroad. I have inserted facts and key concepts throughout each chapter that illuminate events in the Richards' story and give adoptive parents and professionals crucial information they need.

Each chapter ends with parenting tips regarding specific aspects of rearing adoptive children that are pertinent to the scenarios exemplified in the evolving story.

I have written Part II of the book from my perspective as an attachment-oriented therapist specializing in working with adoptive families. These chapters contain a more in-depth look at and discussion of vital information about topics introduced throughout the narrative such as parents' childhood imprinting, attachment, abandonment and neglect, identity, and understanding difficult behaviors. A key chapter outlines the essential elements of therapeutic parenting, which will allow you to learn more about this specialized approach to healing children with wounded hearts. Finally, in the material at the end of the book, you will have the chance to get some of your lingering questions answered as you read the Frequently Asked Questions, as well as an opportunity to look at your own adoptive parenting skills in the Parenting Skills Self-Assessment in Appendix B.

Although especially written for adoptive parents who are raising children with wounded hearts, this book will also serve families of adopted children who are unmistakably thriving in spite of their original abandonment, as it offers a perspective from which parents can validate their skills and their child's emotional adjustment. Because of its foundation in the empathic therapeutic parenting approach, this book is actually useful for *all* parents who are raising challenging children, whether they are being fostered, have been adopted, or are part of the family by birth. Therapists and other professionals will find this book to be a valuable tool in assisting parents who are raising challenging children.

As is true with any book targeting a specific topic, this one is not necessarily comprehensive—instead we intend this to be an offering and an introduction to a perspective that opens hearts as well as minds. What we want to emphasize here is the fact that difficult behaviors constitute the vocabulary of a new language parents must learn in order to understand and translate their child's needs. Once understood, these needs require responses that are not necessarily intuitive for parents. Traditional parenting skills imprinted from childhood experiences rarely prepare parents to meet children's special needs, as the Richards' narrative will demonstrate.

As parents, it is invaluable for us to have a mirror that allows us to see ourselves, our children, spouses, and families more objectively, and with a more understanding eye and open heart. With their story, the Richards graciously offer us that mirror, that opportunity to see ourselves in them. This book will open your eyes as well as give you a map that will allow you to navigate a world the Richards have come to master. Accept the humble hand that the Richards extend here, open their precious gift of experience, and let them guide you into a more compassionate relationship with yourself and your children. Their hope is real—and their hope can be yours.

Kate Cremer-Vogel, MS, LCPC

PART I
The Hidden Faces
of Adoption

*"Mom, if you come on the
roller coaster with me,
I promise I'll bond with you."*

VALERIE

I Preparing to Add a New Family Member

At 27, I was happy, settled in my marriage, and my drive to become a mom was a hunger that bordered on starvation. For me, motherhood was not a choice—it felt as if it was an essential part of my being. Growing up, whether I was playing with dolls, helping with my two younger siblings, or babysitting, I had dreamed about and planned my own family. I *had* to have children.

At 30, my husband, Dan, had a different view of parenthood. He was content with our marriage and serious about his college-level teaching career. Dan agreed that we should have children, yet the desire for fatherhood did not burn in him the way the desire for motherhood did in me. Growing up in a large family, Dan had helped raise four younger siblings. He knew firsthand what taking on children would mean, yet out of his love for me and armed with a practical attitude, Dan was ready and eager to parent.

We were an ordinary college-educated couple unable to conceive; therefore, we adopted our children. We had not read books on adoption, nor did we know other adoptive families. Nonetheless, we felt up to the challenge of raising children based on our combined life experiences.

In 1971 we filed for the adoption of our first child and our journey toward parenthood began. We chose to adopt Korean children out of affection for Dan's uncle, a Jesuit missionary in Seoul. Other than the few facts Lori, our social worker from the adoption agency, told us, we really knew very little about Korea or about adoption. In Korea, a country deeply rooted in paternalism, apparently boys were valued more than girls were. Lori said we would therefore almost surely receive a girl. It did not matter to us whether we received a boy or a girl; we would love either one equally.

During these months, as my mental pregnancy grew, I was already bonding with my future baby—no matter who she or he would be. Long before I ever saw either of my children, I had made the same commitment to each of them that I had when I married Dan. It was for life—no question in my mind.

Prospective adoptive parents may not be able to imagine that their children could have extraordinary needs, let alone be prepared for what it might take to meet such needs. (See chapter 18.)

Finally, one morning we received *the call*. The excitement in Lori's voice felt like a million volts to my expectant ears. She had nearly screamed when she said the adoption agency had referred us a baby boy! After Lori and I hung up, I practically burned down the phone line dialing "Dad." Since I was at work, I tried to remain calm. I scream-whispered the news to him and told him Lori would bring over our baby's file the next morning. Dan, though more restrained than I, was equally jubilant.

That evening Dan and I had a good laugh over the fact that all the clothes we had gotten were for a daughter. "Well," I said confidently, "I'll just save these because our next baby will be a girl by choice." We had considered various names for our son and agreed on Antoine. We would call our son Tony.

I was so excited I could not sit down. I tore around our apartment for hours, drunk with happiness. I caught myself grinning as I pictured dirty diapers and spilled food in our now-childless apartment, and promised myself I would never be crabby. I could not wait to feel my baby's warmth as he and I nestled in the rocking chair. Budding motherhood had cast its spell.

After a night I thought would never end, the next morning I sprang to the door the second the doorbell rang. Lori shared how excited she was—our son was only the second boy she had ever placed. As Dan, Lori, and I settled in with coffee, Lori teased us, holding up the envelope we knew contained pictures of our son. I welled up with thanks to God for this moment in my life, putting my hands over my eyes as Lori reached in for the photos. When I ripped my hands away, there he was, our son, Park Yung Do.

In the first photo, our son was just about 3 months old. With our heads bent close to the table, Dan and I studied two pictures that were not much bigger than postage stamps. Park Yung Do looked distinctly different in the earlier photo in which he was sleeping—a picture of innocence, a beautiful baby with lots of tousled black hair. I could hardly believe I would be allowed to have such an adorable child. What agony his family must have suffered in giving him up, I thought.

In the later photo our son was much bigger. For heaven's sake, they had shaved off all his hair! He was not smiling. His eyes bore directly into the camera lens. If an infant could look fierce, he did. I looked at the long number someone had written beneath his picture like a prison ID. In fact, Park Yung Do *looked* like a prisoner.

A small sob rose inside me. Why did he have to look so rough? I knew they must have had to shave his head to keep the lice away, but in this photo, our son looked so changed from the darling infant with tousled hair. He looked fierce with his arms pressed stiffly to his sides, his eyes steely, and his hair all but gone. I hurt just looking at him in that photo. This was my son! All I wanted was to hold him in my arms.

Being abandoned by one's birth mother can instill an unconscious sense of worthlessness in a child that may become visible in his face and posture as he lingers in a temporary foster home or orphanage. (See chapter 18.)

Not knowing what else to do with my feelings, I focused on getting details about our little boy. Park Yung Do had been abandoned in a basket in the back room of a restaurant where the owner had found him. Seeing that the baby had a badly infected eye, the man had taken him to the American hospital in Seoul. Dan and I listened in rapt attention to our baby's story.

After being treated for the eye disease and jaundice, he had been placed in a foster family. Apparently, Park Yung Do's foster mother had carried him on her back until the day he left Korea. At the time, we had no idea how crucial it was that our baby had received this kind of loving one-on-one care in his first months of life.

Lori told us the reason we were getting a boy was that he had had a serious disease. In the early seventies when Korea was still struggling in the aftermath of war, medical facilities were severely lacking. Lori speculated that knowing that they could not save him, Park Yung Do's family had abandoned him with the hope that a miracle would take place and their son would receive the medical care he needed to survive.

I felt so much compassion for our son's birth family. Even today, I would love to tell them what a beautiful gem they sent us, a baby who was perfect in our eyes—so beautiful, so intelligent, with such a wonderful spirit. I would want them to know how loved he was and is and that we always did our best to raise him with a feeling of honor toward them and their country.

After our meeting with Lori, we received no further news of our son until the day she phoned with his plane number and exact arrival time. As was the custom then, internationally adopted children were flown into this country to be united with their future parents. As we waited to receive our precious 5-month-old cargo from Korea, my excitement was nearly more than I could contain.

Parenting Tips

Prepare yourselves
Before adopting, read and learn all you can about adoption, including information on attachment and the inevitable effects of abandonment. Parenting books specifically aimed at adoptive parents can be helpful to read both pre- and postadoption. Understanding the range of physical, emotional, and developmental problems that an adoptee may have due to genetics, neglect, and/or abuse is essential. For information on the realities of adoption, talk to other adoptive parents and consult with a therapist who specializes in helping adoptive families.

Come to terms with your personal reasons for adopting
Separately and with your spouse, get clear on why you are going to adopt. Some parents adopt because they want more children and want to give a waiting child a home. Some adopt because they aren't able to have children. In this case, there may be significant grief and loss issues

that you need to address and put to rest so that your adoption experience is not negatively affected.

Closely examine your expectations

Again, separately and with your spouse, write down exactly what you are expecting from your adoption experience. Are your hopes realistic, do they focus on the child's needs, and are they achievable? What personal, couple, family, and community issues might arise? What are the best and worst-case scenarios that may happen? What if the worst-case scenario comes to pass? Periodically review and adjust your expectations as the adoption proceeds.

Identify resources and supports

Find out who the adoption specialists are in or near your area. Sign up for adoptive parent training or classes offered through your local state and/or private adoption agencies. For ongoing support, locate any parenting support groups and adoption-specific groups in your area, join online forums, and sign up for adoptive parent seminars put on by nationally renowned professionals. Consider contacting a therapist who offers preadoptive counseling to help you understand and prepare for what is to come.

Secure financial subsidies

Some agencies, especially those that are state sponsored, have a pool of monies available for medical and psychological postadoptive care of the adoptee. If you are adopting internationally, inquire about possible resources that may be available in the event your child needs extraordinary care. Even if you think you won't need these resources, secure them anyway. All too often, adoptive parents are taken by surprise and unprepared financially for problems that arise after adoption.

Prepare to ease the child's transition

With a professional, discuss and plan to provide what your child might need to transition to your care with minimal stress. If possible, obtain at least one personal article of clothing from your child's birth mother and a voice recording so he can be comforted by her familiar odor and sound. Ideally, make arrangements to spend as much time as possible with the birth mother and the baby until he becomes familiar with you.

Discuss the option of open adoption

In an open adoption, the birth mother and/or members of the birth family remain in contact with the adoptee, usually on the adoptive parents' terms. There are pros and cons to this arrangement, inevitably some that are unforeseeable. Talk with families who have exercised the option of open adoption and with those who have chosen to maintain a complete separation from the adoptee's birth family. If parents choose a closed adoption, they still may be able to obtain information about the birth family that the adoptee would need should he choose to contact them in the future. A therapist specializing in adoptions can add to the pool of information you need to make your decision.

2 Imprinting: Parenting Begins in Childhood

Sometimes because of the high demands of our daily lives, as parents we get so used to pushing forward that we forget where we've come from. Indeed, some of us would rather not remember. However, both the acceptable and unacceptable parts of our histories and selves will become exposed in the course of parenting our children. Because the past is so often the hidden driving force behind our actions as parents, we must find some way to come to terms with it as have Dan and Cassie in the following childhood narratives.

Dan's Childhood Imprinting

I was the third born of seven children raised in a working-class family by my father, Pa, and my mother, Mia. Pa was in charge. He brought home the paycheck, set the rules, and meted out discipline.

In addition to bringing my stepbrother, Tommy, into her marriage with my father, Mia bore Pa's six children, kept house, and did the cooking. When any of the kids acted up, Pa heard about it when he got home from work. Pa was not a violent man. He did not beat or abuse us, but he was serious—and that translated as spankings or other consequences. We all understood that Pa was the boss.

I have almost no knowledge about my parents' childhoods. Both Mia and Pa were closed mouthed. There probably were and still are skeletons in the closet. My siblings and I have secrets, too: even today, whenever we have reunions, the best stories are always about antics Pa either never discovered or those we did get away with for a while.

One time, a water department worker inspecting the right-of-way behind our house discovered that someone had cut the strands of barbed wire fence where it crossed a bicycle path through the field. It was pretty obvious that someone in our household who didn't want to keep hopping the fence was responsible. After the truth came out, Pa gave my younger brother and me a good tanning.

In wanting to make it absolutely clear that a line had been seriously crossed in this case, Pa requested that I bring him the offending wire cutters. When he had finished chiseling off one of the handles, he quietly handed the now useless tool back to me. I got the message—I now had to find another way of undoing the baling wire on my daily newspaper bundle.

Aside from such normal kid stuff, for the most part we were obedient—except for Tommy, who was usually in trouble. When Pa and Mia married, Pa had adopted then 5-year-old Tommy but was never able to control him. After repeated brushes with the law that began before Tommy was even a teen, the courts ran out of compassion. Now at 70-plus years old, Tommy remains in prison, where he is serving a life sentence.

The father-in-charge hierarchy is a classic example of what is referred to in this book as traditional parenting, and although effective in general, this approach does not offer the healing component necessary to meet the emotional needs of many adopted children. (See chapter 24.)

One of my earliest boyhood memories is getting out of bed early in the morning so I could have breakfast alone with Pa. As we sat together at the kitchen table, Pa would douse his strong coffee with sugar and cream, then would put a few tablespoons on my cereal. When he would leave for work I would read a book or draw until the rest of the household woke up. This father and son ritual made me feel special.

From the time of my infancy, for some unknown reason, tumors kept growing on my right leg. I had several surgeries but the tumors always came back. Eventually, when I was in the second grade, the doctor said they would have to amputate my leg. Pa would have none of that and he looked for another doctor.

Meanwhile I was sent to a children's hospital for several months for close observation. While I was there I attended the hospital school and managed to have a good time. Confident that Pa would take care of my leg problem, I felt no fear about losing my leg.

I don't remember ever feeling afraid about being away from home, either. I trusted my parents to come on weekends to see me. During the week I amused myself by making puppets and putting on shows for the other patients, doctors, and nurses. The shows were predictably corny, but everyone said how creative and clever I was.

After several months I was released on crutches with a special elastic stocking to improve circulation in the leg. When I got home Mia hailed me as a hero because I had never complained. I remained on crutches many months. Eventually the tumors went away, never to come back again, and I kept my leg, though it remained somewhat atrophied.

I can remember how both Mia and Pa constantly told me that I was intelligent, something that apparently was not said to my brothers and sisters. Indeed, I ended up carrying a lot of responsibility in the home because my parents thought I was smart.

My older sister suffered from a learning disability; therefore the role of "assistant parent" fell naturally to me, the third oldest. Some of my earliest memories center on changing diapers, rounding up kids, and enforcing family rules. To encourage obedience, I took a lesson from my mom and warned my little brothers and sisters what Pa would do if they were naughty.

From the time I was 14, I worked various part-time jobs, beginning with a paper route, then pumping gas and doing mechanical work at gas stations and clerking in a retail store. As I matured and became aware how short the money was at home, I began to pay certain bills for my parents. No one talked about it much. It was just a way of helping the family.

Affirmation of a child's desirable behavior is an effective behavior-shaping tool, especially when used in parenting a child who suffers from attachment disorder. (See chapter 25.)

Our family was Roman Catholic and we would go off to Sunday Mass each week, where we nearly filled a whole pew. It was well understood even by the youngest of us kids that there would be no toilet runs or drinks of water at church. When we were with our parents, we followed their rules.

Friday was the family shopping day. As long as everyone behaved we had free run of the grocery store while our parents shopped. Afterward, Pa took Mia for a beer before picking up chow mien for us. We looked forward to Fridays.

Most often the Richards kids hung out together, both at school and around the neighborhood. My brothers and I were inseparable, fiercely holding our own on the playground, ganging up on bullies who tried picking on one of us. Through our adolescence, we continued our alliance.

Pa used to read the daily newspaper from front to back, including the police reports. One day when I was 18, Pa came barreling into the gas station where I worked, waving a newspaper that reported a recent encounter I had had with the law.

A couple of my buddies and I had sneaked into a drive-in and were enjoying a free movie and some 3.2 beer when the police raided our party. Pa was angry; he never condoned lying, stealing, or breaking the law. When I got home from work that evening, Pa gave me a lecture and then grounded me even though I was really too old for that consequence.

Eventually we brothers left behind our illicit cigarettes and swear words to move on to more manly pursuits like pulling pranks with cars and motorcycles, clandestinely rustling horses, chasing women, and getting our hands on booze illegally. To these ends, I used my artistic skills and became the family forger, crafting nearly perfect fake driver's licenses for my underage brothers.

During my childhood there was not much in the way of individual attention from either parent. There were just too many kids. There were no fishing trips alone with Pa, no shopping for prom dresses for the girls with Mia. The family did not go to visit Disney World or take many vacations.

At Christmas there were no stacks of presents under the tree. There were a few presents, often things Pa had made for us in his shop—like dollies and dollies' beds for the girls and little trucks for the boys. Sometimes Mia rode the bus downtown to work in a department store around the holidays so there would be a little more money. Each year was different.

Our home was noisy with love and commotion, but things ran smoothly. There were rarely ever luxuries but our basic needs were always met.

Pa and Mia lived an honorable life and loved each other deeply, though they were neither verbally nor physically demonstrative of it. They argued sometimes and then made up. They did not have many friends outside of the family. Their social needs were met through work and by enjoying home life with their children.

Over the years the invaluable gifts my parents gave to us were a stable home, good core values, and a strong work ethic. Four out of the seven of us finished college. All my brothers and sisters have established lasting marriages except Tommy, who was divorced twice.

Aspects of traditional parenting such as providing a stable home, instilling good core values, and modeling a strong work ethic are essential for effectively raising adopted children. (See chapter 25.)

As I grew older I continued to hold a privileged spot in the family and enjoyed good self-esteem. Pa had told me early on that I had better plan to go to college. Therefore I worked hard in school to please my dad and graduated first in my class. I eventually went on to earn a master's degree and a PhD in French.

As I moved into adulthood, I had a sound sense of how children should be raised. I instinctively decided I would bring up our children just as I had been brought up. It was what I knew, it was comfortable, and I thought it worked well. Notwithstanding the influence of the many positive aspects of my childhood, the lack of intimacy in my family growing up would set the emotional tone for my future family life.

Experiencing a lack of intimacy in childhood can become a barrier to seeing and meeting the special emotional needs of some adopted children and to understanding and supporting one's spouse. (See chapter 14.)

Cassie's Childhood Imprinting

My own parents' childhood imprinting played a significant role in how they parented me. My French-Irish mom, Elizabeth, grew up in Seattle, and though she recalled few positive memories from her impoverished childhood, Mom was certain that her mother had loved her. My grandmother had married quite young. She had five children, whom she loved passionately.

My grandfather, however, was filled with rage. Tension, fighting, tears, and the relentless Seattle rain took a serious toll on their family life. My mom told me Grandma had lived in fear of Grandpa because she was unable to protect herself and her children from his violence.

One afternoon, my mom heard Grandma scream and ran to the kitchen, where she saw Grandpa holding her down on the table with a knife to her throat. My mom's brother, Bob, came running in just in time to pull Grandpa off Grandma.

My mom's sister, Aunt Margaret, said Grandpa had treated his first three children okay. Sadly, he had not wanted his two youngest children, one of whom was my mom, and he showed it. One time when my mother was little, she had gashed open her knee on a rock and needed stitches. Grandpa refused to take her to the hospital, telling Grandma he refused to spend money on *that child*.

Deep shame about one's self is the core feeling shared by many adoptees. (See chapter 18.)

My father, Hjalmar, grew up on a farm in North Dakota homesteaded by his Norwegian immigrant parents. He was one of 10 children. My grandmother was mute. Her life consisted of cooking, washing, mending, and child rearing. In their home there were no bedtime stories, no birthday cakes, no real holidays. My dad never had a single pair of new shoes while growing up. He wore hand-me-downs throughout his childhood.

My dad and his siblings walked 2 miles to and from school even in the brutal winters. The kids never had enough energy to get into trouble because life in North Dakota was about survival, food, animals, and chores. Even boredom was a luxury.

There were few punishments or spankings in my dad's family. Dad told me that he had had a decent childhood and that they had laughed a lot. His brothers were his best friends. He said what he enjoyed most about growing up was making music and beating up the Russian kids.

Early on, my dad was singled out for his remarkable intelligence. He was also responsible, a hard worker, long on common sense, and held in high esteem by siblings and classmates alike. He graduated valedictorian of his high school class and then joined the Army, a choice that was to form his deepest identity. Dad remained a soldier all his life. True to his ancestry, he was stoic—no whining, no displays of feelings, ever.

My mom and dad had met on a blind date while he was stationed in D.C., where she worked as a bookkeeper. They fell deeply in love, marrying within a month as people did during the war. Mom got pregnant with me immediately. I was still an infant when Dad was called to the European theater for two years.

During the war, Dad served as an Army officer in Germany, where he saw horrors he would never forget. The night my dad came home from the war, Mom cried for joy. She told me the story over and over—when Dad pulled into the driveway, she ran through the yard and threw herself into his arms to kiss him. Instead of kissing her back, Dad peeled her body away from his and said curtly, "For heaven's sake, take it easy."

Mom later said that was the defining moment in their marriage. She felt rejected by her husband just as she had all of her life by her father. Mom said she began thinking she hated men because they always hurt her.

My dad was a man's man: he built a successful business, enjoyed golf with his buddies, and was a member of the Army Reserve. Mom said he paid little attention to her, rarely bought her gifts, and took no interest in helping her raise their children. She had felt deeply hurt by his aloofness.

❧

My mother was my entire universe. I was the firstborn of three children—my sister and brother were 6 and 7 years younger. Mom said I was energetic, fast moving, and never shy. Noisy and gregarious, I got in trouble often, receiving lots of spankings and reprimands. Still, I felt in my heart Mom adored me, and I blossomed.

When I was naughty, Mom would say accusingly in a hurt voice, "Oh, Cassie, you don't love me." I could not bear these insinuations. I would burst into tears, crying, "Mommy, mommy, *please* don't say that. I love you with all my heart, you know I do, and I'm *so* sorry I was bad." I thought I must have been wicked because I always seemed to be in trouble. I never *tried* to hurt my mom.

A parent's inappropriate, incessant need for a child's adoration can become an Achilles' heel that can negatively affect family life. (See chapter 16.)

My formative years were physically as well as emotionally traumatic. I was not taught self-control as a young child, and my impulsiveness resulted in multiple trips to the hospital emergency room. I was also hospitalized twice.

The first time was when I was 2 or 3 and had my tonsils removed. That separation from my mother, coupled with the sterile atmosphere of the hospital, produced a lingering nightmare.

The second time I was hospitalized was at age 6, when I nearly died from polio. At one point, a priest administered the last sacraments to me while my mother wept at my bedside. She was sure I was dying, and I became enveloped by her fear.

I survived, though, and for the next 8 months I was quarantined in a polio treatment center. All day long I received scalding heat packs and endured other painful procedures. When I returned home my mother assumed the role of physical therapist.

Every day for 2 years Mom stretched my back, working the atrophied muscles, until I would cry out in pain. Mom herself often cried during the therapy, stating through tears, "Honey, I'm so sorry I have to hurt you, but I'm going to make you perfect."

After 2 years my back was perfectly healed, which amazed the doctors. The traumatizing experience my mother and I had shared empowered her even more in my eyes—giving rise to a trauma bond that became permanent.

My mother's larger-than-life presence dominated every aspect of my childhood. She had total responsibility for administering discipline. Mom raised us while Dad went to work, and that was that. Because my mother had been hit a lot as a child, she hit me as well. She was severe, and on a daily basis raised her voice, cursing at me to make me obey. I feared her almost more than I loved her.

Therefore, as a child, I lived with constant worry that I would do something wrong and be punished. When I was in fourth grade I accidentally broke Mom's sunlamp and she said I would have to buy her a new one. Since the only money I had was what she gave me for street-car fare—two dimes a day—I had to walk 12 blocks to and from school for weeks until I had paid her back.

My mother seemed to know my every thought. When I lied she would wash out my mouth with soap. She told me there was no use lying because she knew the truth simply by looking at my face.

The way our parents treated us will most likely become the model for how we parent our children, especially if we have had no other training. (See chapter 14.)

Up through fifth grade, whenever I did something bad Mom forced me down into our creepy basement and spanked me on my bare bottom until I cried. As I got older and stubbornly refused to cry, she changed tactics. She made me pick out a willow stick and whipped my bare bottom with it until I finally broke down and sobbed.

From the time I was a toddler I slept with the covers over my head out of fear of fairy-tale monsters that were all too real for me. About the time I turned 9, my mom ordered me to "knock it off," threatening that if I did not uncover my head when I slept, nobody would marry me.

I could not break the habit, though, so Mom attempted to beat the stubbornness out of me with a metal pancake turner, hitting me as I lay in bed on several different occasions. In the end, her tactics were useless—today I still sleep with the covers over my head.

There were other sides to my mother's personality as well. She often could be funny, and I would belly laugh at her antics and rude mouth.

We'd horse around a lot—with Mom chasing me through the house as if I was a 2-year-old, tickling me while I shrieked. She loved celebrating holidays—any holiday. Together we took day trips, played cards, and went shopping.

Mom believed in independence so she taught me to iron, wash clothes, cook, and handle money. She also taught me about God and good values, praised me for high grades, and attended my school events. She gave me an allowance, bought clothes for me, and when there was no money she sewed party dresses for me herself. She told me we were best friends and so I needed to share everything with her. Initially flattered, I obediently reported most of the details of my life.

As I entered my teen years, however, I began feeling uncomfortable around Mom. She would tell me intimate details of her life, which made me feel embarrassed. She often reminded me that I was her favorite child, which made me feel responsible for her happiness.

I began to feel robbed of my privacy. Mom would open and read my mail before giving it to me, find and read my diary while I was at school, and listen in to my phone conversations on the extension line. When I was 14 and started to date, Mom would interrogate me to see if boys were touching me or trying to have sex with me. I felt smothered.

About the time I turned 15, I became aware that my mother actually had three distinct personalities. One was outrageously loud, huge in energy, boastful, funny, and foul mouthed. Another was deeply depressed, spaced out, tearful, and hooked on Valium and Viceroys. The third was professional, confidently well dressed, efficient, religious, and nurturing.

Never knowing which mom I would encounter, I started feeling afraid to come home after school. I would try to adjust to Mom's moods but it was difficult, if not impossible. Those times she decided I was being overemotional she'd force me to take her Valium to calm down. I would object but she'd prevail, saying she knew best. I hated Valium—it made me feel out of it for two whole days.

From the time I was little, Mom had hit me and slapped my face. One morning before school during my senior year, I finally fought back. Mom had slapped me hard in the face to punish me for being "the most selfish kid God ever put on this earth." I lashed out, slugging her with all my might, knocking her flat on the floor while I screamed, "Don't you *ever* lay a hand on me again!"

She whined in a little girl voice, "You hit me. You hit me." I just glared at her while she lay there. Disgusted, I slammed the door and headed for school. She never hit me again.

All the while my mother raised us, my father remained a shadow in our lives. He went to work, came home, read the paper, had supper, and watched TV. On Saturdays and Sundays he went golfing.

Childhood imprinting influences the way we interact with our spouse as we parent our children. (See chapter 25.)

Family outings and vacations were rare. Occasionally Dad would take me golfing, afterward buying me a strawberry malt while he had a beer at the clubhouse. Sometimes, for a good report card, Dad would give me a dollar. He did not tell me he loved me, but I felt he did.

While Dad seemed content in his self-centered world, Mom got sadder and sadder. After 20 years of feeling ignored by her husband, Mom filed for divorce on the grounds of mental cruelty. This blindsided my dad—though he adored his beautiful, spunky wife, he hadn't expressed it to her. Mom threw him out of the house, flushed her wedding ring down the toilet, and never gave her heart to another man.

During the time of their divorce, I was enrolled at the local university and lived on campus. Still I could not break away from my mother's incessant focus, which now took the form of daily phone calls. As well, my parents both continually pressured me to take sides.

Meanwhile Dan and I had met in French class, and gradually built a strong, mutually supportive friendship, leaning on one another through personal turmoil. After 3 years Dan wanted to steer our relationship toward intimacy, but I was not ready. Feeling unable to respond to the demands of either my parents or Dan, I decided I needed a break to sort out my feelings, so I sailed to Europe.

Initially promising that I would return in 6 weeks, I ended up staying in Europe for 2 years—primarily in France and Germany—where I worked a variety of jobs to support myself. To my surprise, I could not overcome my homesickness—in particular missing my mom, to whom I wrote regularly. While Mom wrote back faithfully at first, by the second year she wrote less and less often.

One day I got a letter from my mom saying that her right arm would not move anymore. Despite that strange news, I was still not ready to return home. I did not know at the time that my mother had been diagnosed as seriously mentally ill and that her paralysis was related to her illness. She kept her diagnosis secret.

Finally, after 2 years in Europe, feeling strong and vivacious, ready to take on adult challenges, I returned home. Immediately, members of my family attempted to draw me in to their personal dramas. For the first time in my life, I felt mature enough not to be sucked in. Instead, I pursued my own life.

I accepted an engagement ring from Dan. We were married that November, and I embraced marriage with all the passion and energy of my young, naïve self. Banishing my mother from first place, I put Dan there instead. It would be many years before I gave that place to myself.

Parenting Tips

Examine your childhood

Parents can wait until they find themselves in the middle of a major problem to resolve their old business, or they can be proactive and examine their past before serious difficulties arise. There are many approaches to cleaning out the corners and closets of childhood. Self-examination using self-help books, 12-step and other support groups, and counseling are all ways to address the past. To begin the process, you can use photo albums, old journals, and/or write your history from memory to establish a working childhood map.

Remember, you've already lived through whatever it is that you may not want to look at. You can take the power and choose to meet your unfinished business now, instead of waiting for it to choose when to meet you.

Look at how your parents parented you

As objectively as possible, outline your parents' approach to raising you. Make a list of the basic duties and responsibilities of parents, then characterize the way your parents carried these out. Did you have traditional parenting, where father was in charge and brought home the money, while mother cooked and cleaned and raised the kids? Or was the parenting you received more *laissez-faire,* without traditional structure where everyone was allowed to do his own thing? Was the home atmosphere relaxed or tense? Was there a lot of fighting or was anger forbidden?

Although many of us vow never to parent like our parents did, unless we do a thorough examination of ourselves, find compassion in our hearts for our parents' struggles, and choose to learn alternative ways, we will surely repeat some of their behaviors as we parent. How do *you* want to parent?

Establish and maintain support

Rally family, friends, your community and church, and professionals to support your parenting efforts. Locate and befriend other parents who have been through or who are going through what you are. Ask for help, and ask often, even if it is just for little things. Consider asking people in your support network to read information about the parenting challenges you will have.

3 Attachment: Bonding with Your Adopted Child

Antoine's (Park Yung Do's) arrival, along with nine other Korean babies and young children, was an event we shall never forget. At midnight the plane rolled to a stop and the regular passengers descended. Suddenly the ramp was filled with color as the hostesses left the plane dressed in red, each one carrying a baby dressed either in yellow or white. Most of the people near us were crying as they saw the babies appear one by one at the bottom of the ramp. Antoine was second and Dan recognized him immediately. As each child was delivered into the arms of a crying mother, a thousand cameras exploded to record the joy and confusion of 10 eager families being united.

May 9, 1973
Antoine's baby book

The day our son was to arrive, I was beside myself with excitement. I paced our apartment like a Bengal tiger, arranging and rearranging our cave for our new cub. Even Dan was unable to concentrate and had left work early. Dan and I drove to the airport with our closest friends and my mother for our son's delivery.

As the plane taxied to a stop, my feelings shifted to fear—my heart slamming in my chest. We were about to take on the responsibility for another human being for the rest of our lives. I gripped Dan's hand and we craned our necks, eager for our first glimpse of the babies. Finally a parade of stewardesses came down the ramp, each one smiling and holding a blanketed parcel destined for our cluster of waiting families.

As the second attendant neared, she announced, "Antoine Richards." I crashed through the crowd to claim my baby. She placed my son in my outstretched arms and took Dan aside to complete and sign the papers. Willing myself not to shout out in joy, I forced myself to be quiet.

I stood in shock, holding Tony—*my son*. I was immediately attracted to his sweet baby odor. He had a darling little crew cut and was dressed in yellow. His skin glowed and he looked healthy. His eyes were intelligent and curious. I was amazed by his alert energy. When he squirmed around to look at me, I was afraid he would cry. He did not, but neither did he smile, probably feeling shock, as I was.

Man, was he heavy! At 5 months he weighed 15 pounds, but his weight was nothing compared to the size of his feet. Someday this baby would be a very tall man. As I held Tony to my chest, I thanked God for bringing this miracle into my life. I loved this baby profoundly, absolutely, and passionately from the first second I saw him. I knew he was meant to be our son. Suddenly I was hit by the enormous responsibility I had to shape this child's destiny.

I surrendered Tony to Dan's eager arms and received his papers along with a small pair of green rubber Korean shoes in exchange. It wasn't until later that I realized that aside from the clothes he wore, the shoes were Tony's only keepsake from his first months of life.

Dan seemed right at home with Tony. He looked him in the eyes and used a gentle voice to greet him. I could tell he felt the same sense of responsibility as I did.

Next it was Grandma's turn. My mom began crying as soon as she took him. She held him next to her cheek in a tender gesture and crooned to him how welcome and beautiful he was.

Driving home from the airport, I felt like a queen with her prince. Dan and I shared that first night beholding in wonder the life that had been entrusted to us. I could hardly believe my contentment as I stood in the kitchen in the middle of the night preparing Tony's first meal of rice cereal. I felt full of love and courage. It did not matter that I had not had a pregnancy to ready me.

Tony's and my first days at home together were magic. He was an adorable little brown berry with a crew cut that stood straight up in the air. I held my son close throughout the day, perching him on my knee when I needed a free hand. We began to get to know each other.

Tony's initial visit to Dr. Olander, a pediatrician with a reputation for caring for adopted Korean babies, was a relief. I had brought Tony's sketchy medical records and preflight child report, which stated: "Loves to eat apple juice and sponge cake. Puts her (sic) hands on the bottle while feeding. Sucks finger. Does not feel shy to strangers. Ate like his stomach had no bottom."

After reviewing Tony's medical history and examining him thoroughly, Dr. Olander said our son was healthy and very alert. He advised circumcision so Tony would be like American boys. Dan agreed, and that was that.

Too soon the magic of those first blissful days gave way to distress. Tony cried day and night, flailing all the while. He cried so hard his tears soaked the sheets. I thought a good mother should be able to calm the crying, but nothing I did appeased him. It did not matter that I held him. Discouraged and out of ideas, I phoned Dr. Olander to ask what I was doing wrong.

Even today I remember Dr. Olander's chuckle and advice: "Cassie, give thanks. Your son was deeply bonded to his Korean foster mom. Over there they carry their infants on their back. Your son is grieving for her. He does not feel safe yet. His crying will continue until he adjusts, maybe a few weeks. Then it will stop."

The doctor advised, "Do *not* sit with him or listen to him crying; that will just frustrate you. Leave him in his room, regularly check on his safety, give him lots of water, change his wet clothes, and just let him cry. Sit and read a book a couple rooms away and be patient. Try carrying him in a backpack if you want to. Keep in mind that he can always choose not to cry."

I felt so relieved to hear that I was not doing something wrong. Still, it broke my heart to hear my son crying—once for 5½ hours straight. Although I tried to follow Dr. Olander's expert advice, my instincts did not allow me to follow them completely. I held Tony frequently while he cried and I tried to soothe him, but I knew that it would just take time until he could accept me as his new mother. Over the course of several weeks, Tony's crying subsided as he allowed us to comfort him.

Holding an infant or child through his grief is exactly what one abandoned early in life needs. (See chapter 25.)

During those first weeks when Tony was sleeping, I would creep into his room and watch him, thinking he was the greatest miracle of my life. When he was awake, I rarely took my eyes off him and I held him often. I loved his intense eye contact.

With my white-blond hair, fair skin, and English tongue, I mused over how different I must have looked and sounded from his foster mom, who had black hair, dark skin, and spoke Korean. Whereas she had carried him on her back and smelled like the Korean cabbage-based staple, kimchi, I carried him in my arms and smelled like French perfume.

I had wonderful moments alone with Tony during those early weeks when I would simply hold him in my lap, just loving him. I felt honored and trusted when he fell asleep in my arms.

I lavished corny prattle upon him. He caught on to "So-o-o-o big!" immediately. Tony reacted energetically to my outstretched arms and voice—there was solid communication between us. I gave him "noise hugs"—any odd sound I could think of.

Tony gyrated in his crib with abundant smiles and eager eyes. His little face lit up, gums showing through his grin. With exaggerated gestures and varied vocal tones I gave my son a running commentary about what was going on. He listened and watched me intently.

In stream-of-consciousness fashion, I would tell my son what was in my heart: how beautiful he was, how fun it was to be his mom, and that I was not too good at changing diapers but I would learn. In a soothing voice I let him know when he was tired. In a proud voice I would tell him he was brave when he did something new. I joyfully told him how much I loved to cook for him and prepare all his food from scratch.

Two of the most important tasks of an adoptive parent are to mirror a child's behaviors so he can learn who he is and interpret his experiences so he can make sense of his world. (See chapter 25.)

Tony was eager, sweet-natured, and brave. He absolutely looked smart to me—so alert, so fast, so trusting, especially given the huge interruption in life he had experienced. Aside from his expression of grief at the loss of his foster mom, Tony struck me from the first day as basically secure and happy and seemed to have an extraordinary sense of self.

❧

At 5 months, Tony had a huge presence that he conveyed especially through his eyes, which were bright and curious, even fierce. Tony was highly curious, always looking around intently trying to understand his world.

Dan remembers how Tony used his hands to try to figure out how things worked. If Dan gave him a couple of pieces of anything, Tony would immediately scrutinize them in serious fashion, turning them over, examining all sides and ends, then banging the objects together. If they fit together, his face lit up in a huge smile.

From the start, I read to Tony. My voice taught him the emotions that went with the stories I was reading. He adored *Touch and Feel,* one of our first books. He quickly caught on to pulling the Velcro pieces apart, anticipated the page where he sniffed the cloth strawberry, and loved to run his fingers over the soft cotton pieces.

While I read, Tony listened and would watch my face attentively, even if he had to shift his body around in my lap at impossible angles so he could see me. I knew we were connecting and I soon became confident of my ability to interpret Tony's needs.

The degree to which a child is able to engage in meaningful eye contact with his parents can reveal his present level of attachment to them. (See chapter 17.)

Week by week we delighted in the unfolding of a litany of behaviors in our son. First Tony sat up by himself. Next he began crawling around the whole house, his sturdy little legs acting like wheels as he chugged along in all directions. Then he pulled himself up to the couch, and it was apparent he was very proud of himself. He learned in a stepwise, progressive fashion.

Tony's baby book chronicles typical behaviors of a baby meeting his developmental stages on time during his first year of life. At 9 months he became highly dependent on us and would no longer go to strangers. In fact, at 11 months Tony could tell when I was preparing to go somewhere and would begin to cry even before I left. His strong will returned tenfold, his stubbornness often exceeding ours. Tony did have a temper.

A little before Tony turned one, we moved to Rock Springs, Wyoming, where Dan had accepted a position at the university. Content in our new home I remember peaceful days sitting in the rocking chair giving Tony his bottle. He adjusted well to our initial, temporary quarters in Rock Springs and then again when we bought a house and moved in just before his first birthday.

Tony began walking in earnest at 12½ months, continuing to be on track developmentally. At 24 months Tony was talking a lot, feeling safe inventing his own approximation of words. He confidently called himself "Tinny." He showed initiative by scrambling down from his crib each morning, finding a book, and crawling into bed with us. He was content to sit quietly looking at the pictures while waiting for us to interact with him.

Although he was very much in the "no" stage and quite headstrong, Tony liked to please us more than to have his own way. We felt delighted with the behaviors of our son. We knew we could set limits that he would respect without stifling his initiative. Our being in control provided the security net Tony needed to blossom. Our family life with Tony was going so well that we began thinking of a second adoption.

When a child experiences a nurturing relationship with a caregiver prior to his adoption, his brain begins to develop the capacity for the attachment he will make to his adoptive parents. (See chapter 17.)

From an early age Tony was able to form close friendships with peers. Tony's first best friend was Brad, who lived across the street. We have an endearing photo of the two toddler boys inspecting a single blade of grass. Tony and Brad lived daily life together. When the boys were 2 they both got Big Wheels, in which they charged up and down the sidewalk a thousand times a day.

Tony accepted the boundaries we set for him. Once we knew he understood what he was not to do, we gave him freedom to make choices within our prescribed safety net. I never worried, for example, that he would go in the street, because he knew he had to ask permission for street crossing. He showed no disobedience toward strong rules like that, and he rarely if ever broke them.

From the first, Dan seemed to have a good handle on child anger management. We dealt with Tony's temper on a regular basis. Once when the three of us were at the grocery store, we refused to buy something Tony wanted. He threw a screaming fit right in the aisle. Dan, a very private person, did not want people staring. He told Tony in a firm voice to stop screaming. When Tony did not stop, Dan quickly picked up our furious son and walked out of the store.

I watched them head to our car and saw Dan put Tony in the backseat. Dan told Tony he did not have permission to have tantrums in public, but that he was welcome to have one in the car if he wanted to. Dan said, "I'm going to shut the door now because I don't want to listen to your noise. When you're all done crying, let me know so we can go back in the store."

Dan stood next to the car, keeping an eye on Tony but not engaging with him. Within a few minutes Tony settled down so Dan took him back into his arms and brought him back into the store. We continued to shop as if nothing had happened. This was Tony's first and last tantrum in a public place. When he had tantrums at home, we put him in his room and told him that when he was done he could open the door himself and come out.

Confidence in responding to difficult behavior is a necessary and effective component of parenting success, but healing a child's identity wounds requires the use of therapeutic parenting. (See chapter 25.)

Life continued happily. Dan and I delighted in Tony's love of life and his curiosity. We shared the normal ups and downs but we felt able to resolve anything that came up. Tony was connected not only with us, but from age 1 had demonstrated the ability to form a friendship with someone outside his family. However, when Tony was 2½, his world would abruptly turn upside down upon the arrival of his sister, Suh Mee Jung, from Korea.

Parenting Tips

Keep your child close

Whether in your arms, in a front or backpack, in a portable car seat, or in a bassinette by your bed, your newly arrived child needs to be as close as possible to you most of the time. Since he cannot develop a relationship with you or bond without your presence, you need to hold your child a lot. There is a damaging myth that if you do this, you will spoil the child. However, what actually spoils a child is doing things for him that he can do for himself on a regular basis or giving him material things in place of interacting with him.

Hold him when he cries

Your child needs to be comforted in his distress, both to increase attachment and to regulate his nervous system. Your baby's brain builds neuronal pathways that support self-regulation of bodily functions, emotions, and behavior through direct experience in your arms. He learns how to self-soothe as he experiences you soothing him; he learns how to control his need for instant gratification by you helping him wait; and he learns how to handle his anxiety by being in your arms as you regulate both his and your own anxiety.

Get together with native speakers

Befriend someone who speaks your child's native tongue and learn some baby babble from his country of origin. Ask the friend to read and record stories for the child in his first language. Contact the local college for referrals to students who may be learning your baby's language and who would like to help. Hearing his native tongue can be soothing for your child and engender a feeling of familiarity that can ease his transition.

Limit holding by others

Your child needs to bond with his primary parent and needs to be held exclusively by that parent, if possible, especially at first. Just as your child was bonded to his birth mother by the time he was born due to his 9 months in her womb, he needs to bond deeply with his primary forever-parent now. Allowing extensive holding of your baby by others diluted his attachment experience, patterning his brain for a less-than-optimal intimate connection.

Develop a routine

Feeling secure and trusting come through knowing what to expect. Because of all of the changes your child likely has been through, his anxiety is already running at an elevated level. You can minimize your child's anxiety fluctuations by making his world as predictable as possible. Create a simple schedule that includes the necessities while limiting special activities. Plan to include a lot of lap and rocking time throughout the day. This will benefit both you and your child. If others want to help, ask them to do some of the errands or other activities that would otherwise take you away from your child.

Incorporate daily soothing experiences

In general, we underestimate the need for quiet time in our daily lives. Set aside part of every day for some low-key time for you to spend with your child. Soft light, lullabies, and rocking enhance your child's growth by reducing stress. Quiet baths and massage can be incorporated as well. Once you carve out a time for a daily peaceful ritual with your child, you will find that you look forward to this time, too!

Use "time in"

Traditionally, parents have learned to deal with their child's behavior problems by putting him in time out, either in another room or in a designated chair. However, because he was once abandoned, your child needs you to protect him from the shame that can result from this practice. Using time out can send your child the message that he's bad and unwanted, alienating him when he needs you the most.

When your child's behavior is out of bounds, it is because he cannot yet regulate himself. The way your child will learn to control his behavior is for you to do it for him until he can learn to do it for himself. Using a calm voice, you softly explain to your child that he needs you right now. You tell him that you are going to sit together for a while so you can help him, and then you pull him into your lap. When your child needs redirection, this sharing of "time in" gives him both the regulation and the acceptance he needs.

4 How Early Abandonment Affects Your Child

You looked adorable when you came off the plane and you never were strange with anyone who held you. You were in a fantastic mood and babbled to every-one in sight and even let Tony hold you, though he had you by the neck.
July 16, 1975
Valerie's baby book

When Dan and I felt ready to adopt our second child, we requested a girl. Coasting on the success of our first experience, we felt brave enough to request an older child who might not be picked otherwise. We set our upper limit at 2½ years.

We got along right away with our new social worker, Samantha, who was eager to facilitate a foreign adoption as there had not been many in Wyoming. Samantha watched us interact with Tony at home and asked questions about our approach to parenting. I know we appeared confident because we felt that way. Samantha was clearly pleased to see Tony adjusting so well. She concluded that Dan and I had a solid marriage and a solid home, and approved our application for adoption. We took up our second vigil of awaiting a child.

The magic morning finally arrived. Samantha phoned and in an excited voice informed us that an 18-month-old girl had been selected for us. The referral package with information and a photograph of our daughter was on the way.

I hung up the phone and wondered how I would manage to keep calm or even sleep for 5, 6, or 7 whole days before I got to see the first picture of our child. I raced to the attic and pulled out the box of pink and yellow baby clothes I had been saving for our future daughter. I looked at each outfit, wondering how it would look on her. I started preparing Tony for the eventual arrival of his little sister, but he was not too interested.

Dan and I could not agree on a name for our future daughter, so together we made a list of 10 names, each numbering the possibilities in order of preference. We added up the total points for each name to determine the winner. We hooted at the resultant name, Valerie—not the first choice of either of us. Seeing the name on paper, then hearing myself say it aloud, I loved it. So did Dan. I put the slip of paper with all the numbered possibilities in Valerie's new baby book for her to enjoy someday.

On the day of our appointment, as Dan and I were getting ready to go downtown to see our first picture of Valerie, the phone rang. It was early for a phone call. It was Samantha and all she had to say was, "Cassie. . . ." The tone of her voice told me something awful had happened. "What?" I said. "What's going on?"

She took a breath, then said, "The little girl you and Dan were scheduled to receive is no longer at the orphanage, Cassie. Her mom came and took her back, so I can't place her with you anymore. The adoption agency said they will refer you another child immediately. You've got to be patient."

Dan and I collapsed on the couch while Tony played with his trucks close by, unfazed. My mind was an orchestra of jumbled thoughts. I knew I should have felt happy for that little girl because her mom reclaimed her. I tried to express that thought to Dan, but my voice caught in my throat.

True to their word, the adoption agency immediately referred us a baby girl about 10 months old. We drove to Samantha's office as soon as she had the envelope in hand. No doubt we looked the way we felt— excited, yet cautious and scared from having been burned once. Samantha did not show us anything right away—she said we had to talk first.

Samantha told us that the concept of accepting a child forever when a couple has no say in actual selection was hard for all adoptive families. She said we were extremely courageous to adopt and she knew we could move forward from our disappointment. Finally she grinned and reached for the package.

As Dan and I studied two pictures of our soon-to-be daughter, Samantha watched us in obvious contentment. I could see why. Suh Mee Jung was breathtakingly beautiful. She looked better in her first picture than in the second one, just as Tony had. In her first picture she looked angelic. In the second one she looked . . . what? Squashed, maybe, as if a weight were pushing her down into the chair.

She was not smiling in either picture. I let my gaze fall upon her face, refusing to let myself well up inside. Still hurting from our recent loss, I wouldn't permit myself to have any expectations this time. I looked at her pictures, allowed myself a measured response of happiness, and promised this beautiful baby the deep connection she deserved.

Samantha asked if we were still going to use the name Valerie. We said yes, since we had already come to think of our daughter by that name. Once Dan and I got home and shut the door, predictably my suppressed response at Samantha's office gave way to shrieks of excitement.

As the referral moved toward placement, Dan and I made plans for the summer. Dan had won a National Endowment for the Humanities grant for an 8-week research fellowship in Pittsburgh that would end just before Valerie was scheduled to arrive in mid-August. Tony and I would spend the summer in Minneapolis, where both our families lived, and where Valerie's plane would land. It was perfect.

Successfully raising adopted children who are attached does not fully prepare parents for the challenges of raising a child with attachment disorder. (See chapter 24.)

We drove to Minneapolis in June, arriving at our temporary home, that of friends for whom we were going to house-sit. After the weekend, Dan flew off to Pittsburgh while Tony and I settled in for our 8-week wait. I planned on spending some of that time preparing for my eventual career as a court reporter. For several hours per day, I studied my steno machine theory while Tony played contentedly by my side. Those were good times.

However, just halfway through Dan's fellowship, I got an unexpected call from Samantha announcing that Valerie would arrive in a few days. Four weeks early! I could not believe it. Dan dashed back to Minneapolis for Valerie's delivery. It seemed that practically overnight we were at the airport again waiting for the giant stork.

I stalked the gate area in wild anticipation. I was wearing my best summer dress, as ready for my early delivery as I could be with such short notice. I knew our lives were about to change in ways I could not begin to fathom. I felt excited but apprehensive about the next 4 weeks, when Dan would be back in Pittsburgh and I would have both kids by myself.

At 5 o'clock, the next chapter of our family life began. In much the same fashion as had occurred with Tony, a smiling stewardess came forward, called out our daughter's name, and once again I stepped forward and enfolded my baby in my arms.

In the first pictures Dan snapped of me with Valerie, she looked as though she were perhaps too shy to look at anyone. She made no eye contact with me or with anyone else. Her gaze was fixed. Dan snapped a photo of me holding both Tony and Valerie. She looked composed, not too affected by the extraordinary events. In stark contrast, Tony looked unabashedly worried, refusing even to look at his new sister.

Valerie felt very light in my arms; and, indeed, at 12 months old, she weighed less than 20 pounds. She had arrived on the day of her first birthday, July 15, 1975. As I held her in my arms, she repeated only one word, *u-ma-ma,* the Korean word for "mother." She said it over and over. I was sure she was talking to me.

Children with attachment disorder display signs early on, some of which may be no eye contact, no stranger anxiety, no crying, and marked passivity. (See chapter 18.)

Our family headed for the airport café to celebrate and rejoice. There we first read Valerie's paperwork. The initial social history from Korea had said she had been abandoned. Under her medical history, the report said "no information." We were hoping to hear more about her past, but there was not a word anywhere in this supplemental material about her precious first 3 months of life.

Dan and I went through the papers carefully, trying to glean anything we could about our daughter. There was nothing but a few sketchy background notes. Within her first 7 months of life, Suh Mee Jung had lived in three different places.

At 7½ months, she was 24 inches long, weighed just 14 pounds, and had not yet begun to teethe. She was receiving 200 cc of milk 7 times per day. That meant she had not even received cereal. Wow, no wonder she was so tiny.

The paperwork stated that her physical condition was "fair" and that she had an "asymmetrical, flat right posterior head." I could see her head was not a normal shape. The report's conclusion was contradictory, stating, "Suh Mee Jung stands straight with support and sits leaning. Is normally developed physically for her age."

The remarks regarding emotional development said, "Is not shy of people. Enjoys cuddling by everybody and plays well with arms. Smiles out of joy when soothed. Murmurs. Looks mild by nature. Looks healthy and sound emotionally."

My God, what an act of faith it is to adopt a child. It was a lot to digest emotionally. Dan and I looked at each other, our eyes renewing our commitment to be the best parents we could be. With profound compassion, I held my prized bundle to my breast. I felt outraged at her being so impersonally and ambiguously summarized. I stared in wonder at the tiny red shoes that had arrived with her, knowing I would cherish them the rest of my life.

Valerie looked adorably sweet in her peach dress. I loved her smell. She was even more beautiful than her pictures. Still, it was daunting to adopt a child knowing so little about her. Dan took it all in stride. He could tell I was perplexed by our new daughter's passive reaction to all she had gone through. And I knew he was thinking everything was fine.

Truthfully, I was in shock. I didn't know what to make of Valerie's listlessness and her failure to look at me or reach out for me. What unsettled me most was that she seemed to be having her own private experience, one we were not allowed to share. Optimistically, I told myself she was probably just tired from the long flight. We finished our coffee as Dan and I marveled at our new family addition.

Poor Tony looked undone. No amount of talking had prepared him for a living, breathing sister. He politely offered this peach-dressed person a cookie—his proper behavior belying his anxiety. Valerie held her gaze on Tony while he insisted, "Here. Here's a cookie for you," but she did not reach out for it. She remained detached from us all while we each reeled in our own way in the supercharged reality of her mystery.

Finally we left the airport café and headed to the Richards' house. Joyous introductions were made. Dan's mother said how cute and how small Valerie was. Mia and I both noted that she had the worst diaper rash we had ever seen. She had multiple sores on her bottom that were an angry red color, bleeding and raw. Clearly, she had been neglected.

We stayed at the Richards' for that weekend. The first night went fine. Valerie went to bed with no protest, without even a peep to indicate that she registered all the new things in her life. The next morning, her cries awoke me at 4:30 a.m. After I changed her diaper, she and I had our first *tête-à-tête*.

Lying together on the floor, we shared time if not connection. Though I never took my eyes off her, she did not return my overtures. She was not intense like Tony had been. Instead, she appeared to be a relaxed, self-confident baby who was very well-adjusted. She did not even cry much in spite of what had to be miserable discomfort from her diaper rash.

While we shared that first predawn summer morning in July, I let myself fall in love with Valerie, though we were utter strangers. Tears streaked down my cheeks. I said, "Val, I'm sorry I don't speak Korean, honey." I remember using her nickname for the first time. "Val" sounded intimate.

I said, "Sweetie, it's really a big deal that you're here. Mommy doesn't even know you, but I love you with all my heart." I explained, "You know, Tony's upset that you're here because he's feeling jealous, but he'll love you as much as Mommy and Daddy do when he gets to know you."

I continued, "We're going to see Dr. Olander this morning and he's going to tell us what we need to know about you. Okay? Honey, don't you worry. Mommy is going to clear up that awful diaper rash and diarrhea. Dr. Olander will tell me what to do. Pretty soon it'll be all gone."

Val seemed to listen to me as she looked off in the distance from her prone position on her tummy. It struck me as odd that despite being 12 months old, she apparently did not yet crawl. When I propped her up on her knees, she collapsed to the floor.

Val did not take the toys I offered her. If I put one in her hand she would let it drop. I gave her a bottle, which she accepted well enough, but she did not suck greedily as Tony had. She did not cuddle in to my body but instead lay there somewhat loose in my arms while she drank. She did not hold the bottle, nor did she stare into my eyes.

Children's behaviors can reveal the neglect they experienced prior to adoption. (See chapter 18.)

Though our family arrived at Dr. Olander's office a little early, he saw us right away. I gently placed Valerie into his waiting arms, expecting her to cry. She did not. It was amazing how naturally content she seemed. The entire time I was reporting Valerie's known history and the behaviors I had observed, Dr. Olander remained silent. I sensed that he was not saying something.

I remember how carefully Dr. Olander put Valerie on the table and undressed her, talking to her softly while he smiled. She did not resist him at all. He her held this way and that, turned her over, removed her diaper, examined her eyes, then reexamined her left eye, then her head, her bottom, her arms and legs. She lay on the table in a hush of silence while Dr. Olander finished his exam, lost in thought.

Meanwhile, I was biting my tongue waiting for him to speak. His mood seemed ominous to me. Finally I could not hold myself back. I blurted out, "Why's her head that way?" Then, "How come her eyes don't focus right?" Still Dr. Olander did not respond.

After what seemed like an eternity, he handed Valerie back to me. Choosing his words carefully, Dr. Olander looked me in the eyes and said, "I've seen this before. Her head is asymmetrical because in the orphanage there's not enough help to hold the babies except when they get their bath. So most of the day the babies lie on their side facing the bathing station, where there's activity. Sometimes the babies stay that way so long that eventually the head bones, which are still soft, atrophy, and the head gets flat on the side they're always lying on."

I reeled inside, grief-stricken for Valerie as I stared at her, struggling to digest this truth. I thought of the nurturing care Tony had received, first from his foster family, then from us. Our children had had completely different first years.

Dr. Olander continued, "She'll be able to hide that flatness when she gets older. She can fix her hair so it won't show." He moved on, "Although her gaze is not focused, I don't think she has a vision problem. It presents like a lazy eye right now but may clear up in a couple of months. I wouldn't worry about it, but do have her eyes retested in a few months to see if there's still an unfocused gaze." I nodded obediently, hoping Val would not be cross-eyed.

I said, "Well, what about the missing fingernail on her little finger?" There was no nail there at all, and the tiny stub end of her pinkie was naked and wrinkled. I had never seen anything like it. Dr. Olander replied that while she may have been born that way, it was more likely that she had suffered a traumatic event that ripped out the nail bed, leaving no base for the nail to grow back.

While I was taking in that news, he added, "Your baby has scabies. These are small mites under the skin. It is a mild form of lice, not uncommon in Korean babies. If I were you, I would not mention this to your family, since Americans are not used to it. I'll give you a prescription. The scabies should clear up in a couple months."

Val was below average in both size and weight. Her bleeding, open diaper sores suggested she had suffered from chronic diarrhea. Dr. Olander said quite likely she had been allergic to the milk at the orphanage. If so, then Val's entire diet during her first year of life had been a food she could not tolerate. He told us to buy soy-based formula and not to diaper her except at night. She needed indirect sun, at least an hour each day, to heal her sores.

Even if an infant receives adequate nutrition, if he is not held, the physical neglect can inhibit the production of growth hormones, which are necessary to fully digest his food. (See chapter 18.)

As the doctor told me all these things, one after another, I felt baffled. It was too much for me to comprehend all of these insults to my daughter. What effect would this have on her life, I wondered. Would we be able to make up for it—help this baby thrive in spite of so much neglect?

Dr. Olander looked at me with concern and said, "The reason she has no reaction to any of us holding her is because so many different people took care of her in Korea. For the next few months, refrain from letting anyone hold her except for you and Dan. You want her to bond to you." I nodded numbly. Dr. Olander seemed sad as we left. "Hey," he put his hand on Dan's back, "Good luck to you both. You are good parents. I think she'll do well."

I did not know what to feel. I looked at my daughter in admiration for being so gentle and good natured after such a rough start. I hugged her tightly, vowing silently to protect her from any more hurt in her life.

On the drive home, I wondered how many cribs away from the bathing station Valerie had been in that orphanage. I knew she had been in a room with 25 to 30 baby girls and had been cared for by constantly rotating personnel. At that moment, I imagined what cacophony would result from 25 babies all crying at the same time.

> *The urge to cry eventually gets extinguished in babies who do not get their needs met on demand. (See chapter 19.)*

We returned to our borrowed house. Dan had to leave the following day, his tenure dependent on his completion of the fellowship project. Though I was disappointed about him leaving, I did not feel resentment since I was confident of my abilities to manage alone for the next 3½ weeks.

However, the easygoing schedule Tony and I had enjoyed before Valerie's arrival promptly deteriorated when Dan left. Tony regressed immediately and I could not get him back on track. I did not know how to cope with his jealousy. He cried incessantly, refused to take his nap, was crabby and whiny all the time, and began wetting the bed.

Tony did not want me to pay attention to Valerie. To that end, Tony would tearfully cup his little hands on my face, pulling me toward him and away from this intruding sister. He would call me by my first name, "Cassie," really to get my attention. If that did not work, he would find one of Valerie's little hats, put it on, and come shyly to show me how cute he was, too. Tony was affixed to my hip, pleading to send *her* away on the airplane. He would still not call Valerie by her name.

I tried to be patient with Tony. I made special time for my son, read him stories, talked to him, and played with him. No matter what I did, Tony remained unsoothed. Bit by bit I began to feel overwhelmed. Moreover, I was learning what sleep deprivation could do to me.

When Dan called each night, I would try to sound cheerful, not about to admit I was having a difficult time. The main problem was that lack of sleep was eroding my energy. I finally stopped getting up when Val cried in the night. The truth was that, exhausted and by myself, I was unable to do anything but let her cry. She would cry for a few minutes and then all would be quiet again.

Although I allowed myself to stay in bed at night, during the day, I tried to be a super mom. I bathed Valerie six times a day. She was adjusting to the soy milk and the diarrhea lessened and gradually ceased. Calm as always, Valerie adapted to her new life.

In addition to sleep deprivation, I was experiencing an allergic reaction to pollen. The antihistamine made me even drowsier. However, if I did not take it, I felt sick. It seemed my whole body was betraying me. Without air conditioning, I felt hot, crabby, and depressed. I could no longer find my energy.

Finally things came to a head. On a blistering August afternoon at my sister Carol's apartment, as usual Tony was hanging on me, whining and crying for me to pick him up. After three warnings to leave me alone, I lost my temper and hit him. Carol took over. I worried all afternoon that now I was going to start smacking my kids as my mom had smacked me. I had promised myself never to do to my children what my mother had done to me, and at the first test I had failed royally.

In the quiet of my bedroom, longing for Dan's return, I shed tears of humiliation, admitting how much I needed my husband in this parenting venture. I felt shocked by my emerging behavior. I had been so sure of myself before Dan left. Now I felt lost at sea, unstable, and ashamed.

In the event of a temporary spousal absence, the primary parent needs to have assistance in the home in order to meet the often extraordinary needs of adopted children. (See chapter 25.)

Tony's behavior worsened to the point that even our hard-earned peaceful bedtime ritual disintegrated. Exhausted, I gave in and let him sleep in bed with me at night. I knew Dan would not approve but at least I could get some sleep and feel less like a zombie all day.

On one of my bad days, I drove to my mom's house so she could watch the children while I rested. Tony fell asleep in the car and as soon as we got to Mom's he woke up, refreshed for more whining and crying.

I dissolved into tears, resentful that he had slept at a time not convenient to me. I so much needed a time-out. Now he was awake and crabby, hanging on me, not wanting me to talk to Grandma. I was ready to scream because I needed peace and quiet.

Mom put me in her bathtub and told me to relax, which was exactly what I was doing when she opened the locked bathroom door and barged in, just like in the old days. Valium pill in hand, she ordered me to take it. I flatly refused. She wagged her finger at me, saying the reason I was having so much trouble was that Tony and Valerie were not born of my body.

I turned my face to the wall, heartbroken by the meanness of her remark. She told me again to take the Valium. I bawled through clenched teeth that I was not taking her damn Valium. She left. I have no memory of how the rest of that day went.

Dan's research fellowship ended at last and he returned to the family. Valerie was her usual easygoing self, but during Dan's first night back Tony threw the biggest tantrum of his life because Dan made him go to his own bed to sleep. Tony became hysterical. Dan was astounded at his son's will.

I began sobbing as well because I had never heard that piercing, fear-for-survival voice from Tony before. Dan stood in the hallway watching his family unravel before his eyes. Nevertheless, Dan held firm to his conviction that Tony was not going to sleep in our bed.

Tony kicked and beat on his door, shrieking uncontrollably for me to come and get him. Finally Dan caved in and said Tony could sleep on the floor by my side of the bed. Dan brought Tony into our room, where he fell asleep instantly next to me. Meanwhile, Dan lay in silence pondering all that had happened in his absence.

Children who have experienced significant abandonment often need to sleep near their parents to feel emotionally secure. (See chapter 24.)

The next morning, everyone was in a better mood. I brought Dan up to date on Valerie's development while she sat on his lap. I told him she could actually sit up though she still listed to one side. She knew how to crawl, too, though she did not seem to want to. She could take steps if I held her from behind, but she was not pulling herself up on furniture yet.

I said that Valerie cried, but never urgently. I told Dan that she seemed to be handling her new life incredibly well, while Tony and I were the ones who were falling apart.

When we were ready to leave, we bought a used van in which Dan and Tony made the trip home together. Tony chattered the whole way, so happy to have Daddy back. There were potty stops and many meals at McDonald's. With each mile Tony shared with his dad, his security gradually returned.

Meanwhile, Val and I enjoyed a peaceful flight home. As she slept in my arms, I reflected upon our first few weeks together. The relative ease of parenting Valerie was countered by the tumultuous experience with Tony.

The instantaneous improvement that had occurred when Dan returned from Pittsburgh contrasted sharply with the nearly 4 weeks of discord and frayed nerves the kids and I endured when I was alone with them. I humbly realized my parenting skills needed work.

Upon returning home I was determined to make changes in myself. But in 1975 in our small town in Wyoming, there were no books on adoption available. So I gleaned what I could from Dr. Spock and Dr. Dobson, from parenting classes, and from talking with friends about their toddlers. Dan listened attentively to what I was learning.

Notwithstanding some new information, we found ourselves in uncharted waters. Clearly, we had things happening at our house that were not happening in our friends' homes and we did not know why.

Parenting Tips

Establish in-home supports

Parents need help, especially at times when one parent will be absent or when challenges are running high. It is easy to get overwhelmed with the demands of raising children, especially those with abandonment histories. A parent will not win a superparent award if she tries to do everything herself—she will just wear herself out. In traditional societies, parents were never alone raising children. There were always relatives and village members helping. Today's parents need to create a pool of supporters who are willing to help and then call on them often.

Commit to teamwork

You and your spouse need a unified front to be successful parents. Parents don't always agree about the situation at hand because each parent can have a unique experience of the child. Plan weekly parenting meetings with your spouse in which you review past events and anticipate new ones. Work out any disagreements outside the presence of the children. If an impasse persists, seek professional help.

Mirror your child

If your child missed out on adequate nurturing early on, he didn't have the interaction he needed to learn about his feelings or to discover who he is. Your feedback is essential for your child to learn who he is and what he is feeling: you detect his need, verbalize to him what you perceive, meet his need, and then tell him what you see afterward.

For example, a mother discovers her baby has a wet diaper and she reflects to him, "Oh, I see how unhappy you are in your wet diaper! Let me change you into a dry one." She completes the diaper change then reflects again, "Now, I can tell you like that better . . . you're smiling and happy again." In narrating your baby's life for him, you are teaching him words for his feelings so he can begin to find out who he is, what he likes, and what he doesn't like.

Respect your child's need for "downtime"

It is as important to meet your child's need for disengagement as it is to meet his need for interaction. Parents love to interact with their babies and create mutual enjoyment. However, babies do tire of this intense interaction and need time to look away and take a break from the fun. Similarly, children need an ebb and flow of action in their daily lives—they cannot take constant stimulation. Parents need to orchestrate this for their child by being sensitive to his cues and/or anticipating his capacity for stimulation. This is all part of the continuum of providing your unique child with well-tailored care.

Fill in developmental gaps

If your child was neglected as an infant, chances are his development suffered to some degree. With professional help, establish and implement the activities your child needs to complete his unmet developmental stages. With a thorough assessment, parents can determine what area or areas of their child's development might have been affected—physical, emotional, psychological, and/or social. Parents can work with a specialist on designing at-home interventions that target repairing their child's developmental gaps. This "reparenting" is an essential component of therapeutic parenting.

Take daily breaks

Arrange for daily personal respite time from the responsibilities of parenting, even if it's just a 20-minute shower to begin with. You can't be "on" all of the time. You need a chance to rejuvenate yourself and recharge your energy. This is an indispensable part of successful parenting. Take turns with your spouse, or hire an in-home sitter to be with your child a few hours per week while you rest. Create a plan and commit to it—you'll be more than relieved you did.

Consider parenting your occupation for now

A child needs his primary parent to commit to him above all else. He needs your active presence to develop fully and to reach his potential. Remind yourself of the reasons you adopted and remember that your child will eventually grow up. Save career aspirations until your child has confidently adjusted to school.

5 Early Signs of Attachment Disorder

When we returned home to Rock Springs, our life as a complete family began. Tony settled down immediately. Dad was back with us. Tony's best friend, Brad, was just across the street. Tony was secure again in familiar surroundings, and his tantrums, clinging, and bedwetting all ceased. His cheery self returned and he no longer pleaded with us to send Valerie away. Dan, Tony, and I soon settled into a new routine that included our new daughter.

Val, always self-contained, neither sucked her thumb nor accepted a pacifier. By 14 months, she had begun drinking from a cup at meals and soon gave up her bottle completely. This amazed us and made me wonder why she did not want to be held and given her bottle in the usual ways babies do.

Val's scabies and diaper rash were gone and she appeared to be in perfect health. From the beginning, we observed that Val did not take the tiny steps that usually precede mastery of a new stage. Without much warning she went from sitting to true walking. What we did notice in a striking way was how much she observed things. In particular, whenever she could, she kept her eye on Tony.

Food was an area of concern for us. Val didn't just eat, she force-fed herself. Big squirrel cheeks showed a mouth crammed with food. She would push food down her throat with her fingers. Alarmed, yet not wanting to be overbearing, I hovered nearby like a helicopter to be sure she would not choke.

Val's eating was indiscriminate. She ate everything, nonfood items included. We spent much time opening her mouth to withdraw pieces of rotten apple, pits, stems, bread wrappers, or rocks. We would give her a Popsicle only to watch her turn it upside down and attempt to eat the stick. I realized how great my responsibility was to have her under my eye every second of the day.

When Val began outeating Tony, I consulted our pediatrician. Her body seemed too tiny for so much food. Our doctor said not to worry; her height and weight were in healthy proportion. My fears allayed, I thought she was simply making up for lost time.

Val showed no preference as to who held her, nor did she react much around other people. We still did not allow others to hold her much, remembering what Dr. Olander had said about waiting till she bonded with us. I held her continually, hoping to feel a connection from her toward me, but Val continued to sit in my lap as if by default.

I did not yet judge her behavior in any particular way, nor did I worry about it. Instead I was very, very determined to figure out what to do so that Val would be able to bond with me as I had with her.

I noticed many behaviors in Val that were very different from those we had seen in Tony. In her crib, for example, instead of sucking on a pacifier Val rocked on her hands and knees, apparently to soothe herself.

Tony, in contrast, had depended on me to soothe him. His bombastic nature was in great contrast to Val's, which was quiet and self-contained. Tony had squealed, cried, kicked, fussed, and raged; he had also smiled, cooed, and acted excited. Val, conversely, did not display a wide range of emotions. Even when she cried, it was nothing like the room-piercing cries of Tony at 5 months. She did smile, but it was not exactly personal.

Tony always maintained intense eye contact, whereas Valerie's gaze remained unfocused. Because Tony externalized his feelings, it was easy for us to figure out what he wanted. When we guessed correctly he rewarded us, his body language showing his obvious pleasure.

Valerie, on the other hand, was nonchalant about everything. She gave no cues about what she really wanted. It was almost as if she had no desires. She did not seem to have a noticeable sense of her own identity.

Children with attachment disorder display predictable behaviors that parents can learn to identify and respond to successfully. (See chapter 18.)

My earliest memory of defiance on the part of Valerie remains clear in my mind yet today. One day, all four of us were at lunch. It must have been during a weekend for Dan to have been there. There was a hole in the plastic tablecloth that was near enough for Val to reach from her highchair. She reached over while eating and began to rip at the hole in the cloth with her forefinger. Dan told her "no-no." Val continued to try to make the hole bigger, so Dan said "no-no" a little louder and called her by name. He was sure she understood.

She looked nonchalantly at Dan while she continued to tug on the hole. He reached over and gave her a flick of thumb and middle finger against her hand, not hard but a definitive message nonetheless, and sternly repeated, "No-no, Valerie." That made her cry.

It seemed clear that Valerie understood she was not supposed to rip the hole anymore. Next, to my amazement, while still crying she again attempted to rip the hole even while Dan again flicked her hand. I jumped up, removed the food, and pulled the tablecloth off the table.

This event marks the first time Dan and I disagreed about what had occurred with Valerie. My view was she had not understood what he wanted, while Dan was sure she had not only understood him but was being defiant. In any case, she seemed not to process the pain of the flick as being a reason to stop the behavior. We both agreed about that.

Tony had definitely had a firm grasp of what "no-no" meant by Valerie's age (about 15 months) and he responded predictably. Though at times Valerie would demonstrate clearly that she understood what "no-no" meant, we simply could not predict obedience. Nonetheless, we intuitively began lowering our expectations of her.

By the time Val was 18 months of age, we were thoroughly exasperated. Unlike Tony, who continued to be eager to please us, Valerie seemed to take a certain pride in refusing to observe our rules and instruction. She was still eating all the garbage and plant leaves she could get her teeth into. I'd even had to remove charcoal and ashes from her mouth. We would have Valerie-proofed our house had we ever imagined she would try to eat such things, but each new item was another surprise.

Our attempts to teach obedience to our daughter were not successful. No matter how many times we told Val not to do something, she did it anyway. A small consequence did not influence her either. From the very beginning, when we imposed what we felt were age-appropriate consequences, Val continued right on doing what she pleased.

During this period, Dan and I had a serious talk about our daughter because she got into so much trouble. Once again we disagreed. My take was that she needed a lot of time to adjust and that we should not be too hard on her. Dan insisted that she understood perfectly well and was being headstrong. He came to a conclusion early on that Valerie was a con artist. I argued that was not possible because she was too little. I said Dan was too strict. He said I was too lenient.

A hallmark trait of a child with attachment disorder is the need, thus the determination, to control everything and everyone. (See chapter 19.)

While she was little, Valerie seemed to be living in her own world. I had affectionately nicknamed her my "carefree wild rose." She would pick up a toy only to quickly discard it. Her favorite activity was watching her brother. She learned by watching him. Often she would follow Tony around the house like a shadow, clearly interested in him rather than in his toys or activities. Perhaps Tony was especially appealing to look at because he was Korean. At random times as she padded after him, she would hum when she heard a tune on the radio. It was a refreshing sign of her inner spirit.

Val cared nothing about what was hers, whereas Tony had fully grasped the idea of *mine* immediately and took pride in what was his. Tony quickly figured out how to exploit his sister, asking for anything he wanted. Valerie, of course, would always fork it over so that she could please her brother. Her goal was to be with her brother; however, Tony did not always want his sister around because he usually did not want to share. I wanted to teach Tony how to share, but Dan said we had to let them work it out on their own.

Tony continued to thrive. He was happy, secure, openly friendly, easygoing, and gentle. At home, Tony was curious, explored constantly, and barraged Dan with boy questions about how the world worked. He accepted our limits, followed our rules, and met our expectations.

The behaviors of an attached child contrast markedly with those of a child with attachment disorder. (See chapters 17 and 18.)

Tony's favorite thing was story time at night. He was intensely interested in books and loved us to read to him, especially *Where the Sidewalk Ends,* by Shel Silverstein, and books by Richard Scarry. Tony was helping me cook by age 4 as well as clearing and setting the table.

Around this time, we began to see that Valerie was not only different from Tony but she was actually different from other toddlers as well. In particular, she seemed oblivious to discomfort.

One event that firmly planted this impression in our minds started when we occasionally smelled a bad odor about Val. Finally we figured out that the odor came from her nose. We realized that she must have shoved something up one of her nostrils and we made an appointment with our pediatrician. When he looked in her right nostril, he could see that it was obstructed.

He explained to Val that he was going to put a stick in her nose to get something out and that it was going to hurt a little bit. He pulled out a piece of blue sponge. Amazingly, throughout the entire process Val remained calm, centered, and perfectly silent. Her pain tolerance was uncanny. Most children her age would have noisily resisted. After the procedure the doctor paraded Val around the clinic, raving about her courage. In recognition of her bravery, he gave her *all* the gum in the prize bin.

We observed that Valerie learned new things by seemingly instantly assimilating them. By 24 months, she still hardly said any actual words. Then almost overnight she began speaking in sentences. Potty training was no different. Val went from no interest to fierce interest with quick mastery in just a few days.

∿

Racial identity issues began to bud for Tony. We lived in a white community where the very few children of a different color stood out. Even by 2½, Tony had figured out that he looked different from other kids. At a Halloween party, for instance, he refused to wear a costume because he said he was already in the "costume" of his skin.

When Tony was 4½ and attending daycare part time, his teachers displayed their insensitivity to racial issues by asking the children to line up by their eye shape, calling Tony "Korean eyes." We were unaware of this practice and were shocked one day when one of the teachers called and said Tony had begun telling the kids that when he got bigger his skin was going to turn white and then he would look like everyone else. This teacher was concerned that Tony was ashamed of his race. Dan and I had not anticipated such blatant examples of bigotry when we adopted Korean children into our white community.

That event made us decide to start celebrating Korean Night in our home, cooking and honoring customs from Korea. We had kimchi and other Korean food, sat on pillows to eat, wore Korean clothes, wrote to ancestors on parchment paper, and lit sparklers to conclude the evening.

Our hope was to convey acceptance of our children's racial differ-ence through celebration of their Korean heritage. It was great fun. The children now had their own version of how they fit into the world. Valerie even came to say she was born in Korea, got lost there, and Daddy came and got her in our car and drove her home.

A deep-seated sense of shame about being abandoned by the birth mother is often compounded by physical differences that may exist between adoptive parents and their child. (See chapter 19.)

Despite many pleasant moments in our family, Valerie's defiance continued to disrupt the harmony. I recall that when Valerie was between 2 and 3, no matter how many times we said "no-no" about going in the street, it was the only place she wanted to be. She would deliberately stand in the street as if to taunt me.

Time-outs and words did not seem to matter. Even though she was almost 3, the age when Tony had clearly understood and followed our ground rules, Valerie simply ignored what we said. Once again, I figured it must be too soon for her to understand.

Then the era of lying began. Valerie's first lie occurred on the day I discovered a big "V" in crayon on the wall close to the floor by the stair-way. I pointed it out to Val and asked her if she wrote on the wall. To my astonishment she said, "No, Mommy, I didn't do it. Tony did it." I pointed out that it was a "V" and Tony started with "T." She did not care, insisting that she did not do it.

I then brought Tony in and showed Valerie how tall her brother was, explaining that the "V" was just at her height. It did not matter what theory I advanced. She stuck to her story and adamantly denied doing it. Then I told her the punishment was not any big deal, just to clean the wall. That did not make any difference either. She insisted she did not do it. I was totally confounded.

I stood there scrutinizing my carefree wild rose of a daughter. Though Val's eyes did not meet mine, I noticed she did not act guilty at all. Then, with a casual air, she asked, "Can I go play now?" as though nothing had even happened.

Although flabbergasted, I quietly replied, "No, Val, you can't play yet because Mommy knows you're lying. In our family, we do not lie. I want you to come in the kitchen and Mommy will give you what you need to clean off the wall." I gave her a pail of water and a sponge. She cleaned the wall, said nothing, and then went back to playing.

Tony's preschool lying, on the other hand, had begun and ended when he was 2½ or 3. When he lied the first time, I used the same line my mother had used on me, "There's no use lying because I can see the guilt on your face." After that, Tony quit lying and in fact switched to looking at us with steely eyes when admitting he had done something wrong.

Breaking toys was a new behavior that we did not understand. One time we went to see good friends, and while we were there Val repeatedly broke their daughter's toys. When we confronted her, Val burst into tears and was repentant. She insisted the breakage had been an accident. I was convinced. Other things, however, continued to turn up broken after Val played with them.

When Val was around 3, I bought her a porcelain tea set like the one I had had when I was a little girl. I remember my happiness to give her this gift, hoping it would please her. I explained that it was an inside-the-house toy because it was fragile. For whatever reason, Val never seemed to play with it. I felt so disappointed. Many years later, I found the tea set broken into a thousand pieces. Val had hidden it in Tony's dresser hoping to escape blame.

Lying escalated. One day when Valerie was still around 3, I got a phone call from my next-door neighbor, Sally. I could tell she felt embarrassed. She said she had just seen Valerie picking tulips in her yard. I told her I felt shocked because Val had come home with two tulips in hand, claiming she had found them in the alley. My neighbor said Val had picked nearly all the tulips in the yard. Sally requested that I please ask Val to refrain from any more flower picking.

I hung up the phone, found Val, and said, "Val, Sally just called and told me you were picking tulips in her yard. You told me you found them."

Val said vehemently, "Mommy, I did *not* pick those flowers." I went and got the two she had brought home and showed them to her. She reiterated, "Mommy, I didn't pick them. I *found* them." I looked into Val's face to find the truth. I saw neither guilt nor a lying demeanor about her. It was an amazing performance. I said, "I know you did it, Val, because Sally just told me she saw you." Val replied, "Sally didn't see me, Mommy."

Afterward my confidence was shaken. Her behavior did not line up with anything I had ever seen or known, and I did not know what to do. When I told Dan what had happened, he said in a matter-of-fact way, "She's a con artist, Cassie."

Persistent and "crazy" lying—that is, lying in the face of the evidence—is an extension of a child's determination to feel safe by being in control. (See chapter 21.)

My concern that something was really wrong with Val turned to panic when her behaviors became dangerous. The kids and I had just returned from a morning visit at my friend Janet's house when Janet called. Horrified, she reported what her son, John, had told her. He said when Val had been upstairs playing with him, she found a box of matches. She took out a match, lit it, and then stuck it back in the box with the other matches.

Although Janet sounded relieved that the other matches had not caught fire, she was obviously terrified at the prospect of Val coming to their house to play anymore. When I confronted Val, she promptly began sobbing. She admitted knowing it was wrong to play with matches but confessed she had wanted to do it.

Although Valerie acted out most often when I was alone with her, she also disobeyed the rules and told lies when Dan was there. In such instances, Dan devoted minutes, half-hours, and sometimes entire evenings to getting out the truth.

Even though his methods did not always result in her telling the truth, Dan remained determined not to be conned. I, on the other hand, was beginning to doubt my parenting skills, fearing that Val had already figured me out and sensed my lack of confidence. In fact, this was true. I felt that Val was increasingly gaining the upper hand.

Feeling a lack of confidence and fearing that the child is beginning to take control are common reactions of parents raising children with attachment problems. (See chapter 23.)

Unfazed by either of our approaches, Val continued to lie. She could not see that her lying broke our trust in her, whereas Tony actively pursued our confidence in him and our affection. His transparent honesty was a delight to behold. Tony definitely strove to meet our expectations, not wanting to disappoint us or be in trouble.

Valerie, however, did not care if she was in trouble. Being in our good graces was of little concern to her. While Tony remained a highly curious child, uncomplicated in motive and predictable, Valerie was an enigma. Tony's conscience seemed normal to us, obviously being able to distinguish between right and wrong.

However, Val showed us over and over again that she had little if any conscience. She would simply say or do anything to get her way. While we trusted Tony implicitly, it was impossible for us to trust Val. We did not even know who she was inside.

Val continued to astound us with her mental acuity. Not only could she read and manipulate people at will to get what she wanted, she was also precocious and could perform certain cognitive tasks in ways that were disconcerting.

Reading before bed was a nightly ritual at our house. One night when Val and I were alone, I decided to read *Jack and the Beanstalk* to her. As we sat together in our overstuffed chair next to the stove, I opened the book to begin, when Val uncharacteristically took the initiative and said, "Mommy, I can read it." To humor her, I agreed.

Val took the book, opened it, and shocked me to my core by "reading" it. I am not talking about her pointing to pictures and summarizing the action on that page in her own words. I mean she followed the text nearly word for word, sentence by sentence. Her pronunciation and inflection were very good. She imitated a mother reading to her child. She was not even in school yet.

Unlike other young girls, who spend their early years playing with dolls, imitating their mothers, my Val was not interested in doing so. She did not want to hold a baby doll in her arms and cuddle it. She did not want to feed or bathe it or pretend to read to it. No matter what doll I would give her, even dolls of different races, they remained in her closet untouched. I tried and tried to find one Val would love, but I never did.

During Valerie's preschool years, while she had playmates who came and went, she never developed close friendships with anyone. She experienced nothing like the deep friendship bond between Tony and Brad that was firmly in place by the time the boys were 2 years old.

Playing with dolls and having friends require the ability to be in a relationship—a brain-based capacity that develops only with adequate nurturing. (See chapter 18.)

Parenting Tips

Stay close to home
Parents often feel societal pressure to "enrich" their child's life by taking him to preschool, playgroups, music classes, gymnastics, and other activities. Contrary to popular belief, what your child actually needs is *you* and the simplicity of everyday life—the security of a familiar place. He can wait to explore the outside world until after he has fully bonded to you. His main task is to figure out what your relationship is all about. He does not need distractions from this primary goal. Save special outings until your child is fully adjusted, sometime in the future.

Be playful
Create joy with your child, delight in him, and appreciate him. Not only is interacting playfully with your child fun, it also instills in him a sense

of his own value—"Wow! I am worth spending time with. I am capable of bringing joy to my parents. I am delightful!" Biochemically, play decreases your child's overall level of stress, which enables him to grow and learn.

Address identity
Begin when your child is a baby to tell him the story of his life. Tell him what you know and make educated guesses about what you don't know to fill in the gaps. Include his experiences of birth, adoption, and life with you. In telling your child his whole story, you are conveying your deep acceptance of him—where he came from, the fact that he was born to another mother, and the joy you feel about him being yours. Your child needs a full context for his existence, a way to understand why he might have different eyes, hair, or skin than his adoptive parents. He needs to grow with full knowledge of who he is. Keeping secrets— for instance the fact he was adopted—translates into a message of deep shame for him about himself. Openness equals acceptance.

Honor your child's birth family
Respectfully talk about and value your child's birth mother and family. Your child infers his own personal value from your treatment of his birth relatives. Be honest about the birth mother and her family's circumstances to the level of your child's understanding. Be mindful of the truth while remaining compassionate and without judgment. Express gratitude for the privilege of being your child's parent.

Acknowledge both your child's birth and adoption dates
For adopted children, both birth and adoption dates are significant. Be sensitive to your child's present level of self-acceptance and gear celebrations to your child's present ability to handle them. Surprisingly, many children will be able to tell you if they can handle being celebrated or not. Work with your child in choosing the level of acknowledgment he is comfortable with at the moment.

Address outstanding problems with a professional
At one time or another, all adoptive families will encounter a situation that is beyond their expertise to handle. It is wise to seek professional help

if this occurs because chances are a solution exists to the problem. Putting off seeking help often leads to problems becoming worse, so consult with a specialist sooner rather than later. Taking action proves your commitment and intent to do everything possible to help your child.

Supervise your child

Because of developmental lags, some adoptive children display the behaviors and needs of children who are younger chronologically. Rather than put expectations upon your child that are beyond his abilities to meet, adjust your approach to match his presenting age. Most children need more parental supervision than less. If your child engages in behaviors that often draw you away from other tasks, he is letting you know that he needs more direct help from you in negotiating his world. In gauging your child's need for your close presence, err on the side of higher supervision.

Regulate your child's emotion

Since your child's brain is still developing the capacity for self-regulation, he needs your proximity and attention to help him learn. If you can stay calm and keep your child close when he's losing control, it not only regulates his system in the present, it also teaches him how to do this for himself. It is helpful to describe what you are doing that is helping him to calm down. For example, you might say, "Let's have you sit here on my lap and then let's take five big breaths together right now...one, two, three, four, five."

Employ the empathic healing talk

One of the most powerful tools of therapeutic parenting is the empathic healing talk (see Appendix A for an example using Val's tulip-stealing incident). Your child's behavior and experience need translation for him to learn about himself and to grow his capacity to regulate his choices and behaviors. Regular use of the empathic healing talk also provides multiple opportunities for your child to experience your acceptance and to develop trust in your relationship. Use this dialogue often with your child to address misbehavior as well as to highlight his strengths.

6 Recognizing Core Shame

In the fall of 1979, Tony was in kindergarten and Valerie was still at home. I had stayed home with my babies in what I believed were their formative years. Now the part of me that wanted to have a career blossomed when the opportunity to say yes to a great job presented itself.

Patrick Hennessy, the lawyer who had performed both children's adoptions, ran for district judge, won the election, and asked me to be his official court reporter. Court reporting is difficult both physically and emotionally. In becoming an official for Judge Hennessy, I had taken on the most challenging job of my whole life.

Over the next several years, I hired three different caregivers to look after our children at home as well as start dinner each day. Tony spent mornings at school and afternoons at home, and Valerie was home all day. I wanted my children at home on their own schedules, eating our food and resting, if and when they did, in their own space. Dan, a college professor, had summers off to do research at home, and he could watch the kids then.

Once neglected children may suffer from developmental delays that can be healed most effectively with the uninterrupted presence and care of the primary caregiver. (See chapter 25.)

Tony got off to a good start in kindergarten and had strong reports from his affectionate teacher. It was becoming apparent that he was gifted in many ways. Not only could he assemble, organize, and do good work by instinct, but he was also socially popular, a leader, and eager to do everything. We were happy for a strong beginning in school for our bright, spirited son.

A year later, when Valerie began kindergarten with the same teacher, we also received positive reports about her, especially her personality, her sweetness, and how she shared everything. She appeared extremely bright and was already eager to learn reading. Val was extraordinarily beautiful. She made people smile spontaneously the way we sometimes smile in front of a stunning painting or a particularly harmonious work of art. Life was great.

I volunteered to be the homeroom mother one day for Val's classroom. Class got underway. Val was very shy. She did not say much, but she was doing what she was supposed to do. She did not hang on me at all. I was introduced as Valerie's mommy. A little later one of the little girls came over to me and with no preamble said, "Valerie's a nigger." She turned abruptly and marched away.

I felt as if someone had punched me. I was doubly angry: first, at the prejudice in general, and second, at the inaccuracy of the statement. I ruefully realized that in Rock Springs in the late '70s, the kids were so unexposed to anything except white people that, for them, people were either *white*—like them, or *black*—different. They didn't even know what the word Asian meant. This was the end of my thinking that there would not be prejudice in a small town out West.

During this same academic year, Tony began first grade. He received outstanding report cards in all subjects. The only problem I can remember was a call from his teacher asking for help with a problem that arose regularly in class. Part of the curriculum fostered teamwork. The children needed to be able to work both independently as well as with each other. Tony was having problems working with a group.

That particular week, for example, the assignment had been for groups of four to work together to build a fortress. It was a teamwork assignment using building blocks, towers, and soldiers—many things both big and small. This was apparently the third project where Tony had said his classic line, "Hey, I got a great idea," then promptly told everyone to have a seat while he showed them his idea. When the other children attempted to join in, he stopped them, saying he could do it better by himself.

Tony's teacher assured me that, although it was true he could do it better by himself, the point was cooperation as a team. When the teacher forced Tony to let the other kids help, he ceased participating entirely because he felt ashamed of their work. That night we talked with Tony about teamwork, but it still made no sense to him to work with a team to build a worse fortress than he could build by himself.

> *A child's creations are a reflection of himself, so producing something "less than" confirms the deep-seated sense of unworthiness a once abandoned child may feel. (See chapter 19.)*

In the spring of that year, an event happened that would mark Tony for life. One night at supper, Tony could not eat. His head was down and he would not look at us. This was not normal behavior. I said, "Tony, what's wrong?"

"Nothing." We continued eating. It was clear from his face that something was terribly wrong. I said, "Honey, I can tell you're upset. I know something happened in school. I want you to tell me."

Tony began to cry. Through tears he said, "Paul wrote something on my paper."

"What? What did he write?" Paul was the son of a prominent banker in town.

Tony appeared paralyzed, refusing to speak at all. I knew he did not want to tell me because he was afraid he would get in trouble.

"Tony, did Paul write something mean?"

Tears continued to spill down my son's cheeks. Without looking at me, he nodded his head. I asked if he had the paper. He nodded again. I told him to go get it so we could see what Paul wrote. He cried harder, so I said, "Hey, Tony, this doesn't mean you're in trouble. You are not in trouble. We want to know what upset you."

"Paul will be mad at me."

"Well, we'll see about that. Anyway, go get the paper. We want to see it."

Tony shuffled away while we waited in silence. When he came back, he handed me his school notebook. I saw a yellow smiley face sticker over some writing.

I pulled off the sticker and read: *Roses are red; violets are blue; monkeys are black and so are you.* I was speechless and handed the notebook to Dan, then asked Tony, "Who put the smiley face over that?"

"The teacher." Tony explained that when his teacher had read the poem she had told him she would fix it by placing a smiley sticker over the insult.

I said, "Well, what did she say to Paul?"

Tony said, "Nothing. And then when I went to lunch, Paul told all the boys that I can't eat lunch with them anymore and he said I have to sit at a different table by myself." Tony sobbed openly in shame.

Dan slammed his fork down on the table, grabbed the notebook, stormed out the door to his truck, and drove straight to Paul's house to resolve the situation directly. Dan rang the doorbell, and when Paul's mom answered, he commanded, "You go get Paul and tell him Tony's dad is here to talk to him." Paul's father appeared instead to ask what had happened. Tony's notebook in hand, Dan repeated, "You get Paul out here right now. Don't worry; you're going to hear what happened."

Paul skulked into the living room, saw the notebook, and looked horrified to see Tony's father standing there. Dan said, "Did you write this on Tony's notebook?" Wide-eyed, Paul looked frightened and did not answer immediately. Dan raised his voice, waving the notebook at him. "Paul, did you write this poem on Tony's notebook? Did you?" Paul nodded sheepishly.

Dan went on, "And what's the idea of telling the boys in the lunchroom that Tony can't sit with you anymore because he's black. Who do you think you are, telling him he has to sit alone?"

The family was quiet. Dan continued, "I will not tolerate such cruelty. You have caused enormous harm to my son. He's sitting at the dinner table right now and can't even eat his supper because he is so upset. He's worried that you're still going to be mad at him tomorrow and that you'll make him eat lunch by himself from now on."

Dan then looked at Paul's parents and stated, "Prejudice is learned in the home. If your kid is talking that way, he's learning it here." In the wake of the family's stunned silence, Dan turned on his heel and left.

The next day there was a written apology on Tony's desk and at lunch Tony was included as usual. I called the teacher and told her we thought she handled the situation poorly. She defended herself, saying, "There just aren't racial issues usually and it had never happened before. I thought the best thing to do was just to ignore it."

Tony's deepest concept of himself changed that year, turning a corner that led permanently away from the spontaneous, confident, joyful child he had been before starting school. At home, we observed Tony become more guarded, as though he was afraid to take a risk.

Parents of transracial adoptees must proactively prepare themselves and their children for the likelihood of encountering prejudice. (See chapter 25.)

Valerie began first grade in the fall of 1980, when she was 6. She was quiet at school and was neither ostracized nor particularly befriended. She was always ready to share and appeared easygoing, passive, and easy to please. She was never in trouble at school. Parent-teacher consultations revealed the teacher's deep affection for Val. There were, fortunately, no racial incidents. Valerie received high praise for being at the top of her class in reading. She was strong in all areas.

Later that fall, both children started music lessons and we allowed them to choose their instruments. Tony picked the violin; Valerie picked piano. Since we had no piano then, we asked the neighbors next door if Valerie could practice at their house temporarily. If things worked out, we would buy a piano. They agreed.

A couple of months later, we got a call from next door. Embarrassed, Mrs. Stevens said Val had gone through her daughter Rachel's dresser drawers and used her makeup. Rachel was angry. Mrs. Stevens was very kind; however, she wanted our word that this would not happen again. She had made a new rule and told me Val could only be in the piano room, nowhere else, not even the bathroom.

When I hung up the phone, I exploded at Val. There stood Miss Innocence while I angrily repeated Mrs. Stevens' accusation. Val coolly replied, "Mom, I never did that at all. Whoever went in Rachel's dresser drawer, it wasn't me." I knew she was lying.

When Dan heard what had happened next door, he was even more incensed than I was, because of his own notions of privacy. The news that his daughter had snooped in someone's bedroom was intolerable to him. Dan devoted the entire evening to interrogating Val. Supper came and went. Bedtime came and went. She would not relent. Neither would he. Her staying power was astounding. I left the room; the tension was unbearable to me.

Eventually Dan came and found me. I had gotten ready for bed. It was maybe 9:30. Looking haggard, he said, "She's ready to tell the truth now." I went downstairs.

Val appeared shameless and said in a flat voice, "I went in Rachel's drawer and played with the makeup." It chilled me to see no sign of her being worn out by the long grilling. She looked as bright as Venus.

Dan asked me to take Val next door so she could apologize. I remember my embarrassment at ringing the bell so late. Mrs. Stevens came to the door and I told her Valerie had something to say. Valerie said with an angelic air, "I'm sorry I went in Rachel's bedroom and played with her makeup."

Mrs. Stevens thanked Valerie for her honesty and said she could still come over but she could only be in the living room, not in the kitchen or even the bathroom—only the room with the piano. Val said she understood the rule and we left.

The following afternoon when Val was next door practicing, I happened to walk through Dan's study where the window looked directly into the house next door. I could not believe my eyes. I saw Valerie in the kitchen where she had been expressly forbidden to go. It was not yet 24 hours since the huge harangue with her father, yet she was deliberately disobeying again.

I despaired like a mother in the Irish famine who has no ideas left for getting food. More and more I realized that something new was growing inside of me—it was naked fear about my daughter. I knew we did not have control over her.

When parents discover the power of parenting therapeutically, not only will they regain control but they will also begin to heal the unhealthy independence of a child with attachment disorder. (See chapter 25.)

Another incident took place one night after supper. The kids were already in bed when Dan discovered that the glass door at the rear of the house had wax writing on it. He was very angry and hauled both kids out of bed, herded them to the door, and asked which one had done it. They both said they had not. Then Tony offered, "But that's okay, Dad. I'll clean it up," and he made a move toward the kitchen for a rag.

Dan stopped him, "Tony, did you write on the door, did you?" Tony said, "No, I didn't." Then Valerie promptly said, "Dad, I didn't do it. I never even saw it." Dan got furious. "What the heck's going on with all these things that nobody knows anything about?" No one replied. I could hear Dan's big voice attempting to get at the truth with no results.

Dan marched Tony up to the writing that was at exactly his height. Dan pointed to it, demanding the truth, but Tony merely repeated: "Dad, I really didn't do it. I'm telling you the truth, Dad." Tony began crying, insisting, "Dad, I'm not lying. I can't help it that it's that high on the door."

Now it was Valerie's turn. Dan marched her over to the door, pointed to the wax and barked, "Look at that. It looks like your name to me. Did you write that?" Valerie started bawling. "Dad, honest, I would never lie at our house anymore, so if I did it I would tell you the truth, but I don't know anything about it. That's honest, Dad."

Having gotten no results, Dan finally put both kids back to bed, but before turning off their lights, Dan told them all activities would cease until he got the truth of this thing: no allowance, no friends over, no movie on Saturday, no fun. Nothing until whoever did it told.

When Dan and I were alone, we finally talked. The writing on the door was crazy making. I did not sense that either child was lying. They both looked terrified and truthful to me. However, Tony had offered to clean the door. Did that mean something?

Valerie had been punished so many times for lying I could not believe she would still dare lie. Moreover, her eyes had been entirely truthful. She had not been evasive at all and had looked us both straight in the eyes without a guilty demeanor. If she was lying, God help us. How would we ever be able to tell?

The next morning coming from outside our bedroom door we heard whispered conversation then raised voices, definitely nervous voices, so we knew something was up. When we opened our door, Tony was standing there. Dan said, "Have you got something to tell us?"

Tony nodded, and in that split second, my stomach churned because I thought he was going to say he had done it. But instead, Tony said, "Valerie did it." Somehow, this seemed even worse. I remembered Val's truthful eyes, her poise, and her insistence that she was innocent. Since when had she learned to look so honest when she was lying?

I looked at her face. She at least had the humility to look ashamed now. I asked when she had done it and she said she did not know. Tony piped up, "Mom, I hate to tell you this, but I saw her do it. After school when I walked into the room, she was writing on the door. When she was through, I asked her where she got the wax and she said it was a piece of candle she had found on the floor."

Tony had covered for his sister last night. Why had he done that? Was he that noble? Or was he really just showing us his true colors—his kindness and caring—not wanting his sister to get into trouble? We decided Tony must understand Val and her problems on some level, and wanted to do what he could to help.

Over the next few months, the lying incidents continued. Finally, Dan and I called a time-out to discuss what to do differently. Together we decided we would stop acting shocked when Val lied. We would attempt to act like we were taking her lying more in stride while nonetheless continuing our efforts to make her stop. Dan was worried and said if we could not eliminate the lying, we needed at least to make progress.

Can parents with a tough child ever know how strict is strict enough? All they can do is apply whatever wisdom they have figured out so far in life and do what they know to do. We decided to continue to treat lying as inappropriate but try not to become enraged. Our tools would be groundings, giving Val more responsibility, and providing more quality attention.

We decided to pour out positive reinforcement for anything she did well. We would let her earn money by doing chores around the house. We would talk a lot about trust and how lying wipes that out. We would not compare her to Tony. I would pray. That exhausted our arsenal of tools. We did not know anything else we could do that would not be considered abusive.

> *Effectively dealing with chronic lying includes nonreactively but appropriately consequencing the behavior, increasing positive reinforcement, and teaching how lying destroys trust in relationships. (See chapter 25.)*

The following year, Valerie was in the second grade. While she continued to do well in reading, we were told Valerie also excelled in math. While I was glad to know Valerie was bright, I was worried that her intelligence seemed headed in the wrong direction. I could not help but think of Dan's half-brother, Tommy, whose intelligence had gone the wrong way and had landed him in prison for life.

Val was of course still just a child, but I had read about the importance of the first six years. So far, her greatest talents seemed to be reading, being a con artist, and telling lies. I was concerned enough that I contacted a psychologist, explained her nonstop lying, and asked if it was normal. He told me that many kids lie; we should wait and see. Therefore, we waited. And we saw.

I finally turned to my boss, Judge Hennessy, and asked him to talk to Val, using his influence to alter her behavior. He had five kids and was a seasoned parent. He met with Val and then drew up a legal contract with her that remains one of my treasures of her early years. It said:

> I, Valerie Richards, promise Judge Hennessy that I won't tell a lie for one month. If I tell a lie in the next month, I may lose my friend and admirer, Judge Hennessy. I do not want to lose my friend.

> I, Judge Hennessy, promise Valerie Richards that if she does not tell a lie for a month, I will take her to lunch at McDonald's.

They both signed. However, a lie occurred the very day of the contract, so we made her write to him and explain her behavior. Valerie wrote:

> Dear Judge Hennessy,
> I told a lie on Friday. I'm kind of scared to talk to you in person. But I feel sick because I told a lie, and my mom and dad took away all of my priveliges for one month. It started April 7 and it gose until May 7 and

Sandy one of my best friend's envited me to her birthday and I could-n't go because I told a lie, and I was wondering if you could trust me enough to give me another chance and my dad thought of a cure for lieing. Wheanever I tell a lie and I know and he knows that I'm telling a lie, he will count to ten for me to tell the truth and it works! Dad and Mom soa it happen 2 times. So you tell me if you want to give me another chance.

P.S. I was wondring if I could have another chance on the contrack to patch it up and mabie we could go out to lunch together and I would take you as one of my best friends. Valerie Richards

PSS I care about your frendsihip.

Valerie drew a heart on the note with the word *mabie* inside, trailing it down to a little girl with a sad face. This contract was written at the end of Valerie's second grade school year.

The therapeutic parenting approach not only offers the explanation for such persistent lying but also the tools to address and alleviate the problem. (See chapter 25.)

During the fall of Valerie's third-grade year and Tony's fourth, things had settled down. I cherish memories of family dinners by candlelight, many weekend outings, and birthdays celebrated with cakes and gifts. Both kids joined soccer teams, and Dan and I attended every single soc-cer game. We were so proud of our children, who were making their way just fine.

It was the era of celebrating Korean Night a few times a year with another family who had adopted Korean and Vietnamese children. It was the years of taking Valerie out for tea, one of my most dear mem-ories of time alone with her. We also began our family custom of a fall trip to a bigger city, where we would rent a hotel room, go to the mall to buy school clothes, and take the kids out to dinner. Dan and I were both happy at our jobs. The family was at peace.

In the spring, Val unexpectedly changed directions academically. We were informed that she was no longer working to capacity. She was not following directions. For example, she was adding when it said to multiply, she was doing fractions upside down, and she refused to learn her times tables.

During this time, Val seemed chronically forgetful. For example, she would forget her lines in a school play as well as due dates for library books. Sometimes she would even lose them. If I gave her special jobs to earn extra money, she did them wrong, refusing to follow directions. These traits did not seem logical to me in a child who was intelligent.

Honestly, it appeared as though Valerie was already rebelling. She began raising her voice to me, saying things like, "I heard you the first time." If Dan overheard her and made her apologize, she would roll her eyes at me and choke out an insincere apology, such as, "Mother, I'm so sorry I totally ignored you."

Dan and I went in twice to see Val's teacher. She said if she could pick one pupil to keep, it would be our Val. I could understand what she was saying because I, too, was hopelessly under Val's spell. The teacher said she had been working the whole year on motivating Valerie but had not found a way and felt frustrated. On an intelligence level, Valerie was rated second in the class, but she failed math consistently. Even though she understood the concepts, she refused to follow directions, a task that actually figured into part of the grade.

This news was a surprise to us. What was going on? We decided she needed more time. With a July birthday, she was one of the youngest in the class. Possibly, she was just immature for her grade. When we reprimanded her, she got three 100s in a row in math. Then, the day of the test, she was careless and got 16 wrong out of 25. We did not know what to do.

In contrast, fourth grade had been a good school year for Tony. He was infatuated with dinosaurs and worked hard on his school projects. His teacher loved him. He did good work on everything. Tony seemed to possess a decent grasp of life, loved skiing, and had now discovered baseball.

The summer following fourth grade, Dan and I took Tony on a Boundary Waters canoe trip, which remains one of his fondest childhood memories. We were on the water for a week. Tony had plenty of occasions to gather wood, make fires, and listen to the loons. He helped on portages, read the maps with his dad, helped with cooking, slept like a log, and arose each day eager for what we had planned.

Valerie did not want to come canoeing with us, so she stayed with my sister. Carol was very eager to have her niece to herself for a whole week, but somehow things did not go well. Carol had so wanted a great week of connection and had outdone herself planning a fun week. But Val was not in the mood to do "girl things" with her aunt. Dan and I were baffled.

When a child who suffers from chronic shame is given positive atten-tion, he may feel he does not deserve it so he spoils the occasion. (See chapter 19.)

When Valerie was in fourth grade I finally sought some answers to all of my questions. I was sure something was wrong. I took Val to a psychologist for assessment. He gave her many tests. He said that on the family pictures she drew, Val consistently grouped Dan, Tony, and me together while she drew herself away from us. These drawings were significant, he said, because they showed that she did not feel she belonged in our family.

The psychologist also gave Val an inkblot test on which he based his opinion that she had not bonded with anyone in our family. I asked whether he was sure. He was sure. This was my worst nightmare. I had been so confident our love would be enough. God knew how attached to her we were! I wept uncontrollably. What book was I going to read now? How was I going to fix this? I did not know anyone whose child had not bonded. Who was going to help me? I pitched the report in the trash.

Parenting Tips

Plan to stay home with your child at first

What we now know is that in order to heal a child who has been neg-lected, the primary caregiver must spend as much quality time with that child as she would with an infant. Until he is developmentally on track, this child needs the interaction and mirroring of his primary caregiver to learn about himself and the world. If it is financially feasible for the family, it is best for the child that the primary parent remain at home with him full-time, or at the most work outside of the home part-time, hiring a single, consistent caregiver for her child in her absence.

Prepare your community for your child

Adoptees of different races and cultural backgrounds, especially, need parents to prepare those with whom they will have daily interactions for their differences. Parents can enlist the help of their child's school, church, and community leaders in the task of educating and making the community ready for their child.

Prepare your child for prejudice and give him a place to belong

It is common for adoptees to encounter prejudice, whether it is because they are adopted or because they look different from their parents and the local population in general. Before your child is exposed to potential rejection, you must arm the child with both the knowledge of why others might display prejudice toward him and the means to deal with it. Rehearse likely scenarios and debrief actual events with your child.

Nationally, there are cultural and race-specific weeklong summer camps for adoptive families where the child can interact with other adoptees from his country of origin while having his family's support. This not only gives the child a prejudice-free environment to experience, it also allows him to feel like he fits in somewhere.

In response to disobedience, use both consequences and teaching

Children with neglectful pasts have not developed the cause and effect thinking skills they need to navigate their world. As well, they are unaware of the reasons why they do what they do. Both deficits can be alleviated through consistent parental response that includes natural consequences *and* teaching. Parents need to be especially careful, however, not to introduce shame in the process.

Dan and Cassie handled Val's misbehavior at the neighbor's during the time she should have been practicing piano by employing the logical consequence of Val admitting and apologizing to the neighbor.

Next, Val's parents needed to teach her about her motive as well, which in this case was to sustain her need to *feel* in control—the only power she knew as an infant neglected by adults.

Use instant gratification to shape behavior

Just as a toddler cannot understand the concept of waiting a week for a lollipop, many adoptees, because of developmental lags, cannot respond to promises for future rewards. Parents must *allow the child to choose* to pursue the reward. In schoolwork for example, Val's parents or teacher could have said that Val could either do one problem and then go on to the next, or she could do one problem and put a penny through the slot of a glass piggy bank (so she could see the immediate results of her action) and then go on to the next problem.

Don't require sincerity

Parents need to teach children the proper way to act in a relationship, for instance, having the child apologize for a misdeed. However, requiring a child to be *sincere* about the apology will set up a power struggle. If a child needs to say he's sorry, he has the choice to say it any way he wishes. This approach still allows the parent to shape the child's behavior toward being appropriate, but gives the child his much-needed feeling of being in control.

Recognize your child's shame

Due to their original abandonment, most adopted children carry some shame. For Tony, his creations were a reflection of himself, his worth, and if he had allowed the team to build something even mediocre, an intolerable feeling of shame would have overcome him. If they had been trained in therapeutic parenting, Dan and Cassie would have looked beneath their son's behavior to find its meaning, which was that Tony was trying to prevent his deep shame from emerging by assuring that the castle was the best.

Try not to lay blame

Your child came to you at least 9 months into his development. He carries the genes of his birth parents and the experience of growing within their presence while in his birth mother's womb. Children who are adopted later in their lives have been affected by experiences they had prior to your beginning to care for them as well. Blaming yourself or their previous caregivers for what they may lack is wasting time. Accept your child where he is and meet his needs in the present—this is the most effective use of your energy.

7 A Child's Need to Appear Perfect to Feel Safe

In the fall of 1985, our family traveled to France for Dan's sabbatical year. Dan and I both spoke the language fluently, having majored in French in college. Since we intended to enroll our children in the French school system, Dan and I had devoted 12 months to teaching them survival French. They had made steady progress, accepting that they would need a basic vocabulary to get through their upcoming academic year.

In any event, by the time we left for France, both children could manage rudimentary sentences, ask for directions, describe food, conjugate many verbs, understand and use expressions of cultural courtesy—and if all else failed, they could say that they did not understand.

But how would they cope with total immersion in the French language as well as with all new classmates and teachers? They would be just as Korean in France as they were in Rock Springs. We hoped there would be no prejudice and that our children would be accepted by the French.

To help our children fit in as much as possible in their new surroundings, we had bought them the best school supplies and some new French clothes. Nevertheless, the first day of Tony and Val's school year in France, I had butterflies from imagining how scary this must be for them.

Tony was in the French equivalent of seventh grade with advanced pupils because of high grades on his American transcript. His teacher was a highly verbal, no-nonsense French grammarian. The school had arranged for Tony to have a daily French tutorial in place of the English class the French children attended.

Valerie's fate was kinder. She was placed with pupils who were above average but not superadvanced. Val's main teacher, Madame Elliot, was maternal, gentle, and especially kind. She liked Valerie immediately and said she found her to be extremely courageous. Valerie made a swift integration into Madame Elliot's class as the plucky visiting Korean-American.

Val instinctively adapted to her outer world. Within a couple of weeks she had acquired an older, distinctly un-American look, replicating even the subtleties of French fashion. It was not the new French clothes we had given her that made Val look French; it was her own adroit imitation of style and accessories: a little hair mousse here, a couple of cheap barrettes there, a fake leather belt, used brand-name socks, and a two-dollar purse. What is more, without conscious effort, Val's body gestures became more gathered, more elegant, more womanly—more French.

Valerie was positively charming in social situations. She flawlessly bestowed kisses on the cheeks in a French manner, just the right distance away to suggest intimacy but not invasion. With motherly amusement and admiration, I watched my sweet little girl turn into a beautiful, classy French babe almost overnight. I smiled to myself, "Go, Valerie!"

Children with attachment disorder are generally adept at picking up subtleties in their surroundings, a heightened skill they once needed to survive. (See chapter 18.)

While Valerie dealt with her social challenges in France in a spectacular way, her emotional adjustment was painful. Valerie hid her inner turmoil from the outside world with her clever and realistic French artifice. From what we could tell, Dan and I were the only ones allowed to see our daughter's malaise, which overtook her the moment she entered the apartment.

She was extremely moody, plagued by thoughts of being ugly, stupid, unpopular, clumsy, and uncool, no matter how much we raved to the contrary. For the first time in her life, Valerie's standard mood around the house was one of angry discontent. We could practically feel the anger rising in waves from her body. She and Tony fought constantly.

It seemed that whatever we said, she raced off in elephant sobs, insulted. When we tried to be understanding and explain the inherent moodiness of puberty, she retorted that she did not want to hear that she was normal and doing predictable things. Everything we did to be compassionate seemed only to make her more angry.

Although in public a child with attachment disorder can conceal his stress under the mask of being a model citizen, at home his anxiety often overflows in the form of difficult behaviors. (See chapter 20.)

Tony's beginnings in France did not go well—in fact, he found himself immersed in the worst experience of his life. Tony's effortless success back home did not prepare him for this entirely new cultural and academic milieu. Strong friendships had always come easily to Tony, but he had plunged into a world of anxiety fueled by fear and social challenges. For the first time in his life Tony had to implement a long list of customs, a part of everyday life in France.

Heretofore in school, Tony had earned straight As in every subject with little or no effort. In France it was clear that Tony had to work hard for even minimal grades. As amazing as it was for Dan and me to behold Valerie's instant adaptation, it was equally disheartening for us to watch Tony's world topple.

As the weeks wore on, Tony became completely overwhelmed by his teacher's expectations. In only minimally understanding French, Tony panicked when assignments were handed out. After a while, he did the only thing he knew to do—give up and shut down. Due to the stress, Tony repeatedly fell ill before school and became hostile toward everyone, especially the teacher.

Tony's main challenge stemmed from being placed in the highest academic section, in which even the French students had to work hard. His teacher, a humorless drill sergeant, took an immediate dislike to Tony because he so often said, "Je ne comprends pas" ("I do not understand"). She had little compassion for the fact that Tony began school with only five hundred words of French—a drop in the bucket in comparison with his peers. Tony's lack of adult social skills combined with his authentic guileless self left Tony with no tools to facilitate a smooth integration.

His teacher phoned us regularly to complain about Tony's "impossible attitude." She said she could hear him on the playground at least trying to speak French, while in class he remained mute, insisting he did not understand. She clearly thought he was playing games, trying to act stupid when he really knew what to do. Believing that Tony was perfectly capable, she gave him the same assignments she gave to the other students.

When a child fears he cannot perform up to expectations, his shame can cause him to withdraw or to behave poorly. (See chapter 19.)

Dan and I wanted to do what would best serve Tony. We were concerned that his lack of putting forth effort was becoming a way of life. We also were trying to reshape Tony's habitual response to problems, which was to shut down. We wanted to guide him toward becoming courageous.

In addition to having few work habits, Tony was also handicapped by what we fondly called his social dinosaur syndrome, meaning he had not yet figured out how to deal with adults and social situations in an astute, gracious way. Tony was so wrapped up in his own world that he often made unfortunate impressions on adults.

Dan and I decided it was too soon to rescue Tony. Because he was so capable, we wanted him to experience his own wake-up call. We would allow Tony to find his own way for 3 months to see if he could adapt through his own wits. We told him he had to make a strong effort in school, promising that if he did so and things still did not get better, we would do something. For the time being, we did not say what we meant by that.

At the same time, we began a series of social assignments to improve Tony's rapport with adults. We gave him specific tasks to carry out, just like other schoolwork. At school, he was required to go up to the *Directrice* and greet her with, "Bonjour, Madame," then say, "Comment allez-vous, Madame?" even if he did not understand her answer. If someone invited our family for dinner, Tony had to memorize two compliments beforehand and deliver them even if he felt shy.

We also had Tony write short thank-you notes in French and rehearse the small gestures that indicate in France one is gracious and well bred. He was required to open doors for me, to practice the French kisses-on-the-cheeks greeting and handshaking. We encouraged him to try to adjust to the French teaching style and have a good attitude.

Things went better right away. The *Directrice* contacted me, saying she thought Tony was feeling more comfortable because he shook her hand and greeted her. I cried. When friends had us over for dinner, they praised Tony for his command of French as he rattled off his two memorized compliments. Tony was surprised to discover satisfaction when adults told him he was a gentleman.

One key to diminishing a child's social shame is to increase his competence through rehearsal of social behaviors. (See chapter 25.)

Tony's schoolwork, on the other hand, did not improve much, but we could see he was trying. Tony had a memorization assignment that would have been daunting for either Dan or me, let alone for Tony. Dan and I took turns trying to help him. In the end, Tony mastered a fair amount of the poem and performed it pretty well in class. He had really worked very hard.

Valerie, too, came home with a memorization assignment. She handed it to me in a matter-of-fact way confessing she did not understand a word, then she asked me to pronounce the poem line by line. Within the hour, understanding only a small portion of the poem, Val recited the whole poem nearly perfectly. Her ability to memorize was incredible, remarkable, astounding even.

In the beginning, Valerie's professors had told her to take tests home and do them in English until she got some vocabulary. Dan would translate, and off she would go to her room to take her tests. She dug in. On her first biology test on mammals, she scored 18 out of 20, receiving a standing ovation from the whole class.

Back home, we were always nagging her to do her homework. So we were astounded that by the second month in school in France, Valerie was writing half her answers in French and by the third, reading enough French that she did not even bother with translations. This was totally new behavior.

By the fourth month, Madame Elliot handed Valerie her first French book, which Valerie read to me straight through. Then, she gave Val a second, more difficult book, telling me Valerie was the most gifted for-eign student the school had ever had. Val's school year in France, more than any other year in her life, showed her aptitude for survival under tough conditions.

For a child whose early neglectful experience consists of lying in a crib observing his surroundings, highly developed auditory and visual senses can develop. (See Chapter 20.)

But Tony continued to struggle. Unquestionably, this coursework was over Tony's head. He got low marks on everything despite the extra French lessons he received. His teacher remained intractable. In her view, Tony just was not cooperating.

In addition to feeling humiliated by his sister's academic and social success, Tony was having a difficult time on the playground also, where he was expected to discuss male fashion if he wanted to fit in. Since when did a guy care about how he dressed? Clueless about "in" labels, Tony wore the same jeans and sweater every day, not believing his peers actually cared about clothes.

Tony began getting in fights on the playground and hurt one boy so badly his parents called the school and complained about the "American bully." Inconsistent with his usual honesty, Tony hid this from us. We did not learn about the incident until the school called, at which point Tony broke down crying and could not talk.

Sports did not work out too well for Tony either. Tony's soccer coach reprimanded him for being too independent. Pummeled by so many social, academic, and cultural mishaps, Tony sank lower and lower into gloom. He seemed genuinely depressed. Dan and I anguished over how to handle Tony's situation.

After the 3-month trial period, we clearly saw that Tony needed a complete change at school. Since Madame Elliot was having a grand success with Valerie, the *Directrice* transferred Tony to her also. Madame Elliot was as gentle with Tony as she had been with Valerie. Tony applied himself diligently without complaining and began earn-ing the high grades he was used to.

With his confidence returned, Tony now became remarkably adroit at making friends with the French kids. On the playground, he would join in and do anything the others were doing, relying on his instinctively good athletic ability while not worrying about his bad French. Tony was finally considered cool.

It seemed that now, no matter what he concentrated on, Tony could do it. At the end of the school year, both children passed their equivalent grades in France by French standards and received completion certificates.

During our entire year in France, Tony and Dan had maintained a close interaction through focusing on academics. Tony grew to admire his father as the wonderful teacher he is, and Dan gained an appreciation of his son's intelligence and quick mind. When school was out, we went on a family vacation visiting castles in France, our last hurrah before returning home.

After we got home, we told our kids the sabbatical year in France had been a jewel in their backpack of life. We insisted they had received diamonds; it was just too soon for them to know it. Tony and Valerie, however, were far from convinced. They both breathed a huge sigh of relief when they got off the plane in Rock Springs.

Dan had had a great year overseas, as had I, though I felt sad at the changes between Valerie and myself. For instance, she would not go to tea with me anymore—a ritual we had shared since she was a little girl. I missed sitting across the table listening to her prattle on about this and that.

Val and I had also started fighting in France over small matters. I wanted control; I wanted her to obey me. We butted heads. I assumed her attitude was due to puberty. On the positive side, however, Dan and I had not detected any lies from Val that year. Was lying now a thing of the past? We hoped so.

Parenting Tips

Recognize your child's anxiety

Children express anxiety through their behaviors, and each child communicates it in his own unique way. Because of the stress of abandonment and possible early trauma experienced by many adoptees, these children carry higher levels of anxiety than do most of their peers. Anxiety impairs growth, learning, and all areas of development, so it is essential that you get whatever help you may need to be able to decipher your child's way of showing his anxiety.

You must learn to have compassion for your child, who yearns for safety and security above all else. Compassion establishes the frame of mind you'll need to understand why your child behaves the way he does so you can be with him in his struggles and help ease his angst.

Understand your child's need to appear perfect

Parents get frustrated when they see that it seems easy for their child to behave well in public when he can so readily fall apart at home. Unfortunately, others who only see the child's public face often blame parents for the child's poor in-home behavior. The truth is, however, that for the once-abandoned child who needs to be in control to feel safe, the pressures of navigating the world are immense.

In an attempt to assure his safety in public situations where he is on his own, this child takes control by staying under the radar and not making waves. Especially in school, if a child behaves well, he is left alone by the adults, who are busy spending their time dealing with other students' behavior problems. Home, then, becomes a relatively safe place for this child to let down his guard, and he needs his parents to understand that his consequent acting out is a plea for comfort.

Recognize depression in your child

For many reasons, depression in adopted children is common. Genetic predisposition to depression can be one cause of a child developing a mood disorder. Pre- and postnatal trauma, abandonment, and neglect are possible stressors your child might have endured, each of which overloads the child's stress response system, diminishing the ability of his brain to produce adequate serotonin, which can also lead to depression.

Typical symptoms of depression in children can be excessive irritability, difficulty sleeping, eating problems, lethargy, chronically poor self-image, lack of motivation, hopelessness, helplessness, and suicidal ideation. If you are concerned that your child may be suffering from depression, consult with your family health care provider and ask that your child be assessed.

Advocate for your child in his school

Although many adopted children strive to appear perfect in school, few actually succeed in all areas. Academic and social problems that might arise for your child in school need your attention. A parent is a child's best advocate, particularly in the school setting. Consult with your child's teacher, counselor, school psychologist, and principal to ascertain how your child is doing in all realms at school. Address any concerns by working with school staff members individually or arrange for a team meeting to draw up a plan to help your child. Be persistent if necessary, because often staff are dealing with many other things and may not prioritize your child's needs.

8 Lying, Stealing, and Disruptive Behavior

Our kids resented us for dragging them off to France the previous year. Tony, 13 and starting eighth grade, was mad at us. Seventh grade had been the first year of junior high school and the time when the basketball teams were formed. Our year in France had cost Tony a place on the team.

Moreover, entering junior high a year later than everyone else, Tony was the only new kid; once again he felt like an outsider. Lastly, he resented being short, having buckteeth, and having to get braces. Tony was miserable and going down.

Due to experiencing infant trauma and chronic stress, some adopted children are at risk for developing depression. (See chapter 22.)

Valerie, now 12 and in seventh grade, was potent. She returned from France in a woman's body. She easily looked 16. Her social skills were stunning. She flashed new body language daily. Jumping hormones made her bold, set on getting her way, and ready for male attention. She refused to associate with seventh graders; it was eighth graders or nothing. Dan was adamant that she not cross grade lines for either girlfriends or boyfriends. After all, she was practically the youngest seventh grader in her class as it was.

Overnight Val had resumed lying and sneaking. From the get-go, her schoolwork was abominable. Within a few weeks, Val's behavior toward me shifted and then locked into undisguised coldness. I took it personally. Having been so enmeshed with my own mother, I found it unimaginable, and unimaginably painful, that my daughter was no longer close to me. I analyzed where I might be going wrong. I did so need her to love me.

One day while washing my hands, I studied my hurt face in the bathroom mirror. Suddenly I heard Val's taunting singsong voice, "Oh, there's Mom looking in the mirror, wondering whether she's a good mother or not."

I froze. Guilty. Val had guessed my thoughts accurately. Déjà vu memories of my mother flooded me. My mother's uncanny ability to know what I was thinking was a far worse invasion of my privacy than her barging in on me had been. But Val was only 12. She could not possibly be that psychologically astute. Still, I felt exposed. Bravely, I assured myself that Val had just made a lucky guess.

A child with attachment problems will push his parents' buttons in order to feel secure by attempting to gain control, yet if he is successful, the child will actually feel less secure. (See chapter 23.)

That fall, Tony was caught shoplifting a candy bar. Dan fielded the call and went to the store. I found out after work. We asked Tony many questions. Embarrassed and moved by our concern, he confessed. In the context of his whole life, it was a small thing. We grounded him and let it go.

We had barely processed that event when a new one arose, this time with Valerie. She raced home from school in an ecstatic mood. An eighth grader had asked her out for her first date Friday night. They wanted to go hang out on campus with university kids.

For the time being, I ignored the eighth grade part, saying simply, "Val, of course you can't go. You know darned well you have not earned night privileges yet because of the many trust issues Dad and I have with you."

I was not prepared for her venom. "I hate you!" she hissed. This was a first. Then she fired, "The only thing that stands between me and happiness is you. I had a perfect year going. It was *perfect,* and now you're ruining my social life."

I said, "Valerie, your social privileges are in your own hands. As long as we can't trust you, you won't have night privileges. I guess you'll have to convince the boys that you're worth waiting for."

Though I was hurt by her words, I believed she did not truly mean them. Adolescence was here and she was mad. I decided not to react and instead congratulated myself on being a tough mom. In truth, though, I did not feel tough. I felt sad because Val always got mad at me, never at Dan. Why was I singled out as the bad guy? Since Dan and I decided things together, why did she never get mad at him?

As a result of being abandoned by his birth mother, the adopted child will tend to act out his anger and fears toward his adoptive mother rather than his adoptive father. (See chapter 23.)

Two weeks after Tony stole the candy bar, I came home to a dramatic scene in full swing. Dan was red in the face and both kids looked petrified. Someone had stolen 25 dollars from Dan's pants pocket. Dan had counted the bills the night before, and now a 20 and a 5 were missing. Both kids denied taking the money. Though Dan threatened to ground them both, neither said a word. Dan told Valerie he was going to search her room first. She opened drawers, bags, and private corners, and showed Dan the small amount of money she had. He found nothing.

Dan told Valerie to stay with us while he searched Tony's room. We all went upstairs. My eyes bulged when Dan uncovered a dozen expensive-looking books in Tony's dresser. Dan asked, "What are these?" and Tony replied, "They're *D&D* books." Tony was fond of *Dungeons & Dragons,* a fantasy game involving castles, maps, characters, and even a dungeon master. I whispered softly, "Antoine, you stole these."

Indignant, he blurted, "Mom, I didn't steal them. I bought them when I was earning money, and then I exchanged. . . ." I was not listening. I could taste my fear; I knew he was lying. Dan harped on the missing money until Tony broke down. "Well, Dad, if I confess, what will happen?" Dan said, "Give the money to me immediately."

From his pants pocket Tony handed over 7 bucks and said he had spent the rest in a game room. I was unprepared for this new dark side of my son: Tony sneaking into the bathroom while we slept? Our son's beautiful hands in Dan's wallet?

Dan moved on to the other matter. "How many books did you steal?" Tony lied hoarsely, "Only two. . . ." But Dan had already picked up all the books. He hauled them out to the garbage can. Tony watched, looking sick. He hid in his room the rest of the day.

The second evening, Dan checked the garbage to be sure the books were still there. They were gone. This time I hit the roof. I flew into Tony's room yelling, "Tony, where are those books? And do not insult my intelligence by saying you don't know."

Sheepishly, he told me. I screamed away in my car, retrieved the books from Tony's friend's house, stormed home, called Tony downstairs, and slammed paper and pencil in his hand. "Sit down," I commanded. He sat. I picked up a book, my mouth a slit. "Okay. Write down when you stole these, the store, and the amount." One by one, Tony recorded details.

Tony confessed to stealing on more than 20 separate occasions at two different stores. The *D&D* books were worth over a 150 dollars in all. He had stuffed them in his backpack while a friend watched the aisle.

I made Tony write admission letters to the store owners, asking for appointments to arrange restitution. I drove him to the bank and made him withdraw every cent he had—100 dollars. It was not enough. He asked, "Mom, can I borrow the rest from you?"

I said, "No way. Absolutely not. This is your problem, not mine." I drove him to meet the store owners. He apologized and made partial restitution. Next I drove him to the local paper and turned off the engine. I told him to go in and apply for a paper route so he could complete his restitution. He did so.

I went to Judge Hennessy for advice. I wanted to replicate the judge's procedures for handling stealing. He told me to ask Mr. Hall, the chief probation officer for our district court, to speak with Tony. Mr. Hall met with Tony for an hour.

Mr. Hall called me later to report how controlled and stoic Tony was. He said, "Your kid could sit and listen to my lecturing 7 days a week without flinching." Hall advised me to put Tony in therapy with Mr. Ulrich, who specialized in treating male adolescents.

Tony began seeing Pete Ulrich. My request to Ulrich was that he help Tony understand why he stole and also help him express his emotions. Meanwhile, I worked on accepting that Tony seemed to have two separate halves. He continued to make the honor roll while his "dark side" cast a growing shadow.

> *The adrenaline high that comes with the act of stealing can be one reason children with depression steal. (See chapter 22.)*

During this same time, Val and I were involved in a hurricane of disputes. We argued over her friends, clothes, and study habits. She remained relentlessly disrespectful, deceitful, and untrustworthy. No matter what we said or did, Val hung out exclusively with eighth graders. Nothing at home was right for her. She said it was too clean and she could not be herself.

She was in my face all the time except when she needed something. Then she would switch gears, seducing me with her smile, acting silly, begging me to say yes. I gladly accepted every kindness, but I could not keep up with her. I felt constantly off balance. Sleep, my once-dependable source of renewal, no longer restored me. I felt increasingly drained.

Val provoked fights; I called it "coming after me." She would ask permission to do something she knew was forbidden. When I said no, she would blow up, scream insults at me, slam her bedroom door, and thunder music throughout the house. I was overwhelmed and broken-hearted from her constant rejection. I spent all my energy priming myself for her next assault.

Eventually I figured out that when I got sad, Val got happy. Several times when Val and I were alone at home, she caught me in a moment of obvious depression. Then she hummed and bustled about the house, suddenly content. What was going on in her head? I wondered. She was cunning, though, and rarely let her father see her cruelty to me. Thus, when I told Dan about it, he dismissed me as oversensitive. My confidence deteriorated.

Dan was due to leave for a 4-day conference. I dreaded his absence because Valerie habitually saved her worst behavior toward me for when he was gone. When I would relate my woes to Dan upon his return, Valerie would shake her head in mock innocence as if to say, "Boy, isn't she something? Man, I feel for you, Dad, being married to her." I felt incompetent at such moments. I did not understand her behavior.

Children who harbor deep shame about themselves will often project their self-hatred onto their primary parent—usually their adoptive mother. (See chapter 23.)

Dan left on a Wednesday. The kids had Friday off from school. Friday morning I was in my home office when Val swept in, all smiles, face made up, stylishly dressed. She and her friends had decided as a group to head up to the campus to see what was going on. I told her she had my permission but that she should be home absolutely no later than 2:30.

I went out to do errands, and when I returned home at 3 o'clock, Valerie was not there. When she finally returned, she said she had forgotten our agreement. Pretending to be flustered, she purred, "Boy, excuse me, Mom. I just don't know where my head was. I completely spaced out what you said." There she stood victorious, radiant, telling me what a great afternoon she had had.

I told Val she was grounded and I hoped her memory would improve. She hummed happily to let me know that my punishment had no effect on her great mood. I said, "Valerie, you know what? Your behavior is inappropriate. You're so phony." I walked away and went to take a bath.

Later on, she asked me what video I had rented to watch that night. I said I had a good film for myself but that she could not watch it because she was grounded.

Val left, then returned again a few minutes later, asking, "Can I go and play at Sandy's?" I felt nuts from her relentless attempts to manipulate me. Whenever Dan was gone, Val tried to push me over the edge. I sighed, determined not to lose my temper, then suddenly boomed, *"Get out of here and leave me alone!"*

Five minutes later she returned, pleading in a syrupy voice to let her play with my business typewriter. I got a lot less nice. "Valerie," I said thickly, "I'm warning you, I'm feeling dangerously angry. Get in your bedroom and do whatever you want in there. I do *not* want to see your face again tonight."

Her eyes, pools of disgust and hatred, blazed into mine. She left. I sat and stared at nothing. I was a nervous wreck. Val had won. I turned off the TV and herded my drained body upstairs to the sanctuary of my bedroom and shut the door to find peace.

Not 15 minutes later, Val barged into my room without knocking, asking to borrow my 200-dollar professional court reporter's headset to listen to her music. I reacted without thought, letting rip a string of profanity while I pounded my mattress. At least I did not hit her. I pointed to the door and screamed at her to get out of my bedroom.

Satisfied at last that she had gotten me to lose it, Val turned flippantly, went downstairs, and slammed her bedroom door as the last word. We never spoke about that Friday night.

An insecure child will test his primary parent relentlessly in order to reassure himself that she is strong enough to handle him. (See chapter 23.)

Saturday night I had invited a new friend, Lisa, a lawyer I had met in court and her two children over to watch a video and eat pizza. I told my kids I did not want any fighting. Her daughter was a bit older than Tony and her son was around Valerie's age.

The four kids went off to play while Lisa and I poured ourselves a glass of wine. We had not been visiting 10 minutes when Tony burst into the room. Clearly embarrassed, he blurted through tears, "Valerie just told Lisa's kids that I was convicted of a crime and I'll be going to prison soon."

Stunned, I recalled our family agreement never to mention the *D&D* book stealing episode because it could destroy Tony's reputation. Valerie had given her word of honor, yet here she was violating our family agreement.

Val's intentional audacity shocked me. She showed no fear of consequences. Out of my league but determined not to lose control, I imitated Dan's mom. I quietly told Val we would deal with this matter when her father got home. She fastened hateful eyes on Tony, furious that he had tattled on her.

By Sunday, she was in a lethal mood. That afternoon was Val's piano recital on the college campus. Her teacher had asked her to wear a dress; instead, she put on jeans. She hurled vulgarities at me regarding the dress, the weather, and the piano. I ignored all that and told her to hurry up and change because we had to leave. She put a dress on.

Thirty minutes later, I sat in the audience with all the other proud parents, struggling to overcome my stress, hoping our fights would not affect Val's performance. I need not have worried, however. Val glided like silk onto the stage. Her teacher gave her a big smile. Val played like a pro, then snapped off the stage. Afterward, she remained aloof when her peers raved about her performance. Many of them had been nervous and had made mistakes.

When Dan got home from his trip Sunday night and I told him what Val had done to Tony, he grounded her for 15 days. The next day, because I had to work a friend of mine picked up Val after school. She later phoned me to say that at Val's request she had dropped Val off at one of her friend's instead of bringing her home.

Val lied when she came home, saying she had stayed late at school. That night Dan grilled Val until she admitted her made-up story. He then told her she could spend the whole grounding period in her bedroom, including eating her meals there. She could have no radio, no telephone, nothing.

What could we do next, we wondered. Take away her food? Chain her to a bedpost? What meaningful consequences can parents employ with a child like that? Sometime during those 15 days, we received Val's first report card. All Cs. No surprise—we rarely saw her working.

In order for consequences to work, a child must value the relationship with his parents enough to want to please them so he can remain in their good graces. (See chapter 24.)

My fears about parenting Valerie grew. At home, she was perpetually angry. She instructed me *never* to say I loved her. I was not to hug or kiss her either. When Dan heard this, he told Val, "Well, whatever goes for Mom goes for me too. If you don't want Mom to tell you she loves you, then I won't either." I knew Val would blame me for taking her dad's affection away.

One afternoon when I was in the basement, I heard a crash and raced to the stairway to see my sewing machine cracked in two at my feet. Val stood at the top of the stairs. She said coldly, "I had an accident," and stomped off. I was incensed, and more so when Dan refused to believe Val had done it purposely. Why was Dan unable to see her malice toward me? He calmly suggested that I get a new sewing machine as he thought it would be good for Val to continue sewing. I refused.

A child's underlying unmanageable anxiety can lead him to push harder for what he desperately needs: his parents to stand strong and remain nonreactive so he can feel secure. (See chapter 23.)

I again went to the person whose advice I trusted most, Judge Hennessy, and confided that my life felt out of control, that Val frightened me. To my surprise, he did not support me. Instead, he lovingly told me to shape up and stop feeling sorry for myself. He said, "For God's sake, Cassie, if your knees are shaking, put on a long skirt so Val can't see it." His wisdom was lost on me. I continued to parent the only way I knew how.

Notwithstanding the stealing incident, Tony appeared to be doing so well at school and at home that we began to focus less on his needs while we devoted most of our attention to Valerie. Battles with Val over control issues were a daily occurrence.

After a long contest of wills over the need for winter boots, we finally gave her complete freedom over what she wore. She could wear nylons, heels, any kind of clothing as long as it was not revealing. We allowed her to shave her legs, color her hair, and wear whatever shade of lipstick she wished. We even gave up our insistence that she dress for the weather.

I gave Val a start-up batch of makeup. My only rules were that she not wear makeup to church and not use mine. I soon discovered that she had been sneaking mine regularly. Dan asked her how my makeup had gotten in her room. She replied confidently, "Mom gave it to me." I sputtered, "That is a total lie." Sadly, I felt lucky that day. At last Dan had seen the truth and supported me.

After many discussions on how to build character, Dan and I decided to try something new. Together we drew up an assignment on trust and asked Val to complete it over the weekend. Her response was:

Part One—Things I Like:
(1) I like the fact that my parents don't fight (very often) because if they fought all the time everyone would be sad. (2) I like choosing my friends because I think they're nice. (3) I like my brother because he doesn't get into other people's business. (4) I like my family's friends because they're all nice. (5) I like watching movies with my family because it's fun. (6) I like our fall shopping trip away from home because nobody fights.

Things I Hate:
(1) I hate rules because I can never follow them. (2) I hate myself because I can't ever do anything right. (3) I hate it when Tony's doing well and I'm not because he always says so and makes me feel bad. (4) I hate the fact that my cat Fossette is dead because I miss her company. (5) I hate it when my parents yell at me because I know it's my fault and I don't want to believe it. (6) I hate the fact that I'm the one who always makes everyone mad because I always feel guilty afterward.

Part Two—Trust and Rules:
I'm untrustworthy and can't follow rules. To be trustworthy you have to be able to do things honestly without lying, lying about little mistakes, saying I practiced when I didn't, not wearing my boots when I should have, taking mom's makeup and saying I didn't.

To build trust you could say, "Sorry, mother I didn't do that today" instead of saying—(distrust), "Oh, yeah, mother. I did it today" when you haven't done what you were supposed to. You could build a reputation by always telling the truth and never cheating.

I haven't established trust in any areas. To follow a rule you don't lie about not following it. Also you always follow it. Never disobey a rule. Rules are made to be followed. So I don't turn out like Uncle Tommy and because nobody will like me if I lie when I grow up.

They said to be trustworthy is a very important thing in life and if you're like me, I won't ever get a job because nobody can trust me. And if I do something and lie about it, I might go to jail and nobody will like me and they want people to say, "Gee, Valerie sure is trustworthy. I like what the Richards are putting into their children."

I don't have any disagreements with the trustworthiness. I think it's very important too. And I think I should really work on it. Tell them what my parents have told me. Yes, I do think honesty is important because if people think you lie, then they'll never trust you again.

When Dan and I read what she wrote, we thought she was simply telling us what we wanted to hear. In retrospect, we now believe that Val was telling her truth, and we had missed it.

Though a child with attachment disorder yearns to be accepted and feel worthy, his core shame drives him to act in ways that alienate him, reinforcing his poor self-concept. (See chapter 19.)

In the aftermath of the *Dungeons & Dragons* incident, Tony had started seeing Mr. Ulrich for counseling. After several sessions, Ulrich told Dan and me that Tony was not by nature a thief and would probably never steal again if we could give him something challenging to focus on instead. Ulrich said we had handled the theft incident well.

Then he shifted and told Dan, "You're the one Tony needs now. He will always be close to his mom, but right now he needs to be with you. That's because, like you, he's an introvert. He admires you wildly and now wants to be with you, the other 'dinosaur' in the family, to form the bond of manhood. He needs his dad." Ulrich told Dan to take Tony camping, fishing, and into the wilderness twice a year faithfully from now on. Dan agreed.

In December, Valerie told us she did not know anyone in school who hated their parents more than she hated us. Dan asked why she hated us. She said, "Because of your rules. I hate rules." Dan suggested that she help us make the rules so she would have input. Val protested, "I don't want to cooperate with you on anything!"

By the third week of December, our Christmas tree was up, the presents were wrapped, and the cookies were baking. Val had already reduced the holiday mood to misery. She was acting out right on schedule, just before a festive family event.

Dan and Val ended up in a screaming match about her not keeping her word. When her anger escalated to rage, Val went bonkers, grabbing some Christmas ornaments and smashing them, one after the other, against the wall of her bedroom until Dan grabbed her arm to restrain her.

Val let out a bloodcurdling shriek, at which point Dan smacked her. He took away all of her things for one week—makeup, hairspray, and jewelry. He even took away all her clothing except for one outfit for school, a pair of boots, and her hairbrush.

A few days later, Val threatened to commit suicide by overdosing on aspirin. I found the aspirin bottle in her room and removed it. We had no idea if she really meant it or not, but Dan did not buy her threat. I was not so sure.

Val had seen Mr. Ulrich twice in December and was now in ongoing therapy, so we could at least assure ourselves that we had a professional involved. I felt afraid from morning until night, yet I still could not stop being mad at her.

A child does not threaten suicide in order to manipulate others— at his core, a part of him really does want to die. (See chapter 25.)

On Christmas morning, Valerie raved about all her presents except one. In order to be sure my gift would please her, I had even asked her girlfriends to help me pick it out. When Val opened it, she sighed and commented to no one in particular, "Boy, it's just not me."

To top it off, when my face fell, Val snidely remarked that I always show my hurt. I said nothing. Each time Val tromped on my feelings, it took longer for me to return to normal.

Dan and I were now fighting as well. Having come to the point where he did not trust that I could handle Valerie, Dan came up with an idea. Henceforth, whenever Val and I were fighting, he said he would make us stop and each state our viewpoint to him. Dan continued and said he would arbitrate and decide who was right.

Incredulous, I yelled at him, "Are you crazy? Who do you think you are? For God's sake, Dan, we have to stick together."

The next morning, Dan apologized. Though relieved to hear his words, I declared, "I am going to stop parenting Val until I can figure this out. I'm too mad to even cope anymore. If you can't cope either, then she can just raise herself." I told him I was losing my ability to restrain my reactions and was afraid I might soon resort to my mother's tactics.

Then Valerie began a new assault. She began displaying inordinate affection toward Dan. I said, "Dan, every month it's a new worse thing.

There's never peace. What's going on at our house is not normal. Can't you see that?" Dan said nothing.

Valerie now monopolized Dan. Each night after dinner, Val would run to sit on Dan's lap or engage him with her homework. If Dan and I were talking, Val would race into the room to interrupt us, trying to kiss him, all the while ignoring me or acting ice cold toward me. Dan did not know how to handle her behavior. I could not understand why he did not just tell her to knock it off.

No matter what Dan did, Val poured adoration on him. Even after that time Dan had hit her, she was not mad at him. After he took away everything but one school outfit, she was not mad at him. In fact, she haughtily pronounced that no one at school had even *noticed* she was wearing the same thing every day.

With Dan at the helm, Val took things in stride. She played her new-found role to the hilt, prancing around the house cooing, "Dad, I just can't tell you how much I love you. You've made me so happy. I feel like a beautiful person when you're parenting me instead of Mom."

A child with attachment disorder will also test his father to see if he will set the limits necessary to give him the unshakable security he craves. (See chapter 25.)

On New Year's Eve, as I sipped my wine, I reminisced about the delightful Christmas Eve we had spent with friends—the one reprieve of the season. But, as the wine warmed me, my thoughts returned to reality. I remembered the ending of Steinbeck's *Grapes of Wrath*. I felt like Rose of Sharon, who, defeated by the events of her life, sat in a daze in the empty boxcar passively watching the rising water that would soon consume her.

By the time January arrived, I had no choice but to seek help outside the family. I went to Mr. Ulrich. During my first visits with him, I delivered my perspective on my relationship with my mother, my marriage with Dan, my close connection with Tony, and the hostilities with Valerie. I voiced my concern that according to past testing, Valerie was apparently not bonded to our family.

Mr. Ulrich affirmed my impressions and said we should meet jointly with Dan. His support calmed me. When Dan and I met with him, he offered several suggestions for handling our complicated family issues.

He directed me to figure out what Val set off in me and then learn to detach from it rather than react. He told me to limit my conversations with her to the words "Is that so?" The bottom line was that I needed to learn to manage my sensitivity. He told us to stop worrying about Val's values because they were already a "done deal." He did not feel her lying was pathological since she could admit to the behavior.

Next, Ulrich asked Dan to stop dismissing Valerie's show of hostility toward me. He also insisted that Dan show Valerie neither attention nor affection but simply administration. Dan was never again to allow Valerie to sit on his lap. Evenings were to be exclusively time for Dan and me. He said we needed a unified strategy so Val could not play Dan against me.

Finally, Ulrich suggested a less rigid structure in our home. He said for us to keep things simple, write up a contract outlining chores and consequences, face things as we experienced them, and not talk much to Val. Despite his good advice, my overriding feeling at the end of that hour was negative because I felt helpless to carry out so many radical changes.

Since the therapeutic parenting approach can seem so foreign, parents need step-by-step instructions, ongoing guidance, and practice over time to be successful. (See chapter 25.)

A few days later I met with Val's school principal, Sid Oberg. We were to discuss the possibility of Val skipping the rest of seventh grade. He greeted me and said we had other things to discuss before we got to the topic of changing grades.

Mr. Oberg's tone turned solemn. As he looked me directly in the eyes, he said, "Cassie, seventh grade is often a very rough year for mothers. This is the year when their girls become women. The race of hormones is on."

His confidence in addressing this delicate topic made me respect him immediately. Then he asked, "How are things going at home?" I could sense a ripple of tears beginning and felt mortified. I did not dare speak for fear of a torrent.

I composed myself and related our essential dilemma. In France, Valerie had been the latest wonder of the world. Since coming home, she had refused to work in school, disobeyed us constantly, hung out only with eighth graders, and incessantly asked permission to date much older boys. Her demands were wearing us down. She looked and dressed as if she were 16. Valerie told me she hated me and that it was my fault she was not happy.

My face was hot with shame. Mr. Oberg reassured me that Valerie dressed and acted appropriately at school, a sign of good upbringing. I felt somewhat relieved by knowing that. Then he asked an amazing question, "Cassie, do you and Dan know that raising adopted kids is generally a much harder task than raising biological kids?"

My head jerked up. Wide-eyed, I said, "Absolutely not! I've never even *heard* of that."

Oberg nodded. "That's what I was afraid of," he said. "I want to tell you something I've learned in my many years as a principal at four schools in different states. Throughout my career, I've documented time and time again that adopted kids have a more difficult time emotionally than do other adolescents. That notion is now so firmly fixed in my mind that I can even anticipate what struggles they will likely have."

He explained, "The reason adoptees have a rough time is because they all are abandoned sometime during childhood. That's what makes adoption possible. They suffer a deep wound from their biological parents giving them up—abandoning them—and because of that they feel they are unlovable.

"Most of the time, they take these feelings out on their adopted mom because they fear that maybe she, too, will get rid of them. So they decide they might as well get it over with and act terrible on purpose to see if that's going to happen. These kids will do it over and over again because they're immature and feel worthless and sad inside."

I sat spellbound while my hot tears flowed. As if he were reading my mind, Mr. Oberg said, "Parents of adopted children often have a really hard time even if they are extremely good parents." Maybe I was not some awful mother after all.

When I told him that psychological testing had shown that Valerie had never bonded with us, he said that happened on a regular but unpredictable basis with adopted kids. He reiterated how often he had seen unbonded adolescent girls turn in hatred on their adoptive mothers.

Then Mr. Oberg looked right at me and asked, "Cassie, are you taking it personally?" His sympathy set off a meltdown. Through buffalo sobs, I answered, "Yes, I am. How am I supposed to take it any other way when she tells me it *is* personal!"

He said softly, "Cassie, I have such compassion for you. Let me tell you a few things about Valerie you may not know. First of all, she's a model student here at school. She very much reflects, I'm sure, the values you are modeling at home. She's extremely popular, a class big shot. Your parenting has made her polite around adults, even charming. I really, really like her. I'm so sorry for your pain at home, but let me say that at least you can be proud of her behavior at school."

Mr. Oberg continued, "It's worse when the reverse is true. Some of these kids will act okay around their parents and then at school, all hell breaks loose—they get in serious trouble with teachers, they steal, and get involved with the law." He said kindly, "As hard as it is for you at home, you and Dan should take comfort in knowing that when Valerie is in public, she's a dutiful, respectful, well-groomed, and polite student who is liked very much by both faculty and students."

Finally, Mr. Oberg said, "Regarding Valerie skipping seventh grade, I will not allow that to happen and nothing will make me change my mind. She is way too weak academically."

I insisted, "She's only pretending to be average."

Mr. Oberg shook his head, "Every one of Valerie's teachers agrees that she is incapable of A-level work even in the seventh grade, much less in the eighth. They just do not see her as that smart. Typically a child who skips a grade is one who doesn't fit in with her grade peers, whereas Val fits in everywhere."

Oberg concluded, "Being concerned about grades, earning privileges from parents, negotiating the date scene, dealing with curfews and groundings—all of these issues are standard grist for the seventh-grade mill. What is not standard is that your children are adopted."

He advised, "When your adopted kids eventually feel the wound of abandonment, you can anticipate hard times ahead for them. When that happens, you should ask for help. Try not to take things personally. Do not cave in. All kids need to be disciplined and loved. You're doing a good job, Cassie." He came around the desk and hugged me hard, saying, "Hang in there and believe in yourself. You're a great mom, Cassie. Okay?"

Mr. Oberg's news was an epiphany for me. This was the very first moment in my life as a parent that anyone had given me concrete reasons why I might be having so much trouble with my daughter. I had always felt that I had been the problem. I felt jubilant. Now I had proof that adoption played a role in my troubles with Valerie. I left feeling both supported as a mother and confirmed as a good parent.

I rode the wave of jubilance home only to crash and burn when Dan summarily rejected what Mr. Oberg had said. He simply did not believe that adoption had anything to do with our situation at home. Dan's response felt dismissive to me, and so quickly again, I was all mixed up.

Denial that adoption can have profound effects on children and families limits parents' access to the very help that they need. (See chapter 24.)

That spring I showed up in low spirits for a family session at Ulrich's office. I was still down in the dumps because of Dan's refusal to even consider what Mr. Oberg had said. I wanted Ulrich to support me and get Dan to change his mind.

After a go-nowhere discussion between the five of us, Ulrich proposed a family vote to see if anyone besides me thought the adoption was related to why Valerie rejected me with such hostility. Predictably, Dan, Tony, and Valerie all voted against the notion.

I felt betrayed. Ulrich's stupid poll had the effect of pitting the whole family against me. He had not given me one word of support, and instead just shrugged his shoulders as if to say, "Well, so much for that."

To make matters worse, when we were leaving, Ulrich whispered to me, "Cassie, try to ready yourself for the awful years ahead, possibly worse than you can even imagine. Try to stay away from her. When she talks to you, just say, 'Oh, really?' " Dumbfounded, all I could do was stare back at him. I felt numb.

As I left Ulrich's office, I felt my mental state deteriorate rapidly to a point even lower than it had been before my talk with Mr. Oberg.

That spring, Valerie exacerbated my bottomed-out mood by sabotaging Dan's birthday. He wanted a simple family dinner. Just as Dan poured the champagne for a toast, Val's behavior disintegrated. She turned on the TV and refused to join us.

In an attempt to liven things up, Dan asked the kids to play a little music for him. Tony played two short pieces on his violin, performing beautifully. Val refused to pick a song and told me to pick one. I named a song she knew well.

While Dan and I sat holding hands, Val proceeded to pound on the keys, hit wrong notes, and slap the sheet of music repeatedly. Dan finally told her to stop. That did it. She huffed off to her room, slamming the door, and did not return. Dan opened his gifts in sadness without her.

Afterward, he told me to go tell her she was ruining his birthday. So I dutifully went to her room and said, "You know, you're being really selfish to choose the night of your father's birthday to get ugly." She cut me off, sobbing, "It's incredible how much I hate you."

The level of her emotion was shocking. I yelled back, "I am not interested in your hatred, Valerie. You will be a polite child to your father on his birthday. Now get out there and behave." She did come out but then cried her way through the entire birthday dinner, ruining the special event.

The next day was Easter. Val's foul mood continued even at church. When we got home, Dan raised his voice, "What the hell is going on with you? I want to know."

Val declared, "I hate Mom." Dan insisted that she tell him why. She said, "Mom bothers me in every single way. Mom just being in the house makes me hate her. I wish she wasn't here. I just want to be with you."

Dan said, "Val, you know that would be impossible. Mom is my partner, not you." Valerie burst into sobs. She said, "I already know that. That's why I hate her. It's because of her that I can't be with you." Tony and Dan were hearing the Valerie I knew. Now nobody could say I was exaggerating.

Around the same time, Tony was caught stealing again. This time it was at school. He confessed it to us immediately. He paid back the teacher, who made a hero out of him for having come forward. Because of Ulrich's reassurance that Tony was not a thief, we continued not to overly worry about the stealing. Tony was doing good work in school.

Nevertheless, remembering the recommendation of the therapist to find more challenging tasks to occupy Tony's time, we went ahead and arranged for Tony to spend Mondays after school at an architect's office. He appeared genuinely excited and soon began drafting house plans in his spare time.

In early May, we had another family session with Mr. Ulrich. I don't know why I even agreed to go back to him, but in the end, I was glad I did. This visit, the focus was to be on Val expressing her feelings.

It took Ulrich quite a while to coax Valerie into speaking in front of us. When she finally did, she said she did not know who she was. She wanted above all to hide her intelligence so she would not be different from other kids. She explained that our telling her that it was a dead end to love her father the way she did was pointless; it was what her heart told her she felt.

She said her hatred for me was temporary but that it was not some game and she was not kidding. She explained that her hostility was always tied to something precise and was not a feeling that was there all the time. She said she also felt a great love for me. Finally, she loudly denied that she was jealous or vengeful toward me as some consequence of being abandoned by her Korean mother.

I was shocked by the forthrightness of Valerie's words during this session. She had made enormous admissions. The overall goals of the therapy had been to encourage Valerie to accept herself as she was and to help her build self-confidence. We had hoped it would work.

Following that session, Val's anger seemed to be gone. She actually hummed around the house and appeared content. For a while, we decided, she would continue meeting with Ulrich monthly.

With training and guidance, parents can learn how to give their child the safety and support he needs to speak his truth and to discover what drives his behaviors. (See chapter 25.)

At the end of the school year, Valerie received the school's French award—she had scored the highest marks of any student in the school, even those much older and in more advanced classes. As Val received her award, some guys shouted, "Hooray for Valerie, the most beautiful girl in the seventh grade!" Val beamed a smile a mile wide, clearly pleased at the attention.

As well, out of the 300 students in her class, Valerie had been elected one of two class representatives who would serve on student council the following academic year. Winning this honor meant that the students respected her and accepted her as a leader. Valerie almost passed out when she won.

A few days later, Val admitted to us that because she was now a class representative, she was ashamed of her grades. At the beginning of the year, she had not wanted to appear intelligent, fearing it would not be cool. Now she was changing her mind. Class reps were usually the best students. During the entire seventh grade, even the consequence of missing night privileges because of poor grades had not motivated Val to apply herself, but now she had reason to work hard and she promised a big change for next year. I was so glad these thoughts were her own.

Around this time, Tony truly began adolescence, and we saw many changes in him, including an increase in moodiness. As suggested by Ulrich, Dan attempted a one-on-one activity with Tony. Dan chose a shop project, because for him, shop work gave him a chance to relax and have fun. But Tony approached this project like he did most creative endeavors—with a perfectionist attitude. What was initiated out of hope to be a father-son activity they both would enjoy soon fell apart when Tony began criticizing the way Dan did things. Dan quickly lost his motivation to continue.

Most parents are not prepared to effectively handle a child's need to hide his shame under perfectionism. (See chapter 19.)

That spring Tony was involved in another minor stealing incident. It was then that I insisted he return to individual counseling. Predictably, he did not want to go back. I knew Tony would feel mortified if he had to see Ulrich after promising never to steal again. So I decided it was just as well to make a change. Tony began counseling with a new therapist, Mrs. Gibson.

Parenting Tips

Spend time with your child after school

In the school environment, your child operates in overdrive just to survive. By the time he crosses the home threshold, his energy is depleted. Parents need to accept and prepare for this reality proactively in order to meet their child's needs so he doesn't have to express them with poor behaviors. A positive, low-key parent-child after school ritual such as sharing a snack on the porch works to transition your child.

As well, after being on his own all day at school, it is vital that your child shift his dependence back to you when he is at home to enhance attachment. He needs your help in negotiating his feelings and responsibilities, saving any energy he may have left for just the essentials. If homework becomes a significant source of stress, talk to his teachers about reducing or eliminating it. Your child's primary "job" at home is learning how to be in a relationship with you and how to live well in a family.

Pick your battles wisely

Parents need to win the war, but they don't need to win every battle. Remember that you can't make a child eat, sleep, eliminate on command, be hygienic, or learn, so don't even try. Attempting to make your child do something he does not want to do only increases his need and thus his resolve to maintain control. If you'd really like your child to do something, introduce it as a choice between two things *you* can live with, then stay uninvested in the outcome.

For instance, you can maintain your requirement that your child's bedroom floor is picked up once a week so you can vacuum. You can ask him if he'd like to pick up his room by himself, or if he'd prefer your help. Eliminate all standards except for the bottom line that nothing be left on the floor. If he doesn't want to pick up his room by himself, let him know there are two ways you are willing to help—both you and he can work together or you can work alone, in which case you'll be placing any items left on the floor in a trash bag for him to "purchase" later with extra chores.

Stay firm on social limits

Your child is still developing the ability to self-regulate and to socialize properly. Even if his peers are ready to handle social activities in a responsible manner and without supervision, your child may not be. To support him while he learns to socialize, arrange for him to get together with his friends at your home, or offer to accompany him and a friend to a movie.

Address excessive stealing and lying

Inevitably, children will lie and steal on occasion—this is part of growing up. However, if your child engages in either of these behaviors more frequently or seriously than would seem common, address the problem right away. Excessive stealing or lying means there is something important going on inside your child, and he needs your help to figure it out and resolve it.

Expect oppositionality

As a part of his natural development, a teenager will attempt to assert his authority in many realms. Because of abandonment and a possibly neglectful start, the adopted child tends to be much more oppositional—either overtly or covertly—than the average teen. Again, this is his way of trying to gain the control he needs to keep himself feeling safe. Don't fight with him. Instead, acknowledge and accept his need to maintain control, picking your battles wisely.

Continue to spend one-on-one time with your child

When venturing into the world of teens, your child needs you more than ever. Plan and spend plenty of time with him, doing projects and activities. Give your teen his space, but don't let him isolate from you—encourage him to lean on you when you see his need.

Watch for splitting

A child with attachment issues will attempt to create a rift between his parents so it is easier for him to assert his control. With this "divide and conquer" behavior, the child is actually looking for security. There is no better way for parents to reassure their child that he *is* safe than to stay solid as a team. Together, parents must remain vigilant to any attempt their child makes to split them and remedy it quickly.

Monitor your level of parental confidence

A good indicator of your family's stability is how confident you feel about your parenting. If you are feeling shaky as a parent, it is likely that your child is feeling insecure thus testing for security with negative behaviors. Have daily or weekly check-ins with your spouse about how things are going with your child, and adjust your parenting strategy as warranted to sustain your confidence.

Maintain personal care and supports

Keep active with your established support network—reach out before things get to a crisis level. Maintain personal friendships, make time for your spouse, keep up your hobbies, and continue taking good care of yourself.

9 Handling Your Child's Need for Control

Tony was now in ninth grade. Despite the alienation Tony experienced because of his intelligence and race, he nonetheless earned good grades overall, driven by college aspirations and a sense of personal pride. He also continued counseling with Mrs. Gibson. She gave him another test, after which she reported:

> "Testing . . . indicated Tony is a bright child who does not experience much effective support from others. He uses fantasy . . . to avoid emotional contact with others. Although . . . able to perceive most things accurately, social and interpersonal perceptions are fairly distorted. He appears . . . angry, threatened and paranoid, . . . potential to be assaultive, . . . appears to fear insight, and remains very anxious regarding emotional stimulation. . . . Male-female interactions will become a problem for Tony, particularly in the area of intimacy, as he will fear the loss of emotional control. A male therapist is recommended. . . . Due to the serious . . . long-range effects of these emotional problems . . . , two years of weekly psychotherapy is recommended. With consistent treatment . . . prognosis is reasonably good."

She recommended that Tony continue therapy with psychologist Stan Parks. We willingly made the switch to Dr. Parks and hoped for the best.

In general the atmosphere at home was better. Val, now an eighth grader, was more often in a good mood. Every now and then she even asked me if I was proud of her. I always said I was. She seemed younger, less precocious this year, more vulnerable. She dressed more modestly for school. What she wanted most was to go out at night. We said nothing. Val knew the policy. She felt honored to be class representative but not enough to crack a book.

Actually, Val did read books—just not schoolbooks. One night late, I went in her room to get something out of her closet and surprised her reading a book with a flashlight under the blankets. I saw the cover. It was pornography. I did not take the book away from her. Instead, I told her the book would teach her how women can be degraded and used as objects. I left her crouched over her flashlight.

By addressing difficult situations in a nonreactive, straightforward manner, parents remain strong, resulting in their child feeling secure. (See chapter 23.)

Late in the fall, Valerie stopped talking about boys. Her focus shifted to whether she should start working in school. We gave her space. She seemed to be undergoing a personal crisis. Despite her promises of a new scholastic attitude, the reality was the same old Cs.

We decided to try a new approach, hoping to give her a realistic heads-up on her future. Dan warned, "Val, your life is in your own hands. If you can't push yourself now to be college eligible, you need to understand that you'll still be supporting yourself. It just won't be with the advantages of higher education."

We took turns describing the kinds of future work that would be available to Val if she continued with mediocre grades and as a result was not able to get into college. Dan said enthusiastically, "You know, you could always be a waitress. Since you're so beautiful, I'm sure you would get great tips."

I jumped in. "With your love of fashion, you might enjoy clerking in a department store. I think selling perfume might feel classy."

Dan snapped his fingers as if another thought had just come to mind. "You know, check-out people in grocery stores are unionized. Usually they make enough to live on. Of course, they're on their feet all day, but that might not bother you at all."

I said dreamily, "Hey, you know what? You could find a job at an information desk. You're fabulous at socializing. You'd make a great impression on tourists. Maybe you could even work your way up to manager."

Valerie was visibly irritated by our scenarios. Her self-image was already formed. As Valerie had announced over and over, she expected to rake in megadollars like Connie Chung. However as of yet, she still had not put in the effort necessary to improve her grades.

When a child doesn't put forth effort, it may be because he's trying to hold onto a positive self-view that would crumble if he were to try and then fail. (See chapter 19.)

Although I continued to make attempts to connect with Val, I felt disheartened by my efforts. Gift giving had become a hurtful dance between Val and me. I would always take the first step and buy her something I thought she would love. I would wrap the gift extravagantly, pick the right moment, and then surprise her.

After I hugged Val and handed her my gift, she would get a look on her face that was a mix of surprise and confusion. She would open the gift in a very self-conscious way and then make a profuse statement of pleasure.

Meanwhile, Val's body language clearly stated that she did not like my gift. Feeling hurt, I would berate myself for trying and vow never again to buy her anything. Weeks or months would go by and I would again find an item I was positive Val would love.

One time I went to the mall and purchased several pairs of expensive brand-name socks. Sure of my offering, after school one day I gave Val the socks. She followed right in step, falling over herself with thanks while silently rejecting my gift.

But this time I was sure I must have misread her—I knew the socks were fabulous. I eagerly awaited her appearance for breakfast the next morning to see which outfit she'd matched up with which pair of new socks.

Val showed up in a dingy old pair of white socks. I said nothing. Day after day I hoped to see those new socks on her feet. Finally, I admitted to myself that she would never wear them. Some months later when I happened to see the socks in her drawer, I noticed the price tags were still attached.

Val continued to put a wall between us in many ways. In the fall I bought a new iron. It was on the kitchen counter when Val came home from school. She saw it and said, "Oh, you got a new iron, Mom. Can

I use it?" I said, "No, you can't, because the basement floor is cement. I'm afraid you'll have an accident."

She adamantly told me that she was very capable of being careful with the iron. I caved in. Down the stairs she went. Less than five minutes later, I heard a crash. Val raced upstairs with a horrified look on her face, telling me the iron had accidentally fallen off the ironing board. Dan fixed the iron, and I berated myself for having given in once again.

That year our annual trip to the city to buy school clothes, stay in a hotel, and have dinner out as a family was difficult. Valerie's mood became ugly as soon as Dan and I finished spending money on her. We were exasperated and could not figure out why she always seemed to do this. At dinner that night, we shared the table with a 5-foot hornet.

Unfortunately, Valerie's foul mood continued through Christmas. Not only did she reject every single present from me—Val also rejected the jacket she specifically had asked my sister Carol to sew for her. Though Dan and I had figured out by now that Val must be sabotaging special occasions for some reason, we had no idea why or how to remedy the problem.

A shame-filled child may reject gifts because he does not accept the positive reflection of himself the gift represents. (See chapter 25.)

In January, Val fell into the after-Christmas blues with me right behind her. Though at first I managed to ignore her provocative behavior, eventually I lost it, yelling that I would not tolerate her mouthing off. I did not feel like complaining to Dan, since his official opinion was that everything was fine—Val was merely acting like an adolescent.

I also gave up the idea of getting more counseling, since the previous time I had tried it, the whole family had sided against me. Inasmuch as I would not allow myself to use physical force on my daughter, I was stuck. Because of my deteriorating mood, all I could do was yell back at her. Meanwhile, Val's insults were stacking up inside me like firewood.

Then a new twist—Val began refusing to do her chores. When I reminded her to do them, she eyed me boldly with hatred and told me to shut up. But Val was always careful to shift into a pleasant mood whenever Dan would get home. Without the support of my husband, I began to become obsessed with the idea of maintaining control of myself.

Nevertheless, Valerie and I continued our clash of wills. She would push me away; I would retreat. She would settle down; I would turn around only to feel Val pushing me away again to rid herself of my unwanted affection. If I did not warm up on schedule, Val would actually begin to woo me, cooing, "Mom . . . do you love me, too?"

Since I could not tell if she was sincere, I was unsure what to say or do, but I would take a deep breath, then mumble something like, "Val, I never stop loving you. You know that. My love for you always goes on, but I'm having a hard time with your moodiness, which never seems tied to anything I can understand." Inevitably, hope would wash over me and as nonnegotiable and relentless as Valerie's rejection, my love would return.

> *By rejecting affection, a child can maintain control and avoid the possibility of another abandonment. (See chapter 19.)*

That spring, Dan and I finally figured out how to get some parental control over Val. Ultimatums requiring drastic adjustments in attitude had only brought rebellion. What did work was plainly stating what was expected, what consequences would follow a noncompliant choice, and then following through as promised. When Val complained about consequences, we would say, "Is that so?"

Dan and I also gained a new insight into how to reach Val subliminally—she needed to think our ideas were her own. When a problem arose, if we could restrain ourselves from jumping in, and instead ask Val to suggest a solution, she usually would propose the very plan we'd have suggested.

We learned to camouflage any pleasure we felt over those ideas of Val's with which we agreed. Dan and I would act the part of tough negotiators, and we'd pretend to reluctantly consent to whatever Val would come up with. Also, we found that if we strategically chose our battles, we would win the war in the long run.

When Val spouted off ideas that made our hair stand on end, Dan and I held our tongues and gave her space to come back from the extreme. We strove for wisdom to know when we could ignore Val's words and when we could not. After years and countless confrontations with our fiery, rebellious daughter, we learned that the best way to parent her was, ironically, to let her parent herself as much as possible.

Val now decided what time she went to bed. She could stay up until midnight on school nights, which she frequently did, as long as she was in her room. Val had complete control of her own washing and ironing. She could manage her money any way she wished as long as she first banked one-third of it so she would get used to the idea of the tax equivalent.

Valerie had complete authority to decide her school schedule. We required her to discuss her thoughts with us and for her to listen to our input, but the final choice of classes was hers. This concession was hard because we had strong thoughts about what would be good for Val academically. Our commitment was even stronger, however, to have our daughter learn by making and living with her own choices.

Nonetheless, Dan remained in control of decisions that could lead to pregnancy or death. He would not allow Val to date. He said she was too immature to handle equally immature boys. One day, extremely ticked off and angry about the no-dating rule, Valerie had yelled in Dan's face: "Dad, you know what? I think your secret hope for me is to become a nun!" This remark made us smirk when she left the room.

Dan and I also did not allow Val to give up religious education or music. We felt religion was tied to values, as was music to discipline. We intended to give her a choice eventually, but not right then. Along with this new formula for dealing with Val, for my own sanity, I kept a certain distance from Valerie. I was getting along with her better now that I had ceased trying to please her.

Parents using the therapeutic parenting approach give the child control wherever reasonable, show subdued interest in his choices while allowing resultant consequences to fall, detach somewhat from the relationship, and maintain bottom-line rules for well-being and safety. (See chapter 25.)

While we were figuring out how to be on top of the game with Valerie, to my relief Tony began showing signs of feeling more content.

He was suddenly very serious about life, very goal directed, and extremely responsible. Tony's people skills had improved. He made several new friends in school, skied regularly, and continued to be on the honor roll. He spent hours on the computer, writing programs every spare minute. Predictably, Tony insisted that his counseling was in no way related to any progress he was making.

Valerie's behavior remained enigmatic. Though she placed second in the junior high spelldown and went to the regional competition, her schoolwork continued to be poor. Low grades apparently did not affect Val's social status, however, because she continued to bask in popularity. Her history teacher even mailed us a note saying Val was one of the "neatest, darling-est, most enjoyable students" she had ever taught. Ironically, the day the note came in the mail, Val got an F on a history test for which she had not bothered to study.

Late in the spring, because Dan was so weary of trying to motivate Val where her studies were concerned, they negotiated a new grade contract, which became the first one that ever worked. Val wanted an agreement based on her weekly performance so that if she had failing grades Friday, she could start over again Monday.

Val picked five subjects and asked those teachers for her grades at the end of the week. Dan agreed with Val's plan that she could earn 5 points for an A, 4 for a B, 3 for a C, and so on. She would need a total of 20 points per week to go out on the weekend. That meant if Val got an F in one subject, she could still make her goal if she had enough As to balance it. Valerie's contract included her studying 60 minutes per day at the living room study table.

Dan held Val to her social restrictions per their agreement, reminding her that we were happy to enjoy her company at home if she did not care to work. To our surprise, 3 weeks out of 5 she got her 20 points, and on those weekends she was finally able to join her friends. We let her know we were glad for her that she had become capable of setting realistic goals.

Parents can help their child put the shame of failure behind him by allowing him to start over each day. (See chapter 25.)

Invariably, it seemed, just as one child began to succeed, the other would begin to spin down. In June right before our family vacation, there was another stealing incident. The kids and I were in my office doing some bill paying. Valerie had set her folded 5-dollar bill on the desk, awaiting a last minute run to the store for batteries and candy.

After Tony went upstairs, Valerie suddenly could not find her 5 dollars. Since the office had really been a mess, I spent some time checking the wastepaper basket, reopening sealed envelopes, and looking everywhere until I had satisfied myself that the money was indeed gone.

When Tony stepped in to say he was going to the mall, I said, "Valerie's 5 bucks is missing. Did you take it?" He said he didn't. I asked, "Well, did you see it?" He said, "Yeah, over on the desk." I said, "Tony, are you sure you didn't see it after that?" He was irritated and said, "Mom, I'm sure," and left.

When Tony got home, I went to his room. I said quietly, "Tony, I think you took the money." There was only silence. Then he eyed me sadly, "Mom, I did not take the money. Why would I take money anyway? I don't need it." I said, "Well, you've stolen on three occasions previously." He volleyed back, "Mom, that was *years* ago. I'm not some thief."

I tried to sound compassionate. "It must be disheartening for you to hear me raise this suspicion because it shows you that around here, although we forgive, we do not forget." I then asked again, "Tony, did you take Val's money?" He rolled his eyes and repeated, "No, Mom, I didn't."

I said, "Maybe you didn't realize it was Valerie's 5 dollars. Maybe you saw it floating on the desk and thought it was part of that large business deposit you had just helped me fill out. You probably thought I'd never notice a lousy 5 bucks. Then when you found out it was Val's, it was too late to say anything."

Tony said, "Mom, that never happened."

I replied, "Well, Tony, maybe I missed something. Maybe there's still a spot I didn't check in my office. Why don't you go see if you can find it? I've got my mind made up to find this money because I have to resolve this question mark in my mind."

We went down to my office and I watched while Tony stood scanning the desk area. Suddenly, he dropped down and crawled back to the wall under the desk and said, "Oh, I see something." His hand disappeared and then emerged holding a 5-dollar bill.

I stood in stunned silence—Tony had just planted and retrieved the bill! As I was playing the scene back in my mind, I noticed Tony reading my body language. I saw the hurt in his eyes as soon as he registered that I was not satisfied. Tony then tried making his case, "Mom, I can't account for how the money got behind the desk. It just did, that's all. I didn't plant it because I didn't take it in the first place."

I followed Tony into the living room, and sat down near him. Neither of us spoke. Finally, I broke the silence. "Hey, Tony, I know you did it. You're so afraid of what might happen that you're lying. I don't want you to worry about punishment. For the moment, we're focusing on the truth."

I had his attention so I continued, "All year long you've been saying counseling isn't helping you. Yet here we are, not one week after you've stopped counseling, and you're stealing again. Let me tell you how this all came together in your mind. First, you figured you wouldn't be seeing Dr. Parks anymore, so that made you feel bold. You didn't realize the money was Val's, you thought it was mine and decided I was so rich I'd never even notice." I paused and waited.

Finally, Tony conceded. Head lowering, he said, "Okay, Mom. I did it."

Relieved, I replied, "There, Tony. At last, the truth. Thank you. It was essential that you owned up to this. I think you still have a big problem with stealing. Because of that, I'd like you to continue counseling. To help you understand how serious this is, I'm also going to have you pay your next counseling bill."

Because persistent stealing is a plea for help the troubled child will continue the behavior until someone "hears" him. (See chapter 22.)

Parenting Tips

Be sensitive to your child's ability to receive

If your child experiences core shame, he is not able to feel good about himself. He may reject gifts or destroy them because they represent a positive acknowledgment about him, which does not match how he sees himself inside. In fact, your child may not believe he deserves anything. So, rather than trying to counter your child's negative self-view, accept it, and openly discuss with him how he sees himself and what is behind his beliefs.

Because parents don't see their child the same way he sees himself, they find it difficult to accept that their child can feel so badly about himself. However, when parents *do* accept how their child feels and meet him where he is, he is no longer alone. If parents are able to be with their child when he is in a negative place, they are actually conveying the message that he is tolerable and thus even worthy.

Make praise specific

When you wish to praise your child, hone your comments to very specific and concrete observations since he will likely dismiss any generalized statement you make as being false. For example, if you use the superlative "You're the greatest!" your child will reject the statement (along with you, probably, as well) because the content and your excitement do not match his reality. Although it would be difficult for your child to feel like he is great, he might feel okay about something he's done well. So, be precise when offering positive feedback and say, "I liked it that you got ready for school on time today."

Asking your child how he feels about himself after an accomplishment can often be more effective than giving him direct praise first. Then, if he is able to voice something positive about himself, he is more apt to take in praise from you, especially if you echo the same statement he made—"I think you did a good job, too!"

Allow your child to set his own pace for school

Remember, you can't make your child learn. Therefore, if you try to set up standards for his performance in school, a battle is liable to ensue.

Without expectations, discuss your child's feelings about school with him, allow him to set his own goals, and be supportive of whatever goals he may choose. Assure him that you are there to support him and offer to help him should he want your help, but don't push it on him.

Remember, "It takes a village"

Due to the misguided notion that the nuclear family alone is sufficient for raising children, we have lost the value of sharing the responsibilities of parenting with those in the extended family and community. The nuclear family has never been the basic unit of survival for our species— it is the tribe that has made it possible for humankind to survive for millennia. Therefore, you are not being superparents if you try to raise your child alone—you are depriving yourself of the full resources you need to parent your child so that he can reach his potential.

Recognize that the feeling of being overwhelmed or unable to handle things indicates that you are not utilizing the supports that every family truly needs. Invite extended family members into the fold, call on friends in the community, join support groups, contact Big Brothers/Big Sisters, and/or find a therapist who specializes in the issues of adoptive families. Parents, especially those raising adoptees, cannot parent effectively in a vacuum. Don't wait for problems to arise or for a problem to become a catastrophe to seek the help that is essential for family success.

10 Seeing Hurtful Behavior as a Cry for Security

Tony's mood brightened with the new school year. When we required Tony to join a noncomputer activity that would promote social skills, he asked if we could negotiate. Impressed by his mature approach, we agreed. He dropped religious education and signed up for novice debate.

Overnight, we witnessed in Tony a passion we had not seen since he was young. He embraced the world of policy debate, becoming expert at argument, rebuttal, and logic. Our home floated in 3-by-5 inch cards summarizing pros and cons of euthanasia, abortion, and capital punishment. Intuitive and eloquent, he performed with confidence, remaining poised under attack.

Tony's sense of well-being seemed greatly improved. We attributed this improvement at least in part to therapy and decided, despite his loud protests, that he would continue a while longer. Tony played soccer again that fall and signed up to ski with new friends. He gravitated toward smart kids now, thereby affirming his own academic gifts for the first time. He finally got his growth spurt and walked around in size 12 shoes. Tony would be a tall man.

Valerie, now a ninth grader, got off to a strong start in school but quickly relapsed to finding fault with her teachers. Dan and Val continued their weekly contract, connecting Val's night privileges to acceptable grades. She was her perennial dark self, though, when facing the reality of schoolwork.

One night, Val came to me and said, "Mom, I'm sorry these are such hard times between us. You have to understand I'm just very busy having fun, but I want you to know there is a serious side of me that's beginning to think about the future." She announced her plan to get a 3.7 GPA so she could get a scholarship at the university she wanted to attend. She was running for student council again and had joined Junior Achievement. She said these would look good on her résumé.

Then she said spontaneously, "You know, Mom, I'm sure we'll get along better in 3 years when I'm more mature." Her wide, beautiful eyes were so serious, I hooted aloud in delight. I took her in my arms and said, "Honey, I love you so incredibly much. I know how hard these years are for you because you do not want to be guided. In a few years, these bad times will be nothing more than shadows in our memories."

Many adopted children struggle with knowing who they are at a deep level thus they may "try on" many different personas. (See chapter 19.)

The next morning I awoke feeling especially happy. As Dan and I were enjoying a cup of coffee, Val greeted us cheerfully, then asked, "May I have permission to skip my first class today? I want to do it so I can know the experience of skipping school. Don't worry, there's no test or anything. Can I?"

We sighed the sigh of parents with battle fatigue. Would there ever come a day when she would stop pushing? We agreed to her request mainly as a reward for her being forthright. We said, "One time only." Later we found out she had lied and had missed a math quiz.

For the next several months, there were more explosions between Valerie and me than I could count. Dan was worn out and did not want to hear any more bad news about Valerie. I felt less and less supported by Dan. He stopped meeting my eyes when I would tell him about my day, and he no longer offered feedback when things continued to go wrong. As our connectedness diminished, I slowly withdrew.

One night when Val and I were at each other's throats at the dinner table, Dan exploded. He said the atmosphere in our home was horrible all the time. He was sick and tired of it. His tone shocked me. Later during that same meal, Dan snapped at Val for saying yet another snotty thing to me right in front of him. After supper, I went to my bedroom to be alone and think. I decided once again to stop speaking to Valerie so the fighting would cease.

The next morning when I did not speak, Val instantly showed her delight by switching to engaging behaviors directed at everyone but me. Dan and I could hear her singing in her bedroom while she got dressed. In the kitchen, she whistled while preparing her breakfast. She did all her chores promptly and with grace. Her routine was to giggle around Dan and then walk past me coldly—a sheet of ice with legs.

Parents must stick together as a team so they can reassure their child that they are strong enough to keep him safe. (See chapter 25.)

One evening as I prepared for bed, my eyes began itching like mad for no apparent reason. Within moments, my whole body itched and my nose was running uncontrollably. I scratched desperately, simultaneously grabbing one tissue after another. My head felt so stuffed I was sure this was the onset of a fierce cold. Was the conflict with Valerie finally stressful enough to make me physically sick?

The sadness that had settled into me began spilling over into my job. It seemed as if no matter where I was, there were moments when I would just start crying. Dan, however, was glad that there were no more fights at home.

Friends had invited Dan and me over for a drink one evening. I considered canceling; I knew my face would broadcast despondency. When I went to freshen up, I looked in the mirror and something seemed wrong with my eyes. My upper lip was swollen and I began wheezing.

Suddenly I could not control the urge to scratch. My hands turned beet red, then my entire body was red. Under my right eye, a pouch as big as a walnut hung on my cheek. I began sneezing, and my breathing became labored. Panicked, I ran to find Dan, who screamed when he saw me.

Dan rushed me to the emergency room, where a team of doctors and nurses immediately gathered about me. Voices bumped around me in vague echoes. I heard someone say I was having an anaphylactic attack, words that meant nothing to me. Someone gave me a shot and I started shaking uncontrollably. Two hours later, it was all over.

If held inside, a parent's angst about her child can leak out in the form of serious physical symptoms. (See chapter 25.)

The next day, I went to see an allergist. I told him about the attack and said that the same sort of reaction had also occurred a week earlier but on a much smaller scale. The doctor asked me about everything I had eaten or drunk before the attacks and concluded that nothing I had consumed would cause a systemwide allergic reaction. Given how much the second attack had escalated from the first one, he said a third attack could kill me if I could not get to an emergency room in time. Then the doctor asked, "Is anything going on at home that's worrying you these days?" Incredulous, I asked, "You're not going to tell me this attack was psychosomatic, are you?"

The doctor said no, my allergy was not psychosomatic. He explained that in some people with major depression or anxiety, their brains produce a chemical in response to stress that travels to the blood, triggering an anaphylactic attack. He warned me I needed to clear up the cause of my stress since another attack could be fatal. I drove home feeling as if I had a terminal diagnosis.

Dan arrived at home to find me sobbing. When he asked what was wrong, I spoke in short hiccups. I said, "I feel deserted by you, Dan. All you do is act irritated when I need to talk with you about what's happening. You act as if Valerie is not your problem. I feel like some wild bird trapped in a cage, and I can't fly away nor can I survive if I stay. I hate what Valerie's behavior has done to me and to us."

Dan defended himself, saying he had not realized things were so serious. I yelled, "The problem is you don't respect me. You've been writing me off. What I say doesn't even count because you think I'm exaggerating, so therefore you feel no need to pay attention or to be involved. You only listen when a doctor says I might die. My word alone doesn't mean a thing."

Then Valerie came downstairs, all smiles, wanting to know if we were going out for pizza since it was Friday. Dan said, "Sit down." Val caught the mood and turned hastily to leave. Dan's voice rose. "I *said* sit down." She sat, keeping her head down.

Dan stated emphatically, "Your mother has worried so much over how you act toward her that she's becoming psychologically ill. The doctor warned her that the next time she had one of these anaphylactic attacks it could be fatal."

Dan continued, "So here's what's going to happen. Even though I know you don't want to, you will begin seeing a therapist to understand why you have such negative feelings toward your mother. If you give us the slightest problem about this therapy, if you refuse to cooperate in ending these hurtful episodes that involve all of us, if you continue to be disagreeable at home, then I will have to consider putting you in a boarding school." Devastated, Valerie remained in her room the rest of the night.

We scheduled a family meeting with Tony's therapist, Stan Parks. Feeling detached from everyone, I spoke quietly, saying Valerie either showed me or refused to show me affection based on some formula known only to her. I said I felt like a failure as a mother. I said I was afraid her behavior was eroding my love for her.

Though Valerie admitted she was often mean to me for no reason and that she did it on purpose, she said she did not think she was *that* mean. She looked at me directly and said, "Many of the feelings I feel for you are because you can't handle me. I detest this weakness in you. I'm disgusted at how you are unable to control me. You're always waiting for your hero to come home and fix everything."

She turned to Dr. Parks, adding, "So when Dad comes home, I quit doing that, because I know with him things would get really bad for me. I've never had a good relationship with Mom in my whole life. We've never been close, and I don't think things will ever change." I was flabbergasted by Valerie's nerve to say these things in front of me.

Dr. Parks asked, "Well, don't you think we need to find a solution for the awful situation at your house right now?"

Valerie replied casually, "Well, I suppose so if it's going to *kill* her." Her coldness made me feel sick. However, at least she was showing her true colors. We decided Tony would stop counseling. I would take his place with Dr. Parks. Valerie would begin counseling with his office partner, Sara Gibson.

A child's quest to feel secure in his relationship with his mother along with his deep shame about himself can drive his rejecting behavior. (See chapter 23.)

At my first meeting alone with Stan Parks, he said we needed to talk about the effects of adoption. I was stunned when he said that, because in our first counseling attempt Mr. Ulrich had not supported me in the least when I had stated this very idea. Stan said adopted children made up 25 percent of their office's adolescent clientele. Both he and Sara thought adoption played a significant role in the problems we were having. This included both Tony's stealing and my painful issues with Valerie.

Stan told me many abandoned babies who come from orphanages lose the ability to form normal attachments to other people. They grow up, like Val, in a fog of rage even they do not understand. He maintained that the true target for the rage is the biological mother who has let them go, but that the rage gets transferred to the adoptive mother. Stan said the problem remains a "mother problem" even if there is a dad, because these kids blame their adoptive moms for their original abandonment.

"Later on," Stan explained, "a child who has never attached to her adoptive parents in the way biological kids normally do will act the very way Valerie acts. She will lie, sneak, hide her feelings, and never be able to admit she's not perfect. She feels a deep rejection; therefore, she rejects what's cherished in the family system. She fears her own imperfection which, in her eyes, must be the reason her birth family didn't keep her in the first place."

Stan said, "Kids who don't attach spend their whole lives hiding their faults from everyone in order to appear perfect. Some, like Val, refuse to compete because were they not to win, it would be admitting they're not perfect, whereas if they don't try, no one can judge them. Everything remains a mystery."

Stan went on, "Some children with attachment disorder are haunted by fear that they'll be sent away a second time, so they push relentlessly in order to see how far they can go. 'If I go farther than that, will they still love me?' That's how they think."

Stan said Valerie's rage against me was based in her impoverished, neglectful origins, her inability to accept that she had been abandoned, and her low self-worth. "Children like Val have an identity problem. If their parents cannot find a way to heal them, they can become intolerable, ungovernable, and outright cruel—again, usually to Mom."

Stan said what made the dynamics more harmful in our case was the major battle I had already had with my own mother. He said I had permanent scars from her unintentional harm. Now I had apparently reached a point where I could no longer tolerate being manipulated in another struggle for love and approval.

The reason I took Valerie's behavior so personally was that I had already suffered 20-plus years of my mother's silent treatment, withholding of affection as punishment, and accusing me of not loving her if she did not get her way. Stan said I was incapable of handling any more psychological stress.

I asked why Valerie would appear happy when I was hurting but would turn ugly if things were going well for me. Stan said it had to do with competence; she felt deeply incompetent.

Stan said based on what he knew, my problem was not parenting techniques but was more a question of vulnerability. Because of my own past, I was extra-sensitive about mothering. More than anything else in the world, I wanted to be a good mother.

Stan told me that Dan and I had to figure out how to prevent Valerie from judging me. He emphasized, "The right to judge you must absolutely *never* be given to her. She doesn't even understand what motivates her to be so mean to you, but she'll do it as much as you allow her to, because, just like you, she has deep issues relating to her birth mother. Her problems tag along after her in life just like yours are tagging along behind you."

Stan said that he would help Dan and me to create new ways to handle typical situations at home. I left the session feeling hopeful. I had a lot to tell Dan. I prayed he'd hear me this time.

In order for parents to utilize such profound information, they need time to digest it, reiteration of the key points, detailed guidance in specific therapeutic parenting interventions, spousal support, and much practice. (See chapter 25.)

Suddenly Valerie became as sweet as summer strawberries toward me. I did not allow myself to believe her sugary act for a second. I now saw her behavior as an attempt to keep the upper hand. Knowing how much she abhorred therapy, I knew she would be determined to convince Sara that our problems were entirely my fault.

Around this time, I went in for my annual physical. Dr. Russ Tandy had been treating me for many years. This particular day, when Russ saw my demeanor, he said we were going to have a heart-to-heart talk. I felt surprised by his concern.

Russ said, "You know, Cassie, over my years of experience treating thousands of women, I've seen a pattern that I'm going to share with you. Many families struggle with adopted kids. I am positive of that."

He went on, "I can't tell you how many women have sat in my office crying over the same hurts, the same depression, the same broken hearts. This is just my opinion, Cassie, but to me, you and Dan seem excessively nice to Val. Never in a million years would I allow one of my children, boy or girl, to mistreat their mother."

As my tears flowed, I was thinking that his wife was lucky to have a husband who would stand up for her. In my own case, it had taken another doctor saying I might die before my husband stood up for me.

Russ pointed out, "You've already had a very rough life because of your mom. You're always worried that you're like her, Cassie, and you are *not* like her. It's harmful to you to keep insisting there must be something wrong with you because Valerie acts like she hates you so much."

I looked at him, shocked. It was hard to believe that yet another professional was telling me the very same thing I had just heard from Stan Parks and had heard in the past from Mr. Oberg. It was reassuring, but still I was so exhausted and felt like I was on my own to deal with it all.

At work one day I took the deposition of a psychologist and asked him if we could talk afterward. When we were alone, I told him something was happening in me that I did not understand.

A few days earlier, Dan and I had gone to the movies. An abrupt scene change in the film had shocked me and I suddenly screamed, silencing the whole movie theater. I also told the psychologist I was continually flinching when someone would touch me. I had the jitters all the time and was waking up more and more at night.

The psychologist said I was experiencing a heightened startle response, like a person coming back from war who was suffering from

Post-traumatic Stress Disorder. He said that PTSD does not go away on its own, that both reducing stress and getting therapy were necessary. He assured me that those who have PTSD aren't crazy, just way over-stressed. I went home that night feeling somewhat relieved.

As spring arrived, I slowly realized I was feeling less angry. Because of therapy, I was learning to speak immediately when I felt disrespected instead of storing things up. Each time I did so, I felt better afterward. Valerie seemed to confront me less often. She did her chores better, said thank you more frequently, paid me some compliments, and seemed to be doing well in school. My increasing strength and Val's de-escalation allowed some solid healing to begin happening in the whole family.

That summer we vacationed with friends in Ocean City. The change of scenery from Wyoming was spectacular, and we all loved the ocean. One afternoon we walked along the Ocean City boardwalk. While we took in the nonstop attractions along the way, we ate the local spe-cialty—french fries with vinegar—and eventually headed over to the amusement park. It was a beautiful summer night.

We took turns playing a few games, did some people watching, and after a while we came to the Midway, where we heard raised voices of people thrilled by the exciting rides. It was around 9:30 at night, dusk but not very dark yet. We walked by one ride after another, eating our snow cones, but nobody seemed interested in going on any rides.

Our ears perked up when we heard screams of people taking a plunge on a very high, very impressive roller coaster. Val lit up and said someone *had* to go on it with her. Because of how daunting it looked, no one was willing. But Val had her mind made up and would not take no for an answer. She did not have the nerve to go alone. One by one, she approached the others, begging and wheedling for someone to accompany her, but despite her huge enthusiasm, there were still no takers.

Finally, Valerie turned to me, her face a beautiful display of anima-tion. She grabbed my arm and squeezed me hard. She begged, "Come on, Mom. *Please*. If you go on the roller coaster with me, I promise I'll bond with you." I looked into her eyes and knew I would remember that sentence for the rest of my life.

Parenting Tips

Translate hatred

Children need parents who are bigger, stronger, kinder, and wiser than they are to feel safe and secure (Marvin, Cooper, Hoffman, & Powell, 2002). It is essential that parents understand that their child is seeking security when he says, "I hate you." Cassie took Val's displays of hatred toward her personally, which changed their parent-child equation from the *parent* being in charge to the *child* being in charge. This only reinforced Val's not feeling safe as well as her need to push for control in order to try to feel safe.

Understand your child's identity confusion

The formation of a child's core identity is the result of his brain organizing his accumulated experiences into a pattern, then placing the pattern into memory. Because trauma and stress hinder a child's brain from creating memory, many once-abandoned children lack a continuous narrative, or logical story of their lives. As well, they lack a continuous sense of self over time. Without a sense of self or core identity, children express an array of behaviors, some authentic, some not. While this constant shift can be confusing and mistaken for the child's attempt to take control, it actually represents the fractured inner world of the child.

With the tools of the therapeutic parenting approach, parents can help their child develop a continuous narrative and a core identity. By being a mirror for their child, feeding back to him their observations about his reactions, feelings, likes and dislikes, and needs, parents teach him who he is. As they interpret the world for their child, parents help him organize his experience. Finally, because therapeutic parents are able to help their child regulate his anxiety and stress, his brain can create memory from which he can retrieve a coherent narrative of his life and a solid, core sense of self.

Stick together as parents

To demonstrate the ability to keep their child secure, parents must stick together as a team. Val chose to be pleasant toward her father and brother, while she remained cold toward her mother. Dan might have stated to Val that she needed to treat everyone the same—either pleasantly or coldly, but that she was not allowed to attempt to split her family with her behavior. This would have shored up the parental team, preventing Val from singling out her mother while increasing her feelings of security.

Stay connected with your spouse

You and your spouse had a life that revolved around your relationship before you brought children into the mix. Parents must be partners first before they can tackle the needs of children. They must remain active partners throughout their parenting years to preserve their connection. Along with working as a team when it comes to parenting, the couple needs to make it a point to have a date night at least once a week without the children to sustain and nurture the relationship.

Use humor and laugh!

There is a valid reason for the phrase, "laughter is the best medicine." For us to grow, heal, or learn, our bodies must be in a receptive state. Ideally, that means that we need to be as free of stress as possible. Stress provokes a chemical reaction in the body which decreases one's ability to reason and causes a fight or flight reaction.

One sure way of reducing stress is to engage in pure laughter. If the energy in your household has become negative, stagnant, or even oppressive, stir up some fun. Children will often be more compliant if their environment is positive and the mood of people around them is light and fun. There's no reason why chores, duties, and responsibilities must always be carried out in a serious manner. Blow bubbles while you're doing the dishes!

Keep an eye on your health

Maintaining good mental and physical health takes commitment. Every few weeks, take an inventory of yourself mentally and physically, adjusting your priorities as necessary to maintain your spirits and energy. You can't meet your child's needs if you haven't met your own first.

Revisit the literature

Books about parenting, adoption, and personal growth, as well as your feel-good favorites, can be supportive friends. Remember the good you've gotten from your bookshelf in the past and leaf through some of those books that have helped you the most. As well, check the web or the bookstore for the latest books on topics that will bolster your knowledge and confidence, and splurge on a purchase now and again. Don't forget to tickle your funny bone!

II Hope, Help, and Support for Parents

Even though things had been a bit better during the summer, by the fall of 1989, I had almost reached bottom. Valerie was 15 and in tenth grade. She and I each had been in individual counseling for about 9 months. I was working on detaching myself emotionally from her so she would perceive me as less of a threat. Lately I had achieved exactly that. While I was still committed to her intellectually, I did not react much to the choices she made. My heart felt alienated, and I knew deep down she was miserable, too.

Val's old themes cropped up again: her teachers were dumb, the work they gave was stupid, the tests were unfair—and none of what she was learning in school would help in her future life anyway. Relentlessly she dissected her world, criticizing every person, activity, guy, girlfriend, and rule. One morning when I mentioned what supper would be that night, she attacked my menu.

I was confounded as to how I might help my unhappy daughter. In my ongoing therapy with Dr. Stan Parks, I frequently brought up this topic. He insisted there was not a single thing I could do differently to ease her pain right now. He was adamant that distancing myself emotionally from Val was the right choice, even if it was against my judgment.

At this juncture, he claimed, Val craved coldness. He said the detached kind of mothering I was practicing was totally dissimilar from the manipulative, abusive mothering I had received during my childhood. Stan assured me my treatment of Val was appropriate and was what she needed. He told me to have faith. He predicted that when Val was around 23, she and I would have a good relationship. He had seen it happen before.

When a child does not feel he belongs, he struggles with core shame, which he often projects onto everything and everyone in the form of incessant criticism. (See chapter 19.)

In late November I plunged into a severe depression. I could not get my good mood back. Right after Christmas, Dan left for a conference. Valerie's negativity ramped up as soon as Dan was out the door. I no longer had any ideas about what, if anything, would help.

I stayed home and saw no one. Though Val witnessed my listless state, she remained aggressive and obnoxious toward me. Dan returned home and not knowing what else to do, he made arrangements for Val to stay with friends for two weeks.

I had a talk with Val before she left. Val said she could not understand why I would continue to be committed when she had been sending me messages for years that she did not want me in her life.

Dan reproached Val for the arrogance of her attitude, saying it was contrary to the laws of society. I sat like a limp rag while he went on about her not respecting and honoring me. For the millionth time, I asked Valerie what I had done that had caused her to hate me. She said it was different things she would not enumerate, but that in general it was my whole person.

I said, "How do you think a statement like that would make a mother feel?"

She retorted, "I don't care how it makes you feel. It was stupid of you to be trying so long. I have no intention of working on our relationship in therapy. I'm just working on my own self." She turned to Dan and asked, "When are we leaving?"

After they left, I sat alone in the house and folded camp inside. I felt so overwhelmed and trapped in my life. I had thoughts of hurting myself. In desperation, I reached out to Father Horton, my priest, and told him my feelings. He said I was having a codependency crisis. I did not know what *codependency* meant. Father Horton insisted that I phone a treatment center and seek admission. I phoned a center a good distance from Rock Springs, and within a few days my place was reserved.

Codependency is the need to gain approval and affirmation from those outside one's self. (See chapter 16.)

On a grey morn in February 1990, with tightly clutched admission papers in hand, I gathered up my broken self and closed the door on the world as I knew it. I asked Dan to drive me to the Greyhound Bus station. Wanting to begin the next phase of my life on my own steam without help from anyone, I boarded the bus alone to go to the treatment center.

With my nose pressed against the icy bus window, I stared at overcast skies. Thoughts tumbled pell-mell in disorganized patterns as my breath rhythmically clouded up the window. I felt hollow—a puckered gourd out of which someone had sucked all the pulp.

It is imperative that careworn adoptive parents seek professional help to acquire the tools and compassion they will need to heal themselves and then their wounded child.

Parenting Tips

Don't lose hope

You are undertaking a huge task when you decide to parent adopted children. Because of their often extraordinary needs, raising adopted children can present a more significant parenting challenge than raising birth children. Sometimes you can put things into perspective if you remember that what you are doing is healing a child's wounded heart one day at a time. Allow yourself the reality check of knowing that what you are doing *is* very challenging.

Get support and help

If you do find yourself lapsing into feelings of hopelessness, take action. Go ahead and admit your true feelings to yourself and a trusted other. Allow yourself to feel the depth of the difficulties you are facing, for they are real. However, you don't need to be alone in your pain. Ask your supporters for affirmation and assistance. Call a peer parent, take a break, talk to a therapist, arrange for respite for your child or for yourself, release with a primal scream, and let your tears fall.

It is not the first time an adoptive parent has felt like throwing in the towel, and it won't be the last. Many adoptive parents, whether they are willing to admit it or not, at some point question what they have taken on. Take heart, however, for you *will* get back on track—you need some time off right now to regroup and gather some new tools. When you do get back on the road, take a moment to notice that although the horizon may seem far ahead, you've already come a long way, probably much farther than you could have ever imagined.

12 Therapeutic Parenting Brings Breakthroughs

by Dan

As I put Cassie on the bus that gray February morning, I felt totally disoriented. Our family life was unraveling before my eyes, and I did not know how to stop it. When the bus pulled away, I knew that life would never be the same again. I could not fix Cassie's pain. I did not know if the treatment center could help her, but anything was worth a try.

Right before Cassie had left for the treatment center, in addition to all that had been going on at home, my department had been recruiting candidates for a vacancy in the French Department, and I had chaired the search committee. Thus, I had been busy all of December winnowing out 10 finalists from a field of nearly a hundred applicants for this position. The end of the fall term was also the time I had to grade final exams and papers. To top it off, the day after Christmas, I had had to fly to Washington, DC, to interview the finalists.

I had been angry with Cassie for not being able to keep things calm at home while I was busy with my professional responsibilities. I was convinced that Val's behavior was merely that of an adolescent—a headstrong adolescent, yes, but not abnormally so in my mind. When I had to call our friends to ask them to take Val for a couple of weeks, I was embarrassed, humiliated, and felt like a complete failure at keeping things together at home.

Today, as I reflect back on the events just prior to Cassie's departure for the treatment center, I am amazed at how much that moment marked a watershed between the old and the new—the old codependent Cassie and the new integrated one; the old patriarchal family and the new parental partnership. These changes were not easy nor were they immediate, but there would be no turning back to the old ways. Everything was on a new track.

After Cassie's departure, a vague sort of depression began to set in and hung around me for the next several weeks. Tony and Val hardly seemed to exist. They later told their mother that I had muddled through the month, ignoring them. They said I had been cold and crabby the whole time and barely talked to them except to give them their chores.

Two weeks into Cassie's treatment, I was finally permitted to see her. On Friday afternoon, I left the office early, packed a small bag, and gave Cassie's little Yorkie, Belle, a bath for the visit while I was waiting for Val and Tony to come home. I was feeling very uneasy about having to leave the kids alone, so I wanted to see them before I left.

I was anxious about my visit, not knowing what to expect. It had been two weeks since Cassie had boarded the bus, and I wondered how much had changed in that time. At the center, I was greeted at the door by a staff member who led me to a waiting room while reviewing the house rules for the visit.

When Cassie finally arrived in the waiting room, she seemed subdued and reserved. I was not prepared for this change in her demeanor. She had always been dynamic and talkative, her enthusiasm being part of her great charm. It was almost as if they had turned her into a Stepford wife!

We exchanged small talk, I told her how things were going at home, and she told me the routine of the treatment center. We both avoided eye contact and felt like strangers on a blind date.

When it was time for me to leave, I surprised Cassie, asking her if she wanted to say hello to Belle. Her eyes lit up. She had always treated the Yorkie as if she were her baby, and the dog had returned Cassie's affection tenfold. Belle was so excited to see Cassie. She rolled over on her back, panted excitedly, and tried to lick the skin right off Cassie's face.

When I returned home, I was relieved to find that the house had not burned down and that the kids had apparently respected the rules I had given them. However, home still seemed as cold and gloomy as the February weather outside.

Cassie's treatment required my participation during the next visit I was allowed. During a therapy session, I learned I was in denial about the problems in our relationship. Moreover, I was told that I was a major part of the problem. I apparently tended to be dismissive and had been unsupportive of Cassie's contention that Valerie was unbonded to the family as a whole.

Just like my father, I was used to being the authority figure in the home and having the last word. I was told I would have to make many adjustments in my thinking if our family life was to improve and that Cassie would need to continue therapy for codependency when she came home.

∾

The first several months after Cassie's return were difficult. The family landscape now seemed to be planted with emotional land mines. At first, it seemed as though I could not get through a whole day without doing something to provoke Cassie's ire. Most of the time, I had no idea I had crossed some invisible line. All of a sudden, Cassie would demand that we discuss my behavior and set a time for the confrontation. I would usually spend the interval going over the recent past trying to figure out what it was I did this time.

Cassie had learned a completely new vocabulary and a process for dealing with her life, much of it based on the 12-step process of Alcoholics Anonymous. It was as though a foreign language and culture had infiltrated our home. I would have to master new behaviors to adapt to this new environment. I learned that what I had proudly thought of as tolerance on my part was viewed by others as emotional unavailability.

Cassie began to ask me on a frequent basis, "What are you feeling right now?" or "How does that make you feel when I say . . . ?" She would insist that I describe my feelings in as much detail as possible. Saying just a few words was generally insufficient. I suppose I slowly became a little more comfortable in stating my feelings. Following Cassie's lead, I came to see that there was a certain power in telling your partner how a particular situation or statement made you feel— unappreciated and belittled or, on the other hand, loved.

After several months I was able to begin to use the 12-step principles and vocabulary to explain my feelings to Cassie. I even got to the point where I was able to remind her of the 12-step perspective on problems that arose. Gradually, I stopped giving advice and making unilateral decisions for Cassie. Little by little, I found that I was able to navigate the minefield and even disarm some of the mines.

This was a time of great change in our family life on several levels. Cassie was healing, the kids were on their way to their futures, and I was having some success at being in touch with my feelings. The family mobile began to seem more like wind chimes in a soft breeze than shutters clattering in a windstorm.

Tony was in the second semester of his senior year and had decided on a college. His enthusiasm for team debate continued, and it became an activity that consumed practically all of his time outside of class. Eventually, he took first prize at the state competition and got to compete at nationals held in Chicago. Tony's passion paid off in the form of a college debate scholarship.

Unfortunately, as it turned out, our son had perfected the skill of disappearing from our radar. Tony kept a low profile and was not one to engage in risky behavior. Because we trusted him greatly, we gave him complete independence. However, Tony seemed uncomfortable with so much freedom and continued to check in with us to be sure that everything was okay.

Tony's keeping a low profile, we now can see, was in part due to his inner pain and in part due to our inadvertent neglect arising out of our need to pay extra attention to Valerie. Tony's success in high school had masked both his low self-esteem and his inner struggle with his racial difference.

Tony graduated from high school, and riding the wave of a successful senior year with a debate scholarship, he went off to college in the fall. We would eventually come to discover that our son's off-radar existence was actually a symptom of depression and deep-seated identity issues.

Our attention was still directed toward Valerie's behavior, although we had to admit her conduct had improved dramatically since Cassie had returned from treatment. This improvement was probably due in large part to Cassie's new focus on herself. Cassie's Al-Anon program had finally given her the tools to disengage from Val's behavior. Cassie had learned at the treatment center that Val's opinion of her was none of Cassie's business.

This improved situation was, nevertheless, punctuated now and then by an incident that could not be ignored. One of these incidents occurred one Sunday afternoon at the mall. Cassie and I had been browsing and heard our name being paged over the loudspeaker. When we answered the page, we learned that our daughter had been caught shoplifting cassette tapes at the music store. The manager did not press charges but told Val she could never enter the store again.

To my surprise, when we got home Cassie took charge of dealing with the incident and determined the consequence. Normally, I was expected to carry out that role, but Cassie had acquired useful knowledge about dealing with such behavior from testimony in her Al-Anon meetings and from having worked in district court.

Cassie told Val that once she had made the list of every act of stealing she had done, confessed to the managers, and made full restitution, she would be able to forgive herself and put the event behind her. When Val had completed these tasks, Cassie complimented her and told her that she was proud of how Val had taken responsibility for her actions.

As Val entered her senior year in high school, she embraced her new freedom from Cassie's focus. She seemed to realize that she would need good grades if she were to go to college. Therefore, she did her homework diligently. She was again elected to student council and participated in speech competitions, demonstrating enormous poise and confidence in public speaking, which would serve her well later in life.

However, this improved academic conduct was often complemented at home with a surly attitude. Toward the end of January, after Tony had returned to college from winter break, Cassie and I decided it was time to confront Valerie about her generally sullen manner.

In response to Val's statement that eating with the family made her feel nauseated, Cassie said to Val that she was using us as convenient scapegoats for her unhappiness. Since eating with us was apparently so awful, Cassie told Val she could make her own dinner and eat it in her room until such time as she thought she could enjoy a meal with us.

Val sat in stony silence during the confrontation with a belligerent look on her face while tears welled up in her eyes. Cassie then asked her if she had any comments she wished to make. Val said frostily, "Are you done?" and she walked out of the room.

Cassie and I began having our dinners in the breakfast nook instead of the dining room because it was a cozier, more intimate space. We often watched the deer walk by in the fading light as we ate our dinner at the little round table. Usually we lit candles much as we had done before having our children. We chatted about our day, about a book we were reading, a film we had seen. Valerie stayed in her room.

One evening about 6 weeks later, Val suddenly appeared in the kitchen around dinnertime. Without a word she went to the dishwasher, emptied it, and set the table in the breakfast nook for three. She chose brightly colored place mats, matching napkins, and compatibly colored plates. She selected a new candle and lit it.

Once the table had been set, Val began to chat with Cassie about her day at school. Val kept her eyes on the floor, the table, or the counter, avoiding direct eye contact with Cassie, but cast furtive sideways glances now and then to see if everything was cool.

When I came home from the office and found them together in the kitchen, I immediately turned on my heel and left the room. I assumed we were in for another family squabble and I was in no mood for it. Later when I came down for dinner, I sensed that there really was no dispute. Everyone seemed cheerful.

I cast a glance at Cassie and her eyes met mine with a look that said, "Don't you dare screw this up with some sarcastic comment!" Val was charming throughout the whole meal. She laughed, talked about her life, her schoolwork, and her part-time job. After dinner, she cleared the table and cleaned up the kitchen.

Val ate with us every single evening thereafter until she graduated. She was not sullen. She was not crabby. She did not vary her nice mood. She showed us affection, consideration, and a willingness to accept responsibility for the dishes again, without our ever saying a word.

Val told us about her plans to go to college the next fall. She would move to the West Coast and attend a junior college while she established residency and then transfer later to the university for her junior and senior years. She had asked us to drive her out to college in September, which we did. We told her how proud we were that she was doing such a nice job of getting her life in order.

Meanwhile, Tony had decided not to return to college out of state. Instead, he was going to come home and continue his education in Rock Springs. While away at college, it had become increasingly difficult for Tony to compensate for his buried low self-esteem.

The game had changed—Tony was no longer academically superior to most of his fellow students. Tony had had to work to achieve success, and unfortunately, this was not a skill he had mastered in high school. Moreover, Tony's quick rise to success in high school debate had not prepared him for the competitiveness of the college league.

Once back in Rock Springs, Tony reestablished his personal life on its old foundation. He hooked up again with many of his old friends and then slowly added new ones to his coterie. Many of the members of this group shared the trait of feeling like loners and nonconformists in society.

Tony settled in to his new apartment and college, eventually deciding on a major in graphic arts. When he graduated in 1997, Tony decided to take some time off before seeking a career job. After several months had gone by, Tony still had made no move toward a career. He continued to work at McDonald's.

In February, a friend called to tell us about an opening for a graphic artist on the staff of the state's leading newspaper. She had been so impressed by Tony's portfolio that she had mentioned him to one of the editors of the paper. The editor asked her to have Tony apply. Excited for this stroke of luck, we called Tony and urged him to apply immediately.

Tony got his portfolio in order and sent it off. A couple of days later, the paper called and invited him for an interview. Cassie loaned him her car and off he went. He returned impressed by the operation. The next day, the editor called Tony and offered him the job. Tony asked for the weekend to think about it.

Saturday afternoon, Tony stopped by the house and told us he did not think he would accept the job. I asked him if he had any good logical reason for turning the job down. He replied that he did not want to move out of Rock Springs. This is where all of his friends were. We insisted that he accept the job offer. He was angry at us. We told him we loved him in spite of his anger and would be there to support him.

Tony accepted the job, moved from Rock Springs, and embarked on his new career. His anxiety soon was replaced by a passion for this new world and its relentless, frenetic pace. He did establish new friendships, both in the publishing world and outside of it.

However, as the job became an unchallenging tedium, Tony's boredom deepened. Concerned with Tony's possible career stagnation, we pointed out openings on larger newspapers in other states, but he could not muster the initiative to change. We were witnessing a shutting down in our son but did not know if we could or should do something.

All of the years Tony was growing up we had truly been unaware of his pain. While we had directed most of our concern toward Val, we didn't realize that Tony also needed our special attention to thrive. The result was that our lack of awareness of Tony's inner struggle undoubtedly had led to his experiencing abandonment again.

Meanwhile, away at college, Val was busy exploring her independence and developing her ability to survive on her own. Undoubtedly, the big city presented the perfect venue for her development. When Val graduated with a major in art history, we drove out to visit her and to honor her achievement.

A month after our visit, Valerie moved to the East Coast, where she began preparing for a graduate degree in art history. Once again, her ability to survive in a challenging environment served her well. After some initial setbacks, she managed to find a comfortable apartment in a respectable, affordable neighborhood.

Despite Val's successful new life, over the next decade conflicts continued to erupt between Cassie and Val. During these episodes, which often resulted in noncommunication, I would assume the uncomfortable position of the go-between. The longer these periods became, the more distressing I found them.

Eventually, Cassie would attempt to resolve the situation, usually by letter in which she would own her contribution and invite our daughter to do likewise. When the incident was resolved, light-hearted bantering and gift exchanges would replace the stony cold silence, and I could once again let down my guard in my conversations with them.

One of these episodes began during a visit to Rock Springs one summer about 4 years after Val left home. Val had gotten very angry, then had broken into sobs and told us that she hated coming home. Val said she had nothing but bad memories of growing up in our home and that she was very bitter about her childhood. She told us we were not the family she would have picked to live with. Val left and we were devastated.

Six months later, Cassie finally decided to take the initiative and break the extended silence. Valerie did reply several days later, admitting that writing such letters was very difficult for her. In her letter, she stated that she felt the lowest she had felt since moving from Rock Springs. She was doing a lot of soul searching, trying to find out who she was and what her place was in the world and in our family.

Val said she wanted us to know that she was grateful for all the doors we had opened for her. At the end of her letter Val stated that it was important for her to establish her own home and safe environment. She said that Rock Springs was *our* home and family rather than *her* shared home and family.

Although this and other incidents eventually were resolved, Cassie and I remained at a loss to figure out how to prevent them in the first place. It wasn't until February of 2002, when Cassie attended a groundbreaking lecture in Rock Springs about the effects of abandonment in the lives of adopted children that we finally began to understand what was happening.

After the talk, Cassie had approached the therapist, Kate Cremer-Vogel, who had presented the lecture and made arrangements not only to begin family therapy but also to possibly co-write a manuscript that would be the basis of the therapy. When Cassie came home from the lecture, she could not contain her excitement.

The therapist suggested Cassie begin by writing out the story of raising our kids so our real life events could be used in therapy to help us understand the problems we were having with our adopted children. I told Cassie I wanted no part of any more therapy. I was about to retire and was done with working on family issues. Cassie said she was going to pursue it on her own anyway.

After several months, when I saw that what Cassie was learning in therapy was starting to work for her and our family, I joined Cassie in working with Kate. We were beginning to understand the implications of abandonment in our children's lives.

Kate presented a new perspective on adopted children that considered attachment issues as arising not only from psychological dysfunction, but more importantly, from disrupted development of the child's brain in its earliest formative stages. Kate helped us see that with proper incremental and empathic response to behaviors that were driven by Val's attachment disorder, we could help repair the relationship between our daughter and us.

In therapy, we learned to translate Val's negative behaviors into the meaning hidden beneath them. Slowly, we began to see the core pain that was under Val's disruptive actions, which we had been misinterpreting as hateful, destructive, and disrespectful.

Unfortunately, Val had learned very early in life that the only person she could trust to satisfy her needs was herself. Kate told us that if we could begin to view Val's complex behavior with compassion and verbalize to our daughter our understanding of her inner turmoil, we could help her to develop trust.

In addition to facilitating our ability to see our daughter more accurately, Kate began educating us about the effects of abandonment on Tony. In particular, she corrected our view of Tony as being repressed and said that instead, like many adopted children, Tony was suffering from depression related to his abandonment.

She linked his stealing behavior to his depression as well and said that racial and intellectual differences only exacerbated the problem, causing Tony to feel alienated from his peers. This information was shocking to us, and we became troubled, remembering how we had always assumed Tony was thriving.

Regarding Val's behaviors, we learned that the main drive of a child with attachment disorder is to be in control to feel safe. Val's relentless attempts to control reflected her need to gain a sense of security she had never felt. Kate reiterated what Dr. Parks had told us in the past—that Cassie's childhood trauma prevented her from being objective in the face of Val's neediness, which she displayed in behaviors we once had identified as hatred.

After several months, Cassie and I were getting more comfortable with relating to Val from an empathic therapeutic parenting stance. With our new perspective, Cassie and I felt like we were able to connect with our daughter. We were amazed at her response. Val was opening up and starting to trust us with what was in her heart. This became evident during the holidays that year when the kids came home for a Christmas visit.

Valerie called the night before her flight. Cassie answered the phone, and when she hung up, her face was flushed with emotion and tears were streaming down her cheeks. For years, Cassie had called our kids just before trips to tell them that in case our plane crashed, she wanted the last words that she said to them to be that we loved them. Apparently, Val had just repeated that phrase to Cassie on the phone! We were already reaping rewards from our hard work in assimilating the empathic point of view of our children's true issues.

At first, however, it was very hard to view a provocative situation empathically. This was evident early in Valerie's Christmas visit. To entertain the family, Val had brought the video *Finding Nemo* for us to watch together. It was touching to us that she had done so because of the pertinent themes therein. Not only was it the story of a small fish who had lost its mother, but also it portrayed the fierce devotion of a father. Additionally, the film depicted a hilarious mock 12-step meeting between sharks, a scene that Val had known would make her mom laugh her head off.

The spell was broken, however, as Cassie got up from the couch still chuckling after the video when she went into the kitchen to clean up after dinner. She opened the silverware drawer for something and I saw her freeze. I knew something had happened. At some time unknown to us, the entire drawer had been emptied out and rearranged. It must have taken a long time to reorder this chaotic drawer. Cassie looked stunned to her core, obviously caught off guard. Bewildered by her own reaction, she quietly left the room and called Kate, who helped her figure out what was going on. Val was not trying to invade Cassie's space, but instead was compulsively attempting to control her environment in order to feel safe. Understanding the underlying behavior helped Cassie get right back on track.

More often than not though, our new approach helped us diffuse potential incidents before they escalated. After Tony arrived, we were sitting around the kitchen counter while Val was digging around in our refrigerator. All of a sudden she let out a long drawn-out groan and then stood up a moment later with some green onions in her hand. She said, "Mom. Look. Ugh! These are rotten, Mom. I mean, look at these! I'm going to throw them away."

Cassie tensed, but this time she was ready. In therapy with Kate, we had been introduced to a strategy wherein the parent responds to the child's unwanted behavior in a light manner while being attuned to the underlying needs of the child, which helps to defuse the threat. Cassie took a deep breath and said brightly, "Wow. It's so kind of you to take the time to help me clean the fridge, honey. Boy, I think you're right. Those *do* look old. Here, let me toss them." Cassie fired them into the garbage can.

Val's head disappeared again into the fridge. Now, she stood up and held garden beets, which were in a plastic bag, and said, "Mom, look! These are moldy! Ugh! Mom, look at these beets! I mean, there's mold on them!" She held the bag high so we could view the moldy beets.

This time, pretending to be stern, Cassie replied, "Now, Val, here's the deal. I am extremely fond of those beets because a good buddy of mine grew those in his garden. I mean, those aren't just some old store-bought beets. They're really special. Those are *garden* beets! So, here's the thing. I'm willing to throw them away, but first I want a moment of silence in honor of them because those beets are organic and I'm very partial to anything organic."

Val imitated Cassie, closing her eyes in pretend honor of the beets. Then she handed them to Cassie, who put them in the garbage. Tony stopped peeling carrots at the sink and turned around to stare at the scene with incredulity as though to say, "What the hell is going on here?"

This continued with a few more items, but getting no negative reaction, Val soon ceased her cleaning frenzy. Cassie's newfound ability to cope with such behavior had saved the day. I was amazed, because in the past such incidents would have provoked defensiveness in Cassie and conflict would have ensued between mother and daughter.

We now understand some of the pain our child suffers due to her attachment disorder, her different needs, and her inability to communicate her deep feelings of fear and shame. We realize that we needed to learn a new language in order to be able to understand and respond empathically to Val.

On the morning of Val's return flight after her Christmas visit, we all got up early. Val came downstairs carrying her suitcase and wearing a bright, lime green scarf that stood out as an iridescent exclamation against her black hair and coat. The scarf had been a gift to Cassie from a dear friend.

When Val had admired it on Christmas morning, Cassie had promptly taken off the new scarf, gone over to Val and wrapped it around her neck, saying, "If you love this color, Val, you take it. I want you to have it." Val had protested, "Oh, Mom, I couldn't take it. It's so beautiful, and it's yours." Cassie had replied, "Please take it. It's my way of saying how much I love you." With a big smile, Val accepted the gift from her mother.

While we were dropping Val off at the airport, I told her how pleasant it had been to have her home for the holidays. We hugged, and I left to get the car from the parking lot. When I pulled in front of the terminal to pick Cassie up after she said goodbye to Val, I could see that she had been crying. I was worried that like so many times in the past, something had somehow gone wrong at the end of the visit.

When Cassie got into the car, I asked her what happened. Cassie said, "When I hugged Val goodbye, I said, 'Val, I had such a wonderful time with you, honey. Have a wonderful trip home.' Then I felt like the moment was right, so I asked her something I've been wanting to for a long time, like I used to do when she was little. I looked into her eyes up close and asked, 'Can you feel my love coming into you right now?'"

I asked Cassie, "How did she react?"

Cassie replied, "Val returned my look, hugged me back, then said, 'Yes, Mom. I *really* can.' Naturally, I burst into tears!" Cassie and I drove home in silence, each of us reflecting on prized moments of the Christmas visit.

The therapeutic parenting approach has brought about a miraculous improvement in our relationship with our daughter since we started using it. We are, at last, beginning to establish a connection with Val built on the bonds of attachment. I am confident that this new relationship, although still fragile, will continue to grow. We are finally on the right track with our daughter.

After the success of the Christmas visit with Val, we felt we had the grounding to turn to our concerns about our son. Several disagreements had left us in a state of non-communication with Tony for about half a year. We sent an e-mail message to Tony to reestablish contact. We proposed that we drive up to see him the following weekend. Tony wrote back and suggested that a phone call would be better than for us to drive 6 hours for a 15-minute conversation.

We responded with a second e-mail:

> Thank you for replying right away. On the surface it might seem dumb to drive six hours for a short talk, but actually, we feel connecting with you in person is much more important than a mere six hours. We will arrive around 1 p.m. Please don't bother to dust.

When we arrived, Tony had not yet returned from a pick-up basketball game. He got home 5 minutes later—no hugs or handshakes—just a hello, and we entered his house. Tony took a seat as far away from us as possible. I established eye contact and began by explaining that life is too short to maintain an estranged relationship. If one of us were to die, I said, the other would never heal from the pain of not having made up.

I did my best to apologize for all the mistakes we had made in raising him. I told Tony that we should have been sensitive to his struggle of being a different race in an all-white community, and that we would do it differently now if we were to do it again. Tony refused my apology, saying we had *not* made a bunch of mistakes in raising him. He denied that he had had problems growing up. Realizing we weren't connecting, I backtracked and tried to attune to Tony in the moment.

Cassie shared a few things with Tony. After we had been with him for about half an hour, as promised, Cassie and I stood and said goodbye. It had been good to see him. Cassie approached Tony, her hand extended. He ignored her hand and hugged her instead. Tony did the same with me, even though we usually do not hug. We left without another word.

Cassie and I rode in silence for at least a half-hour, each ruminating to ourselves on the uneasy visit. Then I pulled the car to the side of the road, and we exchanged our thoughts about what had transpired. All in all, we agreed that the visit had been necessary and was relatively positive. We both agreed that the next move should be his.

Eleven days later, we got the following e-mail:

> Hello,
> I just wanted to drop you a quick note to say that I thought the visit went very well, better than I expected. I am glad that you guys made the effort to make contact and I feel hopeful that we will be able to reestablish a relationship.
>
> > Tony

We have a ways to go with Tony, but with our success with Valerie, we are confident we will get there with him too. We now understand more about his struggles and feel compassion for the rough time Tony has had. Though it has been quite a journey, we are thankful for all that has brought us this far and look forward to what the future may bring.

13 Finding Healing and Compassion

by Cassie

One morning not too long ago, I awoke in a depressive funk but could not figure out why. Drawing from years of practice in dealing with this mood, I hauled myself out of bed, had my tea, and then walked 2 miles in the cold of the winter morn.

I had been walking about 10 minutes when tears began streaming down my face. Unexpectedly, I heard myself begin to speak aloud to my mother, who was long since gone. In sentence after sentence of gratitude, I thanked her for the good things she had given me, most notably her profound love.

During that brisk morning walk, I began to feel compassion for myself. I was able to leave my depression along the frozen trail in the snow where it would melt and wash away during the spring thaw. When I returned home I was restored by the warmth and peace of our beautiful home.

As I have come to recognize my own parenting errors, I have become more understanding about how my mother's own imprinting and lack of healing inadvertently led her to harm me. Her emotionally desolate marriage replicated the unresolved abandonment issues of her childhood. When I was born, my mother obsessively bound me to her in order to feel self-worth. Before I got help, our identities were fused together like Siamese twins. Bound by a cluster of emotional chains, I needed professional help to learn to separate myself from my mother's view of me.

Today, I am finally able to compare, contrast, distill, and make sense of my existence through a more balanced perspective. I feel like an integrated woman, wiser because of my mistakes and more compassionate. This is the work I began in treatment and have continued through my 12-step work in Al-Anon.

Today, Dan and I do not berate ourselves for our parenting mistakes, for all parents err. We know we did many things well. Yet when our children were young, we were not sufficiently attuned to their attachment, identity, and abandonment issues. Had we possessed the knowledge, Dan and I could have healed our children's emotional deficits during their childhood. Although Tony's and Val's lives will forever be tied to what Dan and I knew and did not know during their growing-up years, there is hope.

We know that parents really can heal their children's abandonment wounds, even if their children are adults. Now, Dan and I feel equipped to help Val and Tony integrate their past trauma. With effective guidance, we have learned how to channel our parenting strength into supporting the healing of our adult children.

Dan and I believe in ourselves and know we are an unassailable team, united in the power of empathy. Dan's new confidence has made him able to navigate even uncomfortable emotional circumstances with aplomb. And I now have a solid ability to maintain the objectivity necessary to see the true needs of my children.

Recently during a Christmas visit as Dan, Val, and I sat over coffee and tea, Val and I began talking about missing Tony, who had chosen not to come home for the holiday for the first time. Dan followed Val's lead and replied how sad he felt about Tony's inability to let us be near him just now. He said he hoped Tony would let us come up to see him soon.

Dan then began talking about the healing he and I had been doing since both kids had left home. He conveyed how much we wanted to understand what had gone wrong at our house. He explained how we had been studying, reading, going to therapy, and even attending conferences to gather information about adoption issues.

Val's face appeared intense with interest as she listened to her father speak in a tongue she appeared not to recognize as his. Dan confessed our sorrow over missing the boat on some level with both kids. He mentioned Val's attachment disorder, then Tony's identity and depression issues. He said we had remained in the dark for many years until a new therapist moved to town and began teaching parents a new way to understand and talk to their adopted children. Val was captivated by her father's words.

Dan described to Val what we had learned, using terms such as *neuronal wiring, attunement,* and *core shame.* He was relating the concepts we had mastered in therapy to our own family's experience. I was totally in awe. *Go, Dan!* I was amazed to watch Dan remain so carefully attuned to Val's mood while he talked. I was as glued to the couch as Val was to her stool, and the connection between the three of us was palpable.

Dan went on to enumerate several kinds of neglect that Val had experienced during her first year in the orphanage. In acknowledgment, Val immediately raised her pinkie with its exposed nail bed, now painted bright red. Dan told Val how sad he felt inside that her first 12 months of life had given her the idea that she could only count on herself.

Dan then asked Val if she remembered all those times when he had made a huge deal out of her lying. She nodded that she did. Dan apologized for shaming her back then, explaining that he knew now she had only done what she could to take care of herself. Dan added how much he regretted letting her think all those times that she was a bad kid.

This admission seemed too much for Val to bear, and she interrupted Dan to say she knew we had done the best we could. To let us know she needed a break from the spotlight, Val shifted to a less personal topic and asked if anybody knew about this therapy in the '70s. Dan told her that no, it had not yet been discovered. He went on to describe how the approach was now becoming more commonplace because parents were finding that it worked to bring them closer to their children.

Chancing there had been enough of a breather from the intensity, Dan boldly moved on to the topic of the incessant hostilities in the past between Val and me. In a straightforward way, he explained that due to the legacy of problems with my own mother, I had been an easy target for Val's negative behaviors. Dan told Val that her actions were actually expressions of how bad she felt deep down and that I had inadvertently reinforced her belief through my hostile reactions.

I could see this was starting to go over her head, but I was thrilled to know that we were finally beginning to connect with our daughter at a deeper level. I was thankful we would have the rest of our lives to tell

Val her story again, and again, and again, until she developed a continuous narrative of her childhood that she could understand and accept in her heart.

Dan also sensed we had reached a good point to stop for the time being. He then came up with a perfect ending for our serious conversation. Switching gears, Dan said enthusiastically, "Man, can we stop talking about this boring stuff now and go to lunch?"

Upstairs while Dan and I were getting dressed to go out, I came nose to nose with him, a vantage point from which we could each view the relief in the eyes of the other. I said, "Dan Richards, I am so incredibly proud of you. You were so awesome, my whole brain ran away. Val almost fainted to hear you say such soft things. Dan, she was so connected to you when you were talking. Do you have any idea how much you've grown?"

He teased, "Yeah, thanks a lot for ruining 2 years of my retirement making me go to therapy." I actually smiled. Dan paused, then said thoughtfully, "I think things will be okay with Tony, too. I know what to say to him now." My whole body hummed with joy.

The morning of her departure after our holiday together, Val mirrored my giving her the lime green Alpaca scarf the previous Christmas. She went to the coat closet and pulled out a magnificent fuchsia scarf—one that I had never seen her wear.

Val gracefully took the scarf in hand and draped it around my shoulders. She looked coy—shy actually—and said, "Mom, last year you gave me your most prized possession, so this year I'm going to do the same thing for you. Even though I really love it, I want you to have this scarf. It's a color I know you adore, and it would make me so happy to think of you wearing it."

My eyes started filling up as she added authoritatively, "Now, Mom, I'm going to teach you how to tie it. You have to do it a certain way so it will look elegant." It was pretty early in the morning for a scarf-tying lesson, but I did my best. Afterward, elegantly cloaked in dazzling pink, I drove my daughter to the airport. Knowing what we had needed, Dan had decided to let us go alone.

As I helped Val stack her bags at the curbside check-in, we exchanged glances through tearful, happy eyes. I hugged her as hard as I could while we both said how much we loved each other. Then we separated, and I watched as my Wild Sweet Rose whirled away through the revolving doors.

PART II
Finding Answers *and* Getting Help

14 Coming to Terms with Your Past

Childhood experience is the mold that casts our ability to parent. If we come from a family in which our parents were available, appropriately responsive to our needs, and able to provide safety and limits, we will bring those capacities to our own parenting experience.

On the other hand, if we come from a family in which our parents were unavailable, unresponsive, or unable to provide safety and limits, we may not be adequately prepared to parent. No amount of education, information, or advice will affect our ability to parent more than the way in which we were parented. However, *if we have consciously come to terms with our past, we can choose not to repeat harmful patterns* we learned while growing up (Siegel & Hartzell, 2003, p. 1).

The challenge of parenting can be even greater for those adults who have endured past unresolved trauma. Especially if their children are adopted, these parents are likely to encounter difficulties with their children that mirror unsettled personal issues, rendering their job more complex.

Most, if not all, parents enter the world of parenting with some degree of unfinished business from childhood. Those who have had no modeling during childhood for resolving personal problems will have few, if any, tools with which to help themselves or their child. There is no replacement for the experience of having received good parenting in the first place. Unresolved issues actually cloud the ability to *see* a child's needs and inevitably will get in the way of a parent meeting the needs of her child.

Fortunately, there are ways for a parent to resolve leftover issues from childhood. The healing experience that comes from getting support from others who share some of the same challenges is helpful. Knowing they are not alone enables parents to cope better. Parents can resolve issues by engaging in a therapeutic relationship with a professional. No matter how confident parents feel, addressing potential pitfalls will undoubtedly improve their effectiveness.

The opening sketches of Dan and Cassie's childhoods show the development of the parental imprinting they each received. Throughout the narrative we saw the Richards apply their own past imprinting to the parenting of their own children—sometimes with success, and sometimes without. The following childhood summaries point to the aspects of imprinting that affected Dan and Cassie's parenting.

Dan's Childhood

Dan's childhood proceeded with relatively few complications. His family life was straightforward, fairly secure, and predictable. A clear and stable father-mother-child hierarchy was the basis of the family's functioning. The family's life was grounded in consistency, care, security, and structure. Dan, especially, experienced both a solid attachment with his parents and their strong parental commitment to him. All of these aspects of Dan's upbringing lent themselves to providing a solid foundation for Dan's future role as a parent with a few exceptions.

As an adult, Dan replicated his family of origin's hierarchical structure within his own family. He was the boss and the breadwinner, while Cassie was in charge of the household and children. Unfortunately, the demands of raising adopted children required parenting skills beyond those possessed by this couple. Parental unity—operating from a common perspective—was essential for handling the special needs of the Richards' children. Alone, Cassie could not provide the parental strength necessary to meet the challenge.

Another facet of Dan's childhood that proved problematic to his marriage and his family's functioning was the lack of attention paid to emotions. The seeds of Dan's dismissiveness—his general disregard for the emotional aspect of life—had been sown early on in his family of origin. Dan did not learn to value feelings or an emotional perspective because they were not modeled as he grew up. The ability to self-reflect, that is to be able to look inward to examine one's self, was a skill unavailable to Dan until after Cassie returned from treatment.

The emotional nature of the difficulties Dan and Cassie faced as parents was beyond Dan's expertise. Healing identity issues, attachment disorder, and the wounded hearts of his children were all skills that required acute sensitivity, empathy, and a language of emotion that was foreign to Dan. After Cassie's treatment experience, Dan stepped onto a steep learning curve, one that in time would yield the capacity for him to understand and converse in the newfound tongue of emotion. Emotional fluency finally allowed Dan to team with Cassie in parenting their children empathically.

In spite of the fact that he had grown up in an emotionally dismissive environment, Dan did acquire many of the essential skills of effective parenting. Dan's parents, respecting him for both his intelligence and dependability, had given him mature responsibilities commensurate with and sometimes beyond expectations for a child his age.

Due to Dan's hands-on experience with his younger siblings, he became skilled at the basic mechanics of traditional parenting. He practiced keeping his siblings in line, setting limits and following through with consequences, and being the boss—the same things he had watched his parents do. Dan was able to draw upon this skill base when he began parenting. In fact, the parents-in-charge stance he had learned contributed to those successes he and Cassie did have raising their children.

Although Dan had grown up alongside his troubled half-brother, Tommy, who likely had suffered from attachment disorder, Dan was not prepared for parenting a child with attachment disorder himself. Pa's unsuccessful attempts at reigning Tommy in left Dan without the modeling he needed to reach the heart of a wounded child. Dan found that the traditional parenting for which he *had* been prepared did not provide him with an effective set of tools necessary to parent such a child. These he would need to acquire on his own.

Cassie's Childhood

Elizabeth, Cassie's mother, had experienced a childhood replete with deep insecurity, fear, deprivation, and lack of nurturing. Her father was rejecting, scary, and unpredictable, while her mother was emotionally frail and did not provide needed safety for her children. This environment deeply affected Elizabeth. Her core beliefs and behaviors were rooted in feelings of worthlessness.

Predictably, Elizabeth's inadequate parenting model and her sense of being no good led her to repeat damaging patterns with her own children. Elizabeth had received no counseling or treatment to undo the trauma and harmful imprinting of her childhood. Therefore, she passed on to her own children a volatile mix of her mother's powerlessness and neglect along with her father's rejection and rage.

Cassie's childhood was frightening, traumatic, and insecure. She learned early on to be hypervigilant to her mother's moods and needs. Cassie acted out the prescribed roles of "mom's best friend" and "perfect daughter," earning love by doing and being what her mother needed her to be. Elizabeth controlled Cassie the only way she knew how—by withholding affection to ensure obedience. Cassie's early childhood experiences of physical trauma only bound her more to her mother, her only available parent.

Elizabeth's behavior, which in one moment could be attentive and loving while in another abusive and frightening, had created within Cassie a persistent state of high anxiety and vulnerability. During adolescence, Cassie dreaded returning home from school each day because she did not know which mother would be there waiting—the boisterous one, the depressed one, or the even-keeled one.

From any of these states, however, Cassie justifiably feared that Elizabeth instantly could become both verbally and physically abusive. Cassie's hypervigilance returned full force in her relationship with her daughter. Val's complex needs, which she expressed through antagonistic behaviors alternating with sweetness, recalled a pattern all too familiar to Cassie.

For Cassie to survive the relationship with Elizabeth, she had to give full respect and allegiance to her inconsistent, frightening mother. Therefore, when Cassie began parenting, she had no concept of a child being anything but emotionally shackled to her mother. Based on her childhood imprinting, Cassie's expectation that her child would love, obey, and respect her blinded Cassie to Val's needs. Because of attachment disorder, Val's extraordinary needs often manifested in behaviors that were far from loving and respectful. Cassie did not have the training to see her daughter's negative behaviors as a cry for help.

Without success, Cassie relentlessly sought information to better understand how to parent her daughter. Unfortunately, literature and psychotherapy offering effective solutions for treating children with attachment disorder had not yet been developed. Therefore, the lens of her early modeling led Cassie to perceive Val's actions as rejection, which Cassie could not help but take personally. Cassie's enmeshed model of mother-child connection set her up for heartbreak, leaving Val misunderstood.

∾

Eventually, Cassie's issues led her to undergo treatment. In her recovery, Cassie was finally able to parent her daughter more effectively, in part because she had healed her own childhood wounds and also because she had finally found effective psychotherapy that allowed her to see Val's needs more clearly. Through therapeutic parenting, Cassie and Dan were finally able to reach their children emotionally and begin to heal them.

Prior to addressing their own issues, both parents were attempting to parent based solely on the knowledge of parenting they had absorbed during their childhoods. Dan had remained emotionally distant from his children, relying on authoritarianism as his primary parenting tool. Cassie attempted to parent via the power of being in a relationship with her children.

Unfortunately, both authoritarian and traditional relational approaches fell short in adequately meeting the special needs of the Richards' children, due to their past abandonment and trauma. As they acknowledge today, if Dan and Cassie had known and used the therapeutic parenting approach in addition to their other skills, they would have been much more effective.

Today's parents *have* access to the tools the Richards lacked. Now there is more widespread knowledge about treatment of trauma and attachment issues within the professional community, which gives realistic hope for attainable solutions to parenting problems that once were unsolvable. Parents must remain diligent in seeking the specific information and support they need to achieve success. Ask until you receive!

15 Finding Your Strengths and Facing Your Shortcomings

No matter whether we are dealing with adopted children or birth children, our own issues will color our perspective and affect our actions. We bring both strengths and shortcomings to the task of raising children. Since child rearing may be the most important job we undertake, being aware of exactly what capabilities we possess as well as those we lack is essential.

If we are applying for work, for example, we take inventory of ourselves and our skills with respect to the description of the particular occupation. We note our strengths and weaknesses, comparing them with the demands of the vocation. If we lack a particular proficiency but still would like to take on the challenge, we get the training we need to proceed.

In reality, the approach we must take to child rearing is essentially the same. None of us is fully prepared to meet the challenges that may come up in the course of raising a unique child. There is no shame in admitting that we may need to hone skills we have or learn new ones. In fact, it is when we don't have an open mind about our preparedness for parenting that problems can arise.

Therefore, we need to objectively look at what we bring to the task of parenting, including both our strengths and shortcomings. Throughout Dan and Cassie's narrative we have seen both the positive skills and those that were lacking when they were raising their children. We also got a glimpse of how their childhood imprinting either contributed to or detracted from their set of parenting tools.

As a way for you to begin to look at your personal resources, we will look at a chart that outlines the skills useful in raising a challenging child from the perspective of those possessed by the Richards at the outset of their parenting adventure. The checkmarks denote parenting skills they had at the beginning of their adoption experience. Note that each parent had some skills that the other did not and that there also were skills neither parent had that were essential to meeting the problems the Richards experienced.

PARENTING SKILL	DAN	CASSIE
Able to have and keep realistic expectations		
Able to make and keep a commitment	✔	✔
Able to draw upon positive modeling from childhood	✔	
Able to draw upon modeling for shame-free parenting		
Able to maintain appropriate boundaries	✔	
Able to maintain objectivity	✔	
Able to nurture		✔
Able to accurately look at yourself in any given situation		
Able to create and maintain routine and structure	✔	✔
Able to maintain parental hierarchy (parent is in charge)	✔	
Able to convey modest self-assurance	✔	
Able to maintain self-control under stress		
Able to maintain a generalized state of self-control	✔	
*Able to maintain sense of humor		
*Comfortable with giving physical affection		✔
*Comfortable with receiving physical affection		✔
*Ready to comfort the child in his distress		✔
*Able to be playful with the child		✔
*Ready to listen to the child's thoughts and feelings	✔	
*Able to be calm and relaxed most of the time	✔	
*Patient with the child's mistakes		
*Patient with the child's misbehaviors		
*Patient with the child's anger and defiance		
*Patient with the child's primary two problem behaviors		
*Comfortable expressing love for child		✔

PARENTING SKILL	DAN	CASSIE
*Able to show empathy for the child's distress		✓
*Able to set limits with empathy, not anger		
*Able to show empathy for the child's anger		
*Able to give consequences, no matter how the child acts	✓	
*Able and willing to give the child much supervision	✓	✓
*Able and willing to give the child much one-on-one time		✓
*Able to express anger in a quick, to-the-point manner	✓	
*Able to "get over it" quickly after conflict with the child	✓	
*Able to follow through with consequences	✓	
*Able to accept the thoughts and feelings of the child	✓	
*Able to accept and still discipline the behavior of the child		
*Able to receive parenting support from other adults		✓
*Able to acknowledge mistakes in raising this difficult child		✓
*Able to ask for help from trusted people		✓
*Able to not allow the child's problems to become parent's	✓	
*Able to cope with parenting criticism from other adults	✓	
*Able to avoid feeling shame/rage over failures to help child	✓	
*Able to remain focused on long-term goals	✓	

*From "Parenting Profile for Developing Attachment"—a professional seminar handout by Daniel A. Hughes, PhD

Now it is your turn. If you turn to Appendix B, there is a parenting skills self-assessment that includes all of the criteria listed above. This personal tool allows you to rate yourself on your current parenting skills on a scale of one through five. The exercise is meant to serve as both an affirmation of skills you already possess, as well as a guide to understanding those skills that you may need to add or improve. This is not a test but rather a way to look at yourself objectively to assess your present parenting abilities. If you find you are lacking certain skills, you can choose to look for resources available in your community in the form of parenting groups or professional guidance, and you can find pertinent reading materials that will aid you in your growth.

If you were able to relate to the fact that Dan and Cassie had short-comings, then it might be easier to accept that all of us, including you, have them. Again, there is no shame in knowing and admitting we have things to learn. Fortunately, it is never too late to make the changes we need to make to be more successful parents—a truth that was evident in the Richards' story.

16 Needing a Child's Approval Can Be a Parent's Achilles' Heel

In the myth, Achilles' mother dipped him in the river Styx when he was an infant, making him invulnerable except where the water did not touch him—a place on his heel where she held him by her forefinger and thumb. As an adult fighting in the Trojan War, Achilles died from an arrow wound to his only vulnerable spot—his heel. This ancient Achilles' heel myth has become a modern metaphor for succumbing to our weaknesses as we traverse life's challenges.

As in other realms of responsibility, when we take on the job of parenting, we'd like to feel rewarded for our efforts. It's gratifying when our boss recognizes when we do a good job at work or when our spouse is appreciative of our efforts. We also may wish for our children to be grateful for our endeavors on their behalf. The first two kinds of feedback are realistic to expect because such affirmations are a part of those mature relationships. However, no matter how hard we try to remind ourselves that our children are not responsible for making us feel good about ourselves as parents, that expectation can still linger within us.

Sometimes, therefore, we find ourselves in the trap of desiring our child's approval for our parenting efforts. If the want becomes a need, this desire for affirmation from our child can become an Achilles' heel for us. Even a subtle expectation that we should receive kudos from our children for our intentions and efforts can trip us up. Whether we expect actual verbal thanks or good behavior that we then interpret as the child's appreciation for us, anticipating positive feedback from our child will lead us astray and disappoint us.

When we were children, few of us probably said to our parents, "Gee, Mom and Dad, you are working so hard to make sure I have everything I need. You are sacrificing your own wants to give me time and attention. Thank you so much!" It is clear in this rather absurd-sounding example that children being verbally appreciative of our parenting efforts is not a realistic expectation. Yet it can be so easy for us to react defensively to our child's affronts to our authority, to his sometimes hateful behavior, and we interpret these actions as our child's lack of appreciation for us.

As the Richards' story demonstrates, although Cassie's tendency to expect her daughter to treat her with love and respect was greatly exacerbated by her misguided childhood imprinting, to a certain extent it also is representative of every parent's longing for affirmation. While Cassie suffered from a more well-developed and comprehensive form of the need for approval called codependency, she nevertheless wished for the same thing all parents do at some point—their child's admiration. It is precisely because Cassie's Achilles' heel led to her downfall that her story lends us a powerful example and a mirror in which we can see a glimpse of ourselves wrestling with this very human longing for our children to appreciate us.

Codependency: Cassie's Achilles' Heel

Although in general Cassie felt happy, positive, and confident when her children arrived, a problem began to plague her early on that continued to interfere with her intuitive abilities to parent. Cassie's Achilles' heel was *codependency*—a habitual, negative relational pattern that develops in response to having dysfunctional childhood experiences (Mellody, 1989, p. 3). One symptom of codependency is the propensity to allow others to control one's self-impression (Mellody, 1989, p. 46). Seeking self-definition and worth in the opinions of others—a behavior imprinted during Cassie's childhood—interfered with her ability to remain objective as a parent with her daughter.

Codependency can become a life-threatening psychological condition. If the codependent is overwhelmed with negative feedback, he can easily slide into a downward emotional spiral; and if left untreated, the codependent may slip into suicidal ideation. This turned out to be the case for Cassie after years of being unable to handle the rejection of her daughter.

Those who suffer from codependency have a damaged attachment to their primary caregiver, usually their mother. One way the damage can occur is that a mother's love for her child is conditional upon the child meeting the mother's needs instead of the other way around. When the mother is preoccupied with herself, she pays insufficient attention to the crucial task of reflecting to her child who he is. As a result, the child develops only a vague sense of self and concludes his mother's lack of attention means he is unworthy.

Codependency may also result from the primary caregiver's need to live her life through her child. The mother's self-view, in this case, has no personal boundary—her child becomes an extension of her. The child's behaviors, accomplishments, and failures "belong" to his mother. The child learns that he is responsible for the feelings of happiness or sadness of the caregiver and thus forms a codependent identity.

The emotionally enmeshed child grows up to become a codependent adult who looks to others for definition and value, molding his behavior to please others to gain their approval. When he gets attention and praise, the codependent feels good about himself. When the codependent is ignored or criticized, he concludes that he is incompetent and, thus, unworthy of love.

Elizabeth, Cassie's mother, had been overbearing and intrusive in order to hide her sense of inadequacy, which developed during her own sad childhood with a father who did not love her and a mother who could not protect her. To feel like a good person and parent, Elizabeth kept Cassie in awe of and dependent upon her through unremitting criticism.

Thus, Cassie formed a belief about herself that she could do few things right or on her own. As Cassie grew up, because she had been discouraged from having any opinion of her own, she had accepted whatever her mother said as the truth. This is how Cassie learned to look to others instead of to herself for legitimacy.

Cassie had doubts about being ready for or even worthy of motherhood because her mother had given her the message that pregnancy was a prerequisite for being a good parent. After the children arrived, Cassie tended to interpret their challenging behaviors as proof that she was not a good mother. For example, Cassie worried that Tony's inconsolable crying was caused by her own maternal inadequacy, when in fact he was grieving for his foster mother back in Korea. In Cassie's mind, a good mother could have soothed Tony through his crying spells.

Not wanting to feel that she was failing, Cassie sought an outside opinion of her mothering from Tony's pediatrician. Cassie could not think of herself as a good mother until the doctor told her she was. Outside affirmations, however, did not have a lasting effect on Cassie because of her codependency. As time went on, Cassie continued to need others to acknowledge her positively and assure her she was all right.

It is through his relationship with his mother that a child discovers who he is (Schore, 1994, p. 3). Therefore, in receiving exaggerated punishment for typical childish mistakes, Cassie often felt like a mistake herself. Cassie took her mother's mostly negative reflection of her as evidence of her unworthiness.

The mother-daughter relationship that Cassie had learned to expect had no distinct boundaries between the self of the mother and that of the daughter. Val's mistrust of caregivers, which was deeply instilled during her first year of life in the orphanage, prompted her to react in a self-protective manner to Cassie's need for intimacy with her. Val viewed intimacy as a threatening invasion. In raising a protective wall to defend her personal space, Val inadvertently aggravated Cassie's Achilles' heel: Val's self-defense could not help but be considered by Cassie as rejection.

All along, however, Cassie actually had the instincts and intuition of a good mother. For example, despite her own mother's negative modeling and influence, Cassie had been able to give her infant son the nurturing he needed. When she was with Tony, Cassie narrated her actions and feelings to her son, and then reflected to Tony how he was reacting, what he was doing, and how he was feeling. Her needs aside, Cassie had given Tony an accurate mirroring of who he was.

At times throughout her life as a parent, Cassie had been aware of the confidence she felt as she saw that what she was doing was working. However, because of her codependency, Cassie was not able to hold this upbeat self-view for long. The minute she received negative feedback, her confidence would plunge. It was not until Cassie underwent substantial treatment and therapy that she was able to change her core perceptions and finally sustain an affirmative view of herself.

Unfortunately, during Cassie's prime parenting years, confidence and good instincts were not always enough to override Elizabeth's negative messages that ran in Cassie's head like a looping tape when things weren't going well. Cassie could not be sure that she, indeed, was a good mother because she did not solidly know the truth about herself as a person at that time.

Through their interactions with their child and in responding to his self-expression, parents co-create what their child's expressions *mean* (Hughes, 2007, p. 97). A child learns and draws conclusions about himself from these interactions. Parents, therefore, are undeniably powerful in setting into place either accurate or inaccurate reflections of their child that he will carry into adulthood.

Taking your child's disapproval and necessary rejection of you in stride is never easy, especially if you have experienced even a taste of what Cassie faced when she was a child—negativity from your parents. Yet it is your ability to see your child's behavior for what it is that will allow you to react in a helpful rather than potentially destructive manner.

Children disapprove of parents' actions because they are naturally self-centered and unable to see what is in their best interests in the long run. That is why children need adults. I often remind parents that it is not their job to be popular with or liked by their children all or even most of the time. In fact, it is often when parents are doing their job well that their children will express negativity toward them.

Children reject parents, especially during their teen years, because they are striving for individuation, which is their birthright. Being accepted by your teen is not a realistic goal for you as parents. You need to encourage your teen's exploration of himself and anticipate his rejection of you as part of his necessary growth process.

In the case of the adopted child who suffers from abandonment and attachment issues, rejection takes on an additional meaning. As we saw with Val, her relentless negativity toward Cassie was her cry for security. What Val's hateful behavior was trying to communicate was her need for ultimate safety: a mother who could stand strong in the face of anything her child could dish out and not falter or give up on her.

If Cassie would have had this knowledge along with sufficient support during the times Val was testing her, healing might have happened during her daughter's childhood. Years of working with client families in similar circumstances have shown me this is true. What is critical for adoptive parents to have is accurate knowledge and steady, professional guidance as they implement strategies that are designed to meet the profound security needs of traumatized children.

17 How to Know if Your Child Is Attached to You

What is attachment and why is it so important? Attachment is the ability of one human being to be in a meaningful relationship with another. It enables a person to be a law-abiding, productive citizen in society. Attachment allows a person to feel empathy for others, to understand and care about others' feelings, and to value and respect others.

Adequate nurturing by a single primary caregiver is the necessary experience an infant must receive in order to become attached. The intimate, repetitive, interactive process of being tended to by a loving parent creates a template for all future relationships. Inadequate care, frequent change in caregivers, and trauma all compromise a child's ability to attach, and can alter his development significantly.

Importantly, attachment is reflected physically in a fully developed brain that has grown in a step-by-step sequence containing no gaps. An attached child has had the stimulation necessary for his brain to grow all of the neuronal connections it needs to function properly and comprehensively. If we were able to take a picture of a child's brain, with all of the regions visible, we would see that an attached child's brain has all of its parts, and all of the expected links.

How can you tell if your child is attached to you? Observable behaviors plus detailed knowledge of the child's developmental history are the criteria used to determine whether a child is attached. The following is a list of behaviors that, when taken together, describe a child who is securely attached (Cooper, Hoffman, & Powell, 2002–2003). This list is not meant to be used to diagnose a child or anyone. Rather, it is included so that the reader may form a clearer picture of a securely attached child. Parents interested in getting a definitive diagnosis of their child's attachment status need to obtain a professional assessment.

Behaviors and Abilities of a Securely Attached Child

SOLID RELATIONSHIP WITH CAREGIVER

- Shows obvious preference for primary caregiver over all others
- Uses caregiver as a secure base from which to explore and to which to return
- Enjoys playing with or being in the presence of caregiver
- Enjoys receiving and giving affection
- Loves to be held and soothed
- Alternates smoothly between needing to be with caregiver and needing to explore
- Directly seeks closeness with caregiver in times of trouble
- Cries at separation from the caregiver
- Misses caregiver during separation
- Actively, happily greets caregiver after separation
- Is comfortable with and connects through eye contact
- Communicates feelings to caregiver
- Communicates needs to caregiver
- Has confidence and trust in the caregiver

THOROUGH BRAIN DEVELOPMENT

- Is capable of behavioral regulation
- Is capable of emotional regulation
- Is capable of empathy
- Is capable of telling life story with details at developmentally appropriate age
- Can prioritize, filter, and process information—executive functioning of the brain is intact
- Has a conscience
- Acts on and reacts to right and wrong
- Meets developmental milestones in a timely manner

STRONG BOND WITH PARENTS

- Has a generalized dependence on parents
- Imitates parental behaviors when interacting
- Blossoms with parental delight
- Thrives in the glow of mom and dad's attention
- Understands and accepts consistent parental control

SOCIALLY WELL-ADJUSTED

- Shows interest in exploring the world
- Has meaningful relationships with others
- Has age-appropriate stranger anxiety
- Socializes successfully
- Displays both joy and an internalized sense of security in daily life

For the adoptee, his preadoptive experience factors heavily into his level of attachment, and in fact determines his attachment status at the time he is adopted. The good news about attachment status is that it can improve if a child receives the nurturing and interactive stimulation he lacked earlier in his life. Since experience grows the brain, if a previously neglected child who developed attachment disorder is adopted and cared for by an attentive parent—particularly if that parent is trained in therapeutic parenting—he can be given the stimulation that will allow his brain to more fully develop, and his attachment disorder can heal.

If parents get an assessment for their child, they can learn whether he is attached or if he suffers from attachment disorder. This assessment involves parents filling out a rating scale related to the child's behaviors such as the Randolph Attachment Disorder Questionnaire, or RADQ, and having a thorough history taken by the professional who will integrate it with the child's scores on the RADQ rating scale. If it is determined that the child is attached, he may be further assessed and found to be either securely or insecurely attached. The additional assessment for attachment type is observational and typically done in an interactive procedure involving the primary parent and the child.

In Tony's case, because he received adequate nurturing from his foster mother in Korea, he became attached and was able to transfer that attachment to his adoptive parents. However, Tony's attachment status can be considered *insecure* rather than *secure* due in part to his unconscious, lingering fear of abandonment, and in part to his unresolved identity issues.

Although an insecurely attached child can show many of the same traits and behaviors as the securely attached child—we can see many of Tony's traits in the list above—there remain aspects of his capacity for relationship that are lacking. If we look at Cassie's relationship with her mother, for example, she definitely was attached, but that attachment was insecure because Elizabeth used Cassie to meet her own needs instead of her focusing on meeting Cassie's needs.

An insecurely attached parent can at best raise an insecurely attached child because she has not had the parenting she needed to become securely attached, so she cannot pass that level of attachment to her child. An adult, however, can become securely attached through sufficient treatment and therapy, and thus able to relate to her children differently, bringing them with her along the attachment spectrum.

In this book, with the goal of illuminating the narrative in mind, we are only drawing detailed attention to the differences between the attached child and the child who suffers from attachment disorder.

Becoming Attached: Tony's Process

Despite Tony's original abandonment by his birth mother, he developed the capacity for attachment during his first 5 months of life in Korean foster care. Tony's foster mother and family gave him the rich, fertile environment that enabled him to grow. Not only did Tony's foster mother meet his basic physical needs, but she also met his emotional needs by attending to him *when he needed it*. On-demand care gave Tony the sense of being worthy because he got the message that his needs and wants—thus he, himself—mattered. Therefore, he was able to develop a strong attachment to her.

The keen attunement of Tony's foster mother to what he needed was possible because she carried him on her back continually. This closeness allowed her to be aware of his every movement and need. Indeed, this custom provided Tony with the closest possible womblike experience for an abandoned infant.

Tony's emotions, body, and brain developed within his dependent relationship with his foster mother, so his brain became wired for dependency and attachment. Tony's capacity, need, and desire for attachment were firmly in place by the time he came to live with his permanent family in the United States. Thus, he arrived primed to reach out to his new primary caregiver, Cassie.

Even though Tony's positive foster experience gave him the capacity to attach, he nonetheless suffered deeply at times during his first 5 months. Beginning with his abandonment by his birth mother in his infancy, Tony lived through both physical and emotional trauma that left its mark. For the first few weeks of his life and during an eye illness that had required hospitalization, Tony did not have a primary caregiver.

Next, Tony had to move and adapt to his foster family. Just when he had begun to attach and feel safe, Tony was once again moved, this time across the world to another family and culture. Then, during his adaptation to his new family and before he had bonded to them, Tony underwent circumcision, undoubtedly one of the most painful physical traumas he had yet experienced.

Despite the fact that Tony's infancy was scarred with trauma, he came to attach to his adoptive parents. It was highly significant that Tony had developed the brain capacity for attachment while in foster care. What this meant was that he was able to stay on track developmentally, a remarkable feat for a traumatized infant to achieve.

The order in which parts of a baby's brain grow is critical. Much as the stability of a building depends upon the quality of its foundation, the capacity for higher thinking depends upon proper, orderly development of the lower parts of the brain (Perry, 2006, p. 248). Attachment, emotional and behavioral control, empathy, having a conscience, and overall brain-body control are all capacities of the higher brain that grow if there is a solid foundation.

Tony was fortunate during his preadoptive life to have had the nurturing that allowed him to develop a fully functioning brain. This is not the case for many children who have been abandoned and traumatized in infancy. Fortunately, if guided professionally in the use of the therapeutic parenting approach, today's adoptive parents can repair many of the developmental gaps in their child's brain caused by neglect.

Tony's active and intense grieving for his foster mother revealed his depth of attachment to her. In being attached, Tony had paid a price. While adjusting to his adoptive family, Tony expressed his abandonment grief through tantrums and long, inconsolable, tearful protests. In leaving his foster mother, Tony experienced profound loss that included losing the feeling of being safe.

Though it was difficult for his adoptive parents to witness, Tony's grieving was normal and to be expected for an attached child who had been removed from his primary caregiver. In fact, it was absolutely necessary for Tony to complete this active mourning process. Only through his grieving was Tony able to let go of his foster mother and transfer his attachment to his "forever mom," Cassie.

We now know that if Tony's parents had held, comforted, and carried him as much as possible throughout his grieving process, they would have given him more of what he needed at the time. Unfortunately, the family pediatrician gave Tony's parents the opposite advice regarding how to handle the situation. *Nonetheless, even if Tony had received the most perfect care in the world, his two abandonments still would have left an emotional scar.*

Abandonment scars—emotional pain the child may feel in any number of ways—can be permanent and may run deep, whether the child is conscious of it or not. As the adoptee becomes an adult, this lingering wound of abandonment may become a significant issue, possibly manifesting as anxiety and/or depression. Sadly, this was the case for Tony and is frequently the case for many adopted children.

Yet through it all, Tony formed a bond with his adoptive parents. Tony's level of eye contact, his imitation of his parents' behaviors, his dependence on them, and his display of stranger anxiety were some of the key traits that confirmed his attachment. Tony showed intense curiosity and interest in the world within the safety of his parents' care. He thrived in the glow of his mom and dad's attention, loving to be held and soothed.

Tony blossomed as his parents delighted in him. Because of his having become attached, Tony was high functioning and met his developmental milestones on time, despite his early trauma. Tony showed both his joy and his feeling of being safe in his daily life. His understanding and acceptance of his parents' limits also proved Tony's bond to them.

Additionally, Tony's parents had a solid sense of being lovingly in control of him, confirming that they were as attached to Tony as he was to them. Attachment goes both ways. Parents and their child come to a bonded center point through consistent, meaningful, and most importantly, daily interactive experience.

The exceptional contrast between the motivation and the behaviors of an attached child like Tony and a child with attachment disorder like Valerie showed up clearly in the children's early development.

Tony's base motivation was to please his parents and to use his intellect and creativity enthusiastically. His behaviors at home were predictable and cooperative. Tony felt grounded and safe in his parents' care. What mattered most to him *was* his relationship with his parents. Therefore, he oriented his behaviors toward pleasing and maintaining a positive relationship with them.

On the other hand, Valerie's base motivation was to do what pleased *her* and made *her* feel okay. At a core level, she did not value parental approval or a relationship with her parents. Not by choice, but rather because of the neglect she endured in her first year of life, Valerie had not experienced the interaction necessary for her brain to become wired for reliance on parents.

Often, Valerie was a puzzle to her parents. To the untrained eye, her behaviors seemed relatively unpredictable compared to those of Tony. Yet, as Dan and Cassie would come to see later on, the thread of control was woven into every action Valerie took.

Internally, Valerie was comfortable when she was in control and very uncomfortable when she was not. For a child with attachment disorder, control serves to prevent him from feeling anxiety and shame. Being in control equals feeling safe for this child. Since his patterning does not allow him to depend upon anyone but himself, the child suffering from attachment disorder uses any means available to stay safe and in control.

Valerie used lying to maintain safety and inner balance. For Valerie, lying was merely a means to an end, and disappointing her parents by lying was not a concept she truly understood at a basic emotional or brain level.

Valerie's understanding of the effect her lying had on others was limited to that of how she could use the behavior to manipulate their actions. This is because her brain was simply not wired the way Tony's was. He could feel remorse about lying, hurting someone's feelings, and breaking trust, whereas Valerie could not. Valerie did not know what it was to trust anyone but herself. Trusting within an interpersonal connection is not possible for a child who suffers from attachment disorder.

18 Recognizing Attachment Disorder in Your Child

In the crucial first 3 years of his life, if a child has a nurturing, safe relationship with his primary caregiver, his brain develops wiring for attachment and socialization. Without this relationship, the child's brain does not get patterned for attachment and socialization—resulting in the development of attachment disorder. The early events in an infant or toddler's life that may lead to the development of an attachment disorder include:

A TEMPORARY OR PERMANENT SEPARATION FROM THE BIRTH MOTHER
FOR ONE OR MORE OF THESE REASONS:

- Mother's ambivalence toward pregnancy
- Relinquishment of parental rights
- Abandonment
- Neglect
- Abuse
- Drug/alcohol addiction
- Illness/hospitalization (child's or mother's)
- Having more than one change in caregivers or multiple caregivers
- Certain genetic disorders
- Prenatal trauma
- In-utero exposure to drugs and/or alcohol
- Birth trauma
- Chronic maternal depression
- Unprepared mother with inadequate parenting skills

Essentially, attachment disorder is incomplete brain development. Most of the traits associated with attachment disorder reflect a poorly wired brain. The following is a list of behaviors that, when taken together, could identify a child who has attachment disorder. It is included so that the reader can get a clearer picture of what a child who suffers from attachment disorder is like. This list is only meant to be a reference and should not be used for diagnostic purposes—parents *must* consult a professional for an assessment.

Traits of Attachment Disorder

RELATIONSHIP PROBLEMS

- Resists affection initiated by parents
- Is inappropriately demanding and/or clingy
- Does not make eye contact, especially with parents (except when lying)
- Cannot experience reciprocal enjoyment (fun, love)
- Cannot receive comforting
- Fears being vulnerable, intimate
- Engages in intense control battles, is bossy
- Is argumentative, defiant
- Does not respond to consequences (they only work if a child values preserving his relationship with his parent)
- Lacks capacity for empathy
- Has poor peer relationships
- Is superficially charming and engaging
- Indiscriminately "attaches" to anyone
- Disrupts celebrations, destroys personal gifts—can't accept positive reflections because of inner shame

NEED FOR CONTROL

- Excessively needs to control everything and everyone to assure his own safety
- Uses feelings and behavior to manipulate others to attempt to control them to assure his own safety

- Is indiscriminately charming to control others in order to stay safe
- Is indiscriminately affectionate with strangers to control them in order to keep himself safe
- Acts oppositionally defiant to maintain control to stay safe
- Tries to split adults apart (treats one parent as "good" and the other—usually the mother—as "bad") to maintain control to assure his own safety

COGNITIVE PROBLEMS

- Lacks cause-effect thinking
- Lacks a conscience
- Is not capable of guilt or remorse
- Has learning lags or delays
- Has speech and language problems

DIFFICULTY WITH EMOTIONS

- Feels chronic high anxiety
- Has intense negative feelings of rage, terror, and despair
- Actively avoids feelings
- Lacks emotional control
- Is unable to identify feelings of self or others

PHYSICAL PROBLEMS

- Lacks awareness of bodily functions
- Lacks appropriate physical boundaries
- Lacks impulse control
- Is overly concerned about small pain while minimizing big pain
- Has food issues: gorges, refuses to eat, eats strange things, hides and/or steals food

DIFFICULTY CONTROLLING BEHAVIOR

- Hurts others or self emotionally and physically
- Is destructive to property, self, and/or others
- Has poor response to discipline, frustration, responsibility, and/or rules

- Incessantly chatters and/or asks questions
- Steals, hoards
- Is hyperactive

POOR SELF-CONCEPT

- Feels overwhelming shame: "I am bad to the core," "I am worthless"
- Has sense of entitlement, expects demands to be met
- Has no insight into or understanding of self
- Lacks a continuing sense of self, experience, and mood across time
- Feels like a victim
- Feels self-hatred that he often projects onto others

PSYCHOLOGICAL PROBLEMS

- Lies about the obvious, uses excuses and blaming (to avoid shame)
- Thinks in black-and-white terms
- Is hypervigilant
- Dissociates ("spaces out") to avoid feelings
- Frequently does not make an effort—does not want to risk failing because this would prove he is bad, worthless
- Is fascinated with fire, blood, gore, weapons, evil

A child need not have all of these traits to have attachment disorder, nor does a child with only some of these traits necessarily have attachment disorder. There can be other causes for some traits listed above. Attachment disorder can coexist with other problems, such as mood disorders, anxiety disorders, and attention deficit/hyperactivity disorder. A thorough assessment by a qualified specialist, including completion of the RADQ (see chapter 17) and the taking of a detailed history of the child is essential to determine his diagnosis.

How Attachment Disorder Develops: Valerie's Story

Valerie's abandonment at birth led to her placement in two different orphanages. For the first 12 months of her life, Valerie was profoundly neglected. Inadequate physical and emotional care generated chronic problems for Valerie in all areas of her development. Yet though traumatized from the moment she was born, Valerie's incredible will allowed her to survive. The same spirit that kept Valerie alive in spite of her bleak first-year environment, however, became a barrier to bonding. We will now take an in-depth look at the range of effects abandonment and neglect can cause.

Physical Damage

Valerie's trauma began with her birth mother's relinquishment. At the time Valerie was born, there was a male-dominated culture in Korea. The fact that male babies were preferred contributed to Valerie's rejection. In the orphanages, Valerie undoubtedly received less attention than did the more valued males. Valerie shared too few attendants with the 25 to 30 other infant females in her ward.

Valerie suffered from nutritional deficiency, which resulted in her subnormal weight and size. This lack of adequate nutrition had several likely causes. The practice of bottle propping probably led to milk leakage due to Valerie frequently losing the nipple. Without touch during feeding, the release of growth hormones was stymied, so even if Valerie had taken in enough milk, she could not have fully assimilated its nutrition (Perry & Szalavitz, 2006, p. 92). Additionally, Valerie possibly suffered from a milk allergy. This would have likely been the cause of Valerie's chronic diarrhea and severe diaper rash, which was replete with untreated open sores.

As a consequence of the unsanitary conditions of the orphanages, Valerie contracted scabies, which only increased her suffering. To cope with the untreated physical pain, Valerie had but one choice if she were to survive: she had to learn not to feel it. During physically inescapable trauma, the psychological defense of dissociating—mentally going away—often gets triggered as a survival mechanism (Ogden, Minton, & Pain, 2006, p. 105). Valerie's adeptness at dissociating from physical pain was one of the first things Cassie and Dan noticed about their daughter upon her arrival.

The most striking physical remnant of Valerie's early neglect was the asymmetry of her head, which the orphanage had documented by her eighth month. Undoubtedly, Valerie was held so infrequently that her head flattened from constantly lying on one side in her crib. Such overwhelming physical deprivation is responsible for scores of infant deaths in orphanages around the world. Without human contact and love, babies fail to thrive and sometimes die (Erickson & Egeland, 2002, p. 3), a fact that makes Valerie's survival remarkable.

Overwhelming Emotions

Valerie's psychological response to being neglected, although unconscious, was to blame herself. Naturally self-centered, children believe that something is wrong with *them* when a caregiver abandons, ignores, or abuses them. To Valerie, her original abandonment and orphanage staff neglect meant to her that she was unworthy of care and attention. Although the hypothesis that an abandoned baby can feel worthless is not easily verified, as the child develops language, he often will give voice to this feeling. This negative self-view, deeply rooted in the child's infant experience, becomes the core of who he is. Core shame, then, is an identity scar that many once-abandoned children will carry the rest of their lives.

Abandonment terror is the most primal reaction possible to being left vulnerable and alone. Ludwig Janus argues convincingly in his book, *The Enduring Effects of Prenatal Experience,* that ". . . our earliest experiences remain alive and active within each of us" (1997, p. 143). An infant separated permanently from his birth mother, therefore, may carry the fear of abandonment with him as he develops.

As the infant grows, his early association between abandonment and mother may further develop, especially if he lacks a primary caregiver. To solve his dilemma, the abandoned child becomes as self-sufficient as possible and puts himself in control of the caregiver, getting her to meet the needs he cannot meet for himself. This quandary negatively affects the parent's ability to get close to the child as well as the child's availability for attachment. This was the core problem that faced Dan and Cassie when trying to parent their daughter.

The lack of trust in a primary caregiver engendered by her abandonment cemented Valerie's independence at a brain-based level. By the time Valerie was 12 months old, she was a self-contained individual, needing from others only the minimal physical care that she could not provide for herself. Valerie's self-reliance substituted for a give-and-take primary relationship. Sadly, emotionally Valerie needed no one. Valerie's premature independence set her up for intense interpersonal conflict because the adoptive family's world she entered was built for *interdependence*.

Need for Control

The terror and shame of being left alone are feelings the abandoned child cannot tolerate or escape; therefore, he seeks to avoid them at any cost. Indeed, the child may carry some level of fear and shame with him his whole life. Therefore, the child focuses his energy on controlling everything and everyone to keep his terror and shame at bay. Parents often misinterpret their child's incessant need to dominate as defiance or oppositionality, behaviors for which they then issue consequences. This error in interpretation only increases the child's resolve to be in charge.

Dealing with the abandoned child's obsession-like need to control can often become the bane of the adoptive family's daily existence. The ability to see beneath this behavior to its source may take professional support and guided practice. Trained parents understand that the child's drive for power serves to keep him out of painful feelings. Correct interpretation leads the parents to have empathy and compassion for their child, which is the fertile ground they need to connect with him.

Rage

When an experience triggers the child's abandonment terror, he may communicate this feeling directly as fear if he feels safe enough. However, because feeling safe is rare for the abandoned child, he will often express his terror indirectly as rage. The child may also use rage to defend against any threat to his ability to control. It is not always possible for parents to remember that the child's rage is the end result of the actions or inactions of previous caregivers, especially when their child directs his rage at them. Even prepared parents can feel shocked and overwhelmed when their child rages. One of the most difficult challenges that can face adoptive parents is not taking the child's rage personally, a feat that eluded the Richards until they got help.

Because the adoptive mother usually takes the role of primary care-giver, she most often becomes the child's prime rage target. The slightest thing can trigger shame and terror-based rages. Unfortunately, the parent may believe that her child's rage indicates something is wrong with *her*. If a parent makes the child's behavior about herself, she misses the child's true message. When the child rages, he is screaming from his depths for security and acceptance. Rage is often a child's desperate plea to be safely embraced, soothed, and valued to his core. This primal care is what the child has been yearning for since the day he was abandoned.

No Patterning for Attachment
As the child's brain grows, it structures itself around repeated patterns (Perry & Szalavitz, 2006, p. 243). A stable, intimate relationship creates a brain pattern that reflects nurturing and results in attachment. This structure mirrors a world in which people are interdependent. The neglected child's brain, however, assembles itself based on the experience of being alone. In the orphanage, Valerie's brain grew to mirror a relatively bleak world in which infants suffer unmet needs and remain estranged from others. Without the consistent pattern of interdependence, the abandoned child's brain does not develop the capacity for intimate relationships. During her first year of life, Valerie was deprived of the experience necessary for her brain to pattern around attachment.

Multiple caregivers and frequent changes in caregivers disrupt attachment and confuse input to the child's brain. Acquired in pieces, the abandoned baby's overall understanding of life lacks continuity. *Indeed, one of the problems many traumatized children encounter as they grow is their inability to create a solid, chronological narrative of their lives due to compromised memory functioning* (Bremner, 2005, p. 103). Remembering sequential events over time requires a fully developed brain, which results from sufficient nurturing.

In the midst of ever-changing caregivers, Valerie herself was the only constant she knew. It was the consistency of having a singular, albeit lonely perspective that enabled Valerie's brain to create a pattern for her experience. In needing a cohesive outlook in order to remain sane, the abandoned baby turns to self-reliance.

A Limited Worldview

The absence of a primary caregiver hinders the development of an abandoned child's comprehensive worldview. Because Valerie spent day after day alone in her crib in the orphanage, not only did she have to cope with feelings of fear and powerlessness but she also had to interpret the world around her on her own, without input from someone more experienced.

As the neglected infant encounters life, he takes in and stores the information he receives undigested. This infant's thoughts reflect a relatively unsophisticated view of life derived from simple input from his senses. He experiences light and dark, cold and hot, noise and silence, bitter and sweet, soft and hard. The baby was fed, or he wasn't, he got dry diapers or he didn't, his cries were answered or they weren't. Without a primary caregiver's translation and assignment of meaning, the neglected infant's worldview becomes one of simple contrasts—to him, things are black or white.

Poor Brain Development

Within an attached relationship, the caregiver in effect "downloads" her brain into her baby's brain. Via verbal and nonverbal interaction while in his mother's arms, the baby learns about everything (Schore, 1994, p. 76). This maternal downloading enables the complexity of the baby's brain to match that of his mother, giving him the capacity for inquisitive and analytical thought, for self-reflection, and for self-regulation.

Additionally, the attached infant's self-concept grows positively due to the attentiveness of his primary caregiver. Valerie had no maternal downloading during her first year, so her brain did not develop the wiring necessary for complex thought. Her self-concept was limited and shame-based due to her neglect.

Developmental Delays

Upon adoption at one year of age, Valerie had only a partially developed ability to sit up. Her inability and lack of desire to crawl at 12 months suggests that at the orphanage she continually remained prone in her crib. In the institution, Valerie was not given the opportunity to explore her world physically. When she joined the Richards family, Valerie did not suck her bottle greedily, nor was she able to hold it. Valerie did not grasp objects her adoptive mom presented to her—another reflection of lack of early stimulation and one-on-one interaction. Valerie displayed little curiosity. She was not interested in exploring her surroundings in general. Sadly, Valerie did not want to cuddle into her mother's body or look into her eyes.

As a result of receiving little or no response to her crying during her preadoptive life, Valerie learned that crying was useless as a signal for help. Her natural instinct to depend upon others eroded quickly through her orphanage experience. The notable lack of crying and protestation present at the time of Valerie's adoption suggests that her crying instinct was all but extinguished.

Tragically, one of the effects of Valerie's abandonment was that she was unable to receive the love that Cassie and Dan offered to her. Due to her attachment disorder, Valerie lacked the brain structure that would allow her to receive nurturing. It was as if Valerie's parents were trying to send her e-mail, but she had no in-box. Meanwhile, Dan and Cassie's intense parental love hovered, waiting for a receptor to form in their daughter.

Because the mother is usually the child's primary parent and the one who provides the child with direct care, she is apt to misinterpret the child's inability to receive nurturing as rejection—when it actually is a physical, brain-based handicap. Cassie struggled with what she perceived was Valerie's personal rejection until she went through attachment-specific therapy after her children had left home. Only then did she realize Valerie had not been physiologically capable of accepting her love.

In the '70s, when Dan and Cassie adopted Valerie, knowledge about attachment disorder was just beginning to surface. Valerie's pediatrician was aware of a child's basic need to become bonded, thus giving the sound advice to limit Valerie's being held to only her parents at first. However, little was known at the time about development of the brain as it relates to attachment. Consequently, interventions specific to the repair and building of the brain structure associated with attachment had not yet been developed.

We now know that new patterning can change the brain at any time in life, albeit more readily in childhood (Perry & Szalavitz, 2006, p. 29). Effective therapeutic intervention for healing attachment disorder is anchored in meaningful, repetitive, sometimes intense, parent-child interaction facilitated by a specialized family therapist. Pioneering efforts are presently underway to establish a universally accepted therapeutic protocol for interventions intent upon building the capacity for attachment in troubled children. The lack of an attachment experience with a single, primary caregiver from the start creates brain deficits that we now know are possible to repair.

If Your Child Has an Attachment Disorder

If your child is suffering from attachment disorder, he has a developmental disability. Without receiving adequate nurturing from a primary caregiver when he was an infant, your child's brain could not develop properly. When you look at the list of possible characteristics and symptoms of attachment disorder and see some behaviors that remind you of your child, you are seeing things his brain allows him to do and those it does not. His brain is missing some important connections, so he cannot regulate himself in many ways.

Your child does *not* engage in difficult behaviors on purpose. He cannot do any better than he is doing at this point. Parents often find it helpful to think of it this way: if a child's leg bones were broken in many places, he would be in a wheelchair until he healed enough to begin to get up on crutches; then he would be on crutches until he healed enough to walk on his own.

Your child's brain is temporarily "broken" in many places. He needs you to help him in most aspects of living, including those in which an attached child would not need help. You or your spouse will in a sense act as your child's "wheelchair" and be with him almost all of the time until he can learn how to regulate himself. Your child will develop this ability over time if you are consistent, receive guidance, and employ the powerful tools of the therapeutic parenting approach. Results vary, but it is not unusual to see at least some progress in just a few months.

Your child's brain can heal, and he can learn to live and think like other children who are attached. Professionally guided parents who follow a prescribed therapeutic parenting protocol can aid the development of their child's brain. Using a neurosequential approach—that is working to "fill in" the missing parts of the brain from the bottom up—you as parents can heal your child from neglect and trauma (Perry & Szalavitz, 2006, p. 138).

If your child had been yours from the start, you could have taken adequate care of him and his brain would have had the stimulation to form properly. Your child missed out on this nurturing care early in his life. Fortunately, you, as your child's "forever parents," can give him the specialized care he needs and actually facilitate his complete brain development, even if he is no longer an infant.

Expecting a child with attachment disorder to be able to do all of the things that an attached child can do is like expecting a child in a wheelchair to walk with broken bones. Remembering that *the child is really doing the best he can in this moment* may be one of the hardest things to do. Because a child may not *look* like he has a disability on the outside, parents and others may expect him to act as if he does not have a disability.

As adoptive parents, you are healing a child with a developmentally handicapped brain that causes him to do maddening things that even he does not understand. Every morning when getting ready for the day, keep this in mind. Every evening when settling in for the night, remember this. If you can celebrate the behavioral baby steps your child takes each day, before you know it he will be "walking."

19 Understanding Your Child's Struggles with Identity, Shame, and the Need for Control

Those involved in adoption deal with the following seven issues over their lifetime: loss, rejection, guilt and shame, grief, identity, intimacy, and mastery/control (Kaplan and Silverstein, 1982). This chapter will focus on three of these—identity, shame, and the need for control. Children who have been abandoned, neglected, or traumatized reveal their struggle with these issues in their behaviors. Each adopted child is unique, and therefore, the way his personal development unfolds is related to the specifics of his genetics, his past experience, and his temperament. However, many adopted children grapple in some way with the core questions of "Who am I?" and "Am I worthy?" and "Can I trust anyone other than myself?"

If you can look closely at your child and his behavior, you will likely find these questions lurking, either in his conscious mind or just under his awareness. Although it is a rare child that can give voice to these struggles on his own, with the mirroring of an adult using accurate empathy, most children are relieved to be able to acknowledge the pain of their issues of identity, shame, and need for control.

Why is it important for your child to be able to talk about these three core issues? You may question the wisdom of eliciting discussion from your child about difficult topics, especially if your child appears to be doing fine, for fear of "rocking the boat." However, the significance of these questions is such that unless you help your child deal with them, they likely will be the driving force behind future difficulties, if those difficulties have not already appeared.

If you can find a way to feel confident about the process of dealing with your child's core issues, if you feel you have the means to do so, and if you can feel assured of a positive, growthful outcome, then you probably are more apt to proceed. To begin this process, you will need to understand the three core issues—their significance and meaning—and via your understanding, gain compassion for your child.

Identity

A biological need to belong exists between mammals and their offspring that bonds them at the most basic level. For example, in the animal world, sheep ranchers will wrap the pelt of a ewe's dead new-born around an orphan lamb to get the ewe to accept it. The ewe will reject a lamb that she cannot identify as hers (Bowlby, 1982, p. 164). In a similar way, when we are born into our birth parents' care, there is a mutual seamless acceptance at an unconscious, organic level.

In contrast, an infant who is adopted by a nonbiological parent has had that initial bond with his birth mother broken. This child's unconscious, organic sense of belonging has been severed. For him, the only biological remnant of his birth mother might well be her lingering scent on a passed-along sweater.

Even those adopted at birth can carry a life-long feeling of being disconnected at some level. Because it is biological in origin, this feeling cannot be discarded or easily overcome. As Tony did, adoptees often develop depression that relates to their original abandonment. The adoptee can work through this feeling of disconnect in therapy, sometimes aided by an antidepressant, to the point where the depression subsides substantially. When he can acknowledge his core sense of feeling rejected, the adult is then able to address and minimize its impact on his life.

To make sense of his life, an adoptee must somehow reconcile with his past. Often, adoptees will search for their birth parents to reconnect with their biological beginnings. This quest can help them rewrite whatever story they've had to create around their abandonment and bring it closer to a more realistic narrative.

An adoptee born of a culture different from that of his adoptive parents carries an additional burden to bear regarding identity. His race may make him easily distinguishable within his adoptive family and his community. This only increases the complexity of coming to terms with the past for him. Like all adoptees, the trans-racial adoptee is different from his adoptive family biologically. Additionally, he also will have to deal with having a different skin color or facial appearance from his parents, which sets him apart even more.

It is helpful to keep it in your mind and heart that your child may experience a feeling of not belonging at some level, regardless of his cultural origin. Ignoring or diminishing the child's differences negates him and the importance of his reality. When you are able to proactively address your child's differences openly and directly with him at his present ability to understand, you avoid inadvertently shaming him and increase the likelihood of bonding. You may need to talk with your child many separate times as he grows about his uniqueness in the family and community.

In being interested in your child's feelings about his differences and in responding empathically, you convey acceptance and understanding. Your parental empathy leads to your child's ability to fully integrate his past, thereby freeing himself from its bonds. Although he can never be biologically connected to you (unless, of course he is kin), if you emotionally embrace your adopted child, he can feel a deep and genuine closeness to you that feeds his need to belong. Honesty, straightforwardness, and the desire to be with your child in his struggles will build trust between you and your child.

You must also pave the way for your child in the community, preparing those with whom he'll interact for his uniqueness. This is especially important in the school setting, as we saw in the case of the Richards' children. Equipping your child to cope with any prejudice he may encounter by having him rehearse deflective responses, as well as teaching him how to personally handle the rejection, is essential to your child's adjustment.

If your child is racially different, you cannot take away his hardship, but you can ease his pain by staying attuned to him. What a visually unique child needs most from you is your unconditional acceptance and assertive guidance as he enters the world outside the family. Without your parental interface, the child may be a prime target for further rejection. Differences must be addressed head-on and dealt with as the real hurdle they are for a child in a dissimilar culture.

Shame

Primal separation of a child from his birth mother can bring with it a deep-seated sense of shame of not being wanted. Even if your child's birth mother loved him with all her heart and placed him out of necessity, your child's feeling of being unwanted by her is to be expected. In not feeling wanted, your child may assume there is something about him, personally, that must be the cause of his birth mother's rejection. Your child may feel abandoned because of *who* he is; therefore, he may conclude he is worthless. It is this innate feeling of shame of self that can endure well into adulthood for an adoptee. Some adopted children carry this shame like the ugliest of secrets and cannot help but be emotionally influenced by it, though they may be reluctant to talk about it.

As his parent, you cannot talk your child out of this feeling of worthlessness. Unfortunately, you cannot simply say to your child that he is valuable and change his core sense of self. You must acknowledge your child's feelings of unworthiness and stay with him in his shame in order for him to trust that you understand him. Only then can your child take your hand and begin to step out of his dark cave of negativity about himself. Of course, this is a process and the work a therapeutic parent does, both informally in the moment and through the empathic healing talk (see chapter 25), often with guidance of a professional.

We all seek congruence—to be in harmony with our environment in order to be at peace. The discord that results from our insides not matching what is outside of us can become unbearable. Presumably, most of us feel worthy and positive about ourselves most of the time, and we therefore behave in ways that elicit a reflection of our worthiness from those around us. We seek positive environs and company that match how we feel about ourselves at a core level.

Contrastingly, shame will often be at the root of the negative behaviors displayed by your child. He may become desperate for his life to make sense from the inside out. Since he feels powerless to change the sense of worthlessness he feels deep down, your child may try to get the outside world to reflect the worthlessness within him. Thus, he may behave in ways that elicit negativity from the environment and from those around him. Your child's negative behavior says, "See, I *am* bad, aren't I?" What your child is also saying in his behavior, however, is, "Please help me feel better." Remember that your child's behavior is always a plea for help and relief from very difficult feelings.

Again, similar to the way you approach identity issues with your child, you need to begin by acknowledging for him his feelings of shame about himself. If you are able to communicate your true understanding and acceptance of your child's shame—and *not* that you want to *fix* it—you can reduce his discord with his environment. The result is that your child will likely settle down behaviorally. This is not to say that you are *settling* for your child feeling worthless, rather you are meeting your child where he *is* in order to really *be* with him. Just the act of you *being there* with your child in his shame begins to instill in him a sense that he is worth *something*, shame and all. What your child will reason at some level is that if you, his *parent*, can stand to be with him in his darkest place, then he must be of some value.

Empathy is the conduit you are using when you "feel with" your child—not to be confused with sympathy, which is to "feel for" him. It is your commitment to be with your child in his every feeling and mood that will transform his intrinsic sense of shame into worthiness. Practically, what this means, is that you need to stay exquisitely attuned, or "tuned in" to your child. This may sound questionable, or even overwhelming, until you understand *how* to do this in a practical way.

Throughout the day, you continue to translate your child's behaviors into the messages that even he, himself, may not know he's sending. For example, when Val expressed her hatred of Cassie through words and angry glances, Val's real message was, "I don't feel safe when I can get to you." When you recognize your child's behavior for what it is and understand its meaning, you can actually say out loud to him what he is trying to convey behaviorally.

In Val's example above, to translate her daughter's behavior, Cassie might have said to her: "Val, I know that what you might be saying to me right now with your hateful behavior is 'Mom, please be strong and realize that what I need to know is that you will never abandon me, even if I am bad.'"

Therapeutic parenting at its core is just this: realizing that your child's behavior, no matter how negative, is a signal that he needs you to come to him, understand him, accept him, explain him to himself, and comfort him. Just as a parent of an infant responds to his every coo and cry, you, as the parent of a once-abandoned child, must recognize his behavior as his expression of a need that you must meet. The hardest part of this process for you—and for most parents—may be reminding yourself that your child's behavior is always a *message*. The problem is that your child's behavior can be off-putting, aggressive, taunting, and even cruel, making it difficult for you to stay objective. However, being objective is exactly what it will take for you to be able to depersonalize your child's behavior in order to see beneath it to his true need.

Next, you, like most parents, may find it difficult at first to begin translating your child's behavior into his *need*. For parents, translating their child's behavior into its meaning is like learning a foreign language. It takes time, practice, and sometimes specialized guidance to learn to stay objective enough to interpret and respond to the child's behavioral messages. Fortunately, the needs your child will be expressing with his behaviors will be *core needs*, and these are limited in number. Children's core needs are these: security, safety, physical and emotional regulation, and comfort.

In our Val example above, Cassie could have asked herself, "Is Val being hateful right now because she is feeling insecure, unsafe, physically uncomfortable, or emotionally out of control?" Cassie then could have run through the possibilities, one by one: "Hmm, well she seems to be quite in control! She doesn't look like she needs food or warmer clothes. Maybe my taking her attacks personally is making her feel insecure." Therapeutic parents usually find that with lots of guided practice, once they get the hang of it, translating their child's behavior gets easier.

Control

We use the word, "control," in this book to describe one of the hallmark behaviors of a child who suffers from attachment disorder. Although it is an accurate description of an observable behavior these children display, the label "control" is not empathic. For the child with attachment disorder, the need for control is linked to his need to feel safe and secure. Being safe is a prerequisite for just about any venture we pursue in life, whether it be sleeping, playing, or learning something new.

Neglected infants do not feel safe and secure. Once they discover that their needs are unmet more often than not by the adults who are supposed to be taking care of them, they begin to take charge. Whether it is by self-soothing, dissociating from pain and hunger, or becoming hypervigilant, a neglected child learns to meet his own needs the best way he can. He manages the interface between himself and the world—he takes control, and that makes him feel safe.

Meanwhile, the adequately nurtured child learns to rely on his parents to be that buffer between himself and the world. His experience tells him that when he has a need, his parents will take care of him. Being taken care of by his parents allows the child to feel safe, and he learns to trust adults and yield to their control, subordinating his own need to control.

The key to meeting the needs of a previously neglected child is to first understand exactly why he seeks to control everything and everyone. Having compassion for the child because his experiences forced him to learn to survive by his own wits can be a beginning point.

The following narrative is an opportunity for you to put yourself momentarily in the neglected child's world:

> Imagine being alone in a crib with a wet diaper, a diaper rash, feeling cold, and being hungry. You cry to get someone to come to you to make you dry, warm, and full. No one comes. You cry for a long time and still no comes. You're exhausted from crying, so you fall asleep for a while.
>
> When you wake up, you're even wetter, colder, and hungrier. You cry again, but again, no one comes so you stop crying. In fact, you give up crying altogether because it does no good. Still, no one comes.
>
> You begin to stare off into space. At times, you turn your head from side to side trying to see whatever you can see from your crib while lying on your back because you can't roll over yet. The nurse at the bathing station has just picked up a baby from the tub and is wrapping him in a towel. She turns from the station and walks out of view. Once again, there's nothing to see, so you go back to staring into space. You stop believing anyone will come and help. You drift off to sleep.
>
> Suddenly you awaken because someone is there stripping off your wet clothes and diaper. She quickly replaces them with dry ones. She

gives you a bottle, propping it near you with the nipple in your mouth. Then she leaves—5 minutes and she's gone again for hours. The nipple slips from your mouth and you struggle to reach it. Meanwhile, your milk is leaking onto your crib mattress and is beginning to soak your fresh, dry clothes. You manage to latch onto the nipple and suck greedily, but the milk has nearly all leaked out. The bottle slips away again and you lie there, staring.

All you have is your eyes and ears so you watch and listen to anything there is, anything at all. When there's nothing to see or hear, you stare and space out into a place all your own. This unfocused gaze, this looking, this listening are your only powers, your only control. This is how you begin to take your life into your own hands.

As you grow, you greedily acquire the abilities that allow you to do more for yourself. Everything you do is for yourself. You can trust no one to take care of you. You take care of yourself and do whatever is necessary to get what you need and what you want. Other people are a means to an end. You find you can get people to do things for you by being cute or by throwing a tantrum until they give in.

Your power to take care of yourself increases as you learn how to control others. You do anything you can to feel safe, if only for a moment here or a moment there. You allow no one to be in charge of you, because that feels very unsafe. You've never been able to trust anyone to be there for you consistently. Now you only trust yourself.

Your brain has grown in response to your experience of independence and has formed neural pathways that are patterned around taking care of yourself. There *are* no pathways for the experience of feeling safe in another's care. So you really don't know what that is like, and it would be terrifying to let go of being in charge to find out. What if you were to let go and no one is there after all? You might get hurt, you might even die. So you stay safe. You stay in charge. You don't let anyone in. This is how you carry on—in control.

This is the world of the neglected infant who eventually becomes the child with controlling behaviors. Perhaps now you understand something about why he needs to have control. Respect him for it. Feel compassion for him. He survived.

20 Why Your Child Might Behave Well with Others but Not with You

More often than not, children with attachment issues are able to control their behavior while outside the home environment. Behaviorally, they seem to put on their "Sunday best" while in school and in the community. Predictably, therefore, adults in the outside world find it hard even to imagine that these children and their families are struggling. Therefore, when outsiders encounter exasperated parents, they understandably, but erroneously, conclude that the child's difficult behaviors at home are due to something the parents are or are not doing. Parents are easily blamed if their child has negative behaviors at home, while his real problems—attachment deficit and identity issues—remain unseen by others.

Children with attachment disorder can, and often do, partition their personalities so that the positive, easy-to-deal-with side is displayed within nonintimate relationships, and the disturbing, hard-to-deal-with part is reserved for caregivers and families. One reason for this is that the intimacy of the home environment can overwhelm a child with attachment disorder, who copes with this anxiety by using defensive and oppositional behaviors. Another reason these children are able to "change their stripes" and behave in the changing circumstances of the public arena is that early on they had to learn how to match their surroundings to fit in.

In looking at the Richards' family story, we saw that Valerie readily mastered her life in France in a comprehensive, astonishing way. Although it is not the case with all children with attachment disorder, many are highly proficient at adapting to a new environment. This primitive survival skill develops when a child undergoes life-threatening neglect and abuse, and it may be reactivated when the child encounters a new circumstance.

At the orphanage, Valerie's observational acuity increased each day as she lay in her crib. Confined there, all she could do was listen and watch whatever activity she could hear and see. As a result, her observational skill became her primary adaptive tool. Valerie was adept at replicating even the smallest of details. For example, her capacity to memorize instantaneously—first fully demonstrated as a toddler when she "read" *Jack and the Beanstalk*—displayed the accuracy and precision of her acute listening skills.

Thus, when Valerie encountered an entirely new culture and daily spoken language in France, it did not take her long to integrate competently. She was like a human chameleon, capable not only of changing her appearance but also her behavior, speech, and affect at will to match her surroundings.

Valerie was rarely afraid or anxious when she stepped into new situations. In fact, unfamiliar surroundings activated her highly attuned adaptive ability, which squelched any fears that may have been triggered. This adaptability served her well—as it does most children with attachment disorder—in dealing with challenges of the relatively *impersonal* kind. In these less personal situations, the child's anxiety is kept at bay, quelled in part by focusing on adaptation.

On the other hand, when faced with the possibility of interacting on a more personal level, children with attachment disorder experience intense anxiety—which wells up inside them, creating angst that disables their adaptive ability. Valerie therefore avoided any situation that might require her to interact with others on a more-than-surface level. She remained aloof from her peers and relied upon accurate imitation to survive in the new culture.

For Valerie, learning and excelling in school in France were motivated in part by her deep need to remain inconspicuous and not call attention to herself in a negative way. Her newfound academic motivation was further stimulated by her surprising discovery that, for the first time in her life, she could outshine her brother. The confidence that Valerie's adaptive tools instilled gave her a distinct advantage.

Additionally, for a child like Valerie with a damaged emotional core, achievement and performance can *become* "the self." *Doing* instead of *being* is what created security and self-worth for Valerie. Because intrinsically she felt worthless, Valerie had to *do* something notable to *be* someone. Thus, in wanting to feel as confident as possible in her new situation, Valerie performed academically like never before.

When faced with novel experiences like the year in France, Valerie relied almost entirely upon herself while Tony, like most attached children, turned to his parents for both guidance and emotional support. Tony's need to rely upon his parents was magnified in France by the obstacles presented by the foreign culture and language. Unlike Valerie, Tony valued a connection with his parents and his community, to which he sought to belong by developing relationships with his French classmates. Valerie's almost complete lack of dependence upon her parents and lack of need for friendships seemed remarkable by comparison. Independently, Valerie transformed herself into a full-fledged French girl.

Although Valerie was fully competent at controlling her external environment via her assimilation of the French culture, she was unable to take command of her internal world. Her inner turmoil overflowed into her home environment, the only place where her success in managing herself broke down. However, even though she suffered emotionally, Valerie clung to her independence, incapable of accepting help or support from her parents. Her brain was not wired in such a way that she could reach out to someone to relieve her internal pain. Therefore, Valerie suffered in isolation, her parents rendered as helpless as their daughter was by her attachment disorder.

The tendency of children with attachment disorder to isolate from meaningful connections with others often leads to significant issues of loneliness in adulthood and a difficulty in developing intimate relationships. This would be the case for Valerie until her parents began to connect with her when she was an adult using the therapeutic parenting approach. Only then did she begin to trust her needs to others.

If your child tends to isolate from meaningful relationships with you and others, there is hope. If you are a parent of a child who behaves for everyone else but you, take heart. There is good news in that at least you have "only" one frontier upon which you need to focus—your rela-tionship with your child. If you begin using the therapeutic parenting tool—the empathic parenting talk—with your child regularly, you will not only increase your child's understanding of himself, but you will give him a safe forum in which to practice intimacy. Appendix A gives an example of the empathic healing talk as well as an outline of its structure.

21 What Lying is Really About

All children lie sometimes. Parenting books and classes commonly inform parents that lying is a normal stage of a toddler's ego development. Generally, parents are not alarmed by this behavior and work with the child to help him learn to tell the truth. As parents become more effective, they often ignore the lie, giving more weight to telling the truth than to the misbehavior, which builds trust.

When a child can admit guilt, he reveals a conscience that has developed over time through consistent, corrective parenting. The child's conscience holds his internalized concepts of right and wrong, which his parents taught to him. When parents are sure their child's conscience is solid, they feel comfortably in control.

A child who is bonded with his parents finds that when he lies, he disappoints the most important people in his life. This child has learned that being in his parents' good graces and having them trust him is more important than anything he may lie about. Trust hinges both on the child being truthful with his parents and his parents being truthful with him.

As trust develops, the attached child discovers that he can't really get away with a lie. Parents develop the ability to read a lie on their child's face. For the securely attached child, chronic lying is not an issue. Most importantly, by the end of his formative years, the securely attached child knows that no matter what wrong he has committed, he will remain safely in his parents' care.

While the dynamics involved in lying for the attached child are relatively simple and easy to comprehend, chronic lying remains one of the most frustrating and misunderstood behaviors of children with attachment issues. The "crazy" and persistent lying of children with attachment disorder is clearly distinguishable from the attached child's developmentally expected lying. Relentless, untrustworthy lying behavior becomes truly alarming to parents because it suggests that their child may not have a conscience. This fear may drive parents to become obsessive about trying to stop their child's lying.

Without knowing what is at the root of the lying behavior of a child with attachment disorder, you may try to use the traditional parenting methods you are familiar with to try to deal with it. However, as you discover you can't reach your child with this approach, you may become frustrated and anxious. The inability to trust your child and your frustrations about trying to stop his lying may bring you to feelings of fear, powerlessness, and even panic.

If your child proves to be truly untrustworthy, you may tend to distance yourself from him emotionally. When someone lacks a conscience, his very presence can be disconcerting. Feelings of dislike for your child may emerge, triggering guilt for not liking your child.

Indeed, the unconditional love you once felt for your child may begin to wane. Worry replaces optimism, and good will disintegrates. At this point, without the intervention of a skilled professional, your confidence may even collapse to the point where you fear you might be incapable of raising this child.

So why does an attached child lie only occasionally while a child with attachment disorder lies repeatedly? As far as children with attachment disorder are concerned, lying has connotations that fundamentally differ from not telling the truth. For one, he may be motivated to lie in order to protect himself from falling into his core shame. Admitting to a wrongdoing is a surefire way for this child to feel he is repugnant. This is why he may even resort to "crazy lying" and deny he ate the candy when the chocolate is dripping down his chin.

Secondly, lying is a tool this child may use to control his impression of himself. Through lying, he can remain perfect to himself by denying his misconduct. He reasons that if he can make others think that he is good, then he won't be rejected. This child may believe he can remain in control of his image using a lie, and when he feels in control, he feels relatively safe for that moment.

The ease with which the child who suffers from attachment disorder lies reveals his lack of conscience, a result of his inadequately developed brain. Without having had a trusting relationship with a primary care-giver early on, this child's brain was deprived of the one-on-one interaction essential for its proper development. Therefore, unlike the attached child, the child who suffers from attachment disorder is not able to trust anyone but himself. In this child's mind, taking care of himself has always been up to him, so he does whatever it takes to meet his perceived needs. This makes any behavior, including lying, seem right to the child if he deems it is necessary for getting what he needs or wants.

Looking back at the countless times Val lied, we can see that her motivation had everything to do with remaining in control. Through lying about playing with the neighbor child's makeup, Val controlled her image as being a good girl who was diligently practicing the piano. When Val picked the tulips, she was satisfying her wants and lied to cover up her actions. Val lied about writing on the glass door with the red wax to deter punishment.

Yet Val's innocent countenance was so convincing each time, especially to Cassie in the beginning. Dan began to see right through his daughter's lies early on, referring to her behavior as that of a con artist. He was picking up something in Val's demeanor that told him she was lying outright each time. I like to help parents of a child with attachment disorder tune in and notice that their child is actually comfortable looking them in the eye when lying. This is not the case for attached children, generally. The attached child will look away from a parent's face when lying, averting his guilty eyes.

In the world of a child with attachment disorder where rules mean nothing because there is no trust in others—especially those who have made the rules—lying is easy. A child like Val doesn't care about pleasing parents in order to remain in their good graces. The child does not understand the value of intimate relationships—he sees others as a means to an end. With rare exceptions, this problem is neither a matter of the child's will nor a matter of genetics. As in Val's case, a child with attachment disorder has a brain that is handicapped due to neglect and will remain this way without specialized intervention.

Via therapeutic parenting (see chapter 25) and over time, you as parents can establish the crucial connection with your child that allows him to begin to trust in your care. You begin by taking your child back to the place where he got off track in establishing a relationship with a primary caregiver, and reparent him from there through the stages of proper childhood development. Your relationship with your child becomes pivotal to him learning the difference between right and wrong. It is within and because of his nurturing relationship with you, in the present, that neural pathways will form in your child's brain which will allow him to learn to understand right from wrong.

As a result of your diligence toward healing your child, he actually will grow and learn to care if he disappoints you with his behavior. Your child will come to understand the value of behaving well to please you. This will increase your trust in your child and allow him to begin to feel worthy.

Your child will begin to be able to see right and wrong in terms that are absolute and as separate from himself as a person. Right and wrong will no longer be a reflection for your child of his good or bad *self*. Nor will right or wrong be considered strictly from the point of view of your child's needs or wants. Instead, your child will come to understand that morals and laws are the basis for whether an *action* is right or wrong. The therapeutic parenting process you engage in with your child will actually change his brain physically so that his conscience can take form. Within your attuned parent-child relationship, neural pathways grow in your child's brain that will allow him to feel empathy (Schore, 1994, p. 353), so he will be able to truly care how his behavior affects you and others.

22 Deciphering the Message Behind Stealing

Whereas all children steal sometimes, it is not a chronic behavior in those who are securely attached. However, persistent stealing behavior in children who suffer from early neglect, abandonment issues, or attachment disorder is common. There are many reasons a child may be motivated to steal, and these reasons can be conscious or unconscious. When we look at a child's past experience and his present level of emotional functioning, his motivation for stealing can be unmasked, exposing the need it disguises. This translation of behavior is the approach taken in therapeutic parenting. Parents learn that behaviors are cues for important needs their child cannot express verbally for lack of words or awareness.

A child's prior physical and emotional deprivation can be the impetus for him to steal because of the suffering he endured as a result of insufficient nutrition or nurturance. Even though the child may now be properly fed and nurtured, his imprinting continues to tell him he still does not have enough, or that he had better get what he can now because there may be none later. His brain continues to send him signals of deprivation. Having developed in an environment of caregiving deprivation or instability, once-neglected children's brains are not wired to fully depend upon others. These children learned early on that they needed to meet their own needs the best they could. So, in the present, they steal to "fill their coffers," whether it is with food, money (security), or things.

Emotionally, a child who was abandoned or neglected in infancy likely developed a sense of emptiness that has never gone away. Stealing may momentarily satisfy this child by giving him a sense that he is filling up the emotional hole inside. The empty child also gains a sense of power in fending for himself to alleviate a terrible feeling of emptiness or loneliness. For this child, the stealing is a more reliable way to get what he wants than asking for it. Stealing becomes habitual because the satisfaction that comes from a single act of stealing inevitably fades.

Through learning and using therapeutic parenting, parents can acquire a comprehensive approach to helping a child who chronically steals. One of the first things parents learn is that having too many precious, one-of-a-kind possessions in the home can be a setup for a child to steal. Parents are encouraged to store such items while the child is developing. Regular use of the empathic parenting talk is the vehicle through which parents teach their child about his needs, how his particular behaviors express those needs, and that reliance on them as caregivers is in the end, the best way to get his needs met. Slowly over time, through these repetitive interactions with parents, the child's brain builds pathways that support his dependence on them.

Poor self-regulation can be the cause of a once-neglected child not being able to stop himself from stealing even if he wants to. This child's stealing behavior is biologically based in that it is reflective of his poorly developed brain. This child will likely continue to steal, not necessarily to spite his parent but rather because he literally cannot help himself yet. If this is the case, the task of a therapeutic parent is to help rewire the child's brain so that he can begin to self-regulate. The approach involves the parent providing the regulation for the child in the form of close supervision until the child begins to "absorb" the ability to self-regulate from this supervision. Over time, with good support from a specialist, parents actually can effect such a change at a brain level.

Another reason children may steal is that they often feel powerless due to their original abandonment and subsequent placement(s). This feeling is probably unconscious for the child but can manifest when a child acts out through stealing. The child will probably not, by himself, be able to connect his deep-seated feelings of powerlessness with his stealing. When he steals successfully though, the child will feel the safety of being in control and powerful for a short time.

The feelings of rage or passive-aggressive anger are sometimes expressed through stealing. Once again, these volatile feelings are usually not conscious or identifiable by the child. As an attempt at getting back at the abandoning birth parent or in some cases "the system" for causing his deep despair, the child's stealing is often directed at the target most available to him—his adoptive parent.

Sibling jealousy can often drive a child to steal. Afraid that there might not be enough parental care and love to go around, the child may steal his siblings' things. Whenever a parent gives something emotional or material to another child in the family, the sibling who suffers from attachment disorder fears there is less for him. The concept that there is *enough to go around* is an abstract thought for a child who is only capable of thinking concretely. This child believes that when his parents pay any kind of attention to others, *his* supply is being used up. Through chronic stealing from a sibling, the child also gains his parent's attention, taking it away from another child momentarily. In a multi-sibling family, many parents discover an unspoken wish common to each of their children—that each one wants to be the only child.

The once-neglected child may feel different than his peers, and often, he truly is handicapped by comparison, socially, emotionally, intellectually, or physically. If he feels *less than,* this child may have a difficult time making a place for himself in the world of his peers. When he finds he cannot do things the way other children can, the child feels he is not on par with them. Therefore, in the moment, stealing gives this child a feeling of being capable, of being powerful, and of being able to accomplish something. Stealing may allow the child to feel more at the level of his peers in the realm of *can do.* For a brief time, the child can feel like he matters.

In the case of Tony, stealing was probably the expression of a fantasy persona as well as a means to an end—acquiring an expensive collection that he could not otherwise afford. Tony had learned to satisfy his need for a powerful identity by escaping to a world where he felt safe. In this world he was able to fashion both the environment and his character. Within the realm of *Dungeons and Dragons* Tony adopted a role as a powerful dungeon master, in which he orchestrated the fate of others. Obsessed with the game and emboldened by his new persona, Tony found it an easy next step to steal in spite of the risk of being caught.

The therapeutic goal in this case is for the child's parent to help him connect his powerlessness and sense of negative identity with his stealing behavior. The child will learn that stealing stems from his drive to attain power over his original abandonment and from his need to feel a more positive identity. He will begin to understand that in feeling less than his peers, he was trying to "be somebody" through stealing and having things. With the guidance of a therapist if necessary, the parent helps the child learn to identify his feelings verbally so he can avoid acting them out.

Stealing is a risky behavior, and engaging in risky behaviors causes the release of feel-good chemicals in the body and brain (Goldman, 1997, p. 163), which can be highly energizing. If a child wants more of this feeling, he begins to steal more often. Because of this sought after "adrenaline rush," stealing can become an addictive behavior for some. This stimulating, feel-good state gives a depressed child a sense of well-being that normally is not there. Parents concerned about their child's chronic stealing may find depression at the root of the behavior.

Stress from early abandonment and neglect may cause a child to become biochemically depressed. The presence of a high blood level of the stress hormone cortisol is associated with depression and can cause some of its symptoms as well (Kramer, 1997, p. 116). Therefore, parents need to remain attuned to their child's mood state. Any chronic state of repression, depression, or being shut down in a child warrants professional attention. Clinical depression in children is a more common problem than is often recognized, especially in children from neglectful backgrounds, and treatment with medication may be needed.

If a child is stealing food, particularly food that is high in carbohydrates or sugar, not only is he trying to fill himself up due to being deprived in the past, but he also is self-medicating. Carbohydrates and sugary foods metabolize into glucose, which stimulates the release of serotonin in the child's brain (Katherine, 1996, p. 25). In stealing and eating foods that promote the production of serotonin, the child creates an experience of pleasure for himself that he wants to repeat. The drive to feel better leads the child to take and eat whatever he can find that will make him feel calmer and happier in the moment. The child feels he can control both his mood and his food supply if he both steals and hoards food full of sugar and carbohydrates. These behaviors can be common in families raising once-neglected children.

Through therapeutic parenting activities, adoptive parents can actually use their child's junk-food drive to strengthen attachment. After the child has had adequate nutritious foods, therapeutic parents may give their child sweets during cuddle time, which can help the child form an association between feeling good and being close to the parent.

In summary, whatever the need chronic stealing may represent, this behavior is *always* a message from your child. Ongoing stealing is your child's cry for help, a subconscious plea for relief from suffering. Your commitment to understanding your child's message and meeting his underlying needs is essential to his growth and healing. Since stealing behavior is often so triggering for parents, a professional consult may be helpful. You will need objectivity when approaching this problem so you can set aside your own reactions in order to focus on what your child is saying with his behavior. Also, you may need an outside point of view to help you decipher your child's message, which may range from simple to complex.

23 Finding Compassion When Your Child is Being Hateful

Because it is so easy to take a child's expression of hatred personally, it can be one of the most disturbing behaviors to deal with. Your child may communicate his hatred in words, body and facial expressions, violence toward others or himself, abuse of animals, or destruction of property—oftentimes his own. However clear your child's expression of hatred may appear, understanding its actual meaning and remaining compassionate in the face of the behavior can be difficult. If you are not the target of the child's hatred, remaining objective is more possible, as we saw in the case of Dan Richards. However, if you're the parent who *is* the child's target, as was Cassie Richards, it can feel impossible not to take his hatred personally.

For sure, it is highly distressing to be the recipient of hatred. A child's hostility seems to be tailored to attack his parent's every insecurity, weakness, and vulnerability. It's as if the child knows exactly how to "get" the parent in any given situation. This can make it even more challenging for a parent to understand that the child's hatred is not really about her.

A child's hatred can originate from two major sources. One of these is the insecurity instilled by the child's original abandonment. The deep, unconscious terror and the total lack of safety the child experienced as an infant when he was taken away from his birth mother eventually may surface as hatred toward any subsequent primary caregiver. At a deep level, the abandoned child can associate fear with caregivers in general, because ultimately, they have the power to abandon him.

This problem is much worse for a child whose parents do not provide sufficient authority for him. When a child feels more dominant than his parent, he cannot trust that parent to take care of him. Fear masquerading as disgust emerges in the child whenever his parent shows weakness. Powerlessness in adults draws out the child's contempt for caregivers in general. In the Richards family, part of Valerie's hatred grew from not feeling safe with her adoptive mother because Cassie was unable to stay objective in the face of her daughter's relentless hostile attacks. Thus, Val's ability to overpower her mother emotionally resulted in Val feeling more powerful than she perceived her mother to be. A child who can overpower the parent develops a conviction not to trust or respect any adult he can "conquer." A nontrusting child will remain entrenched in a self-care mode while freely expressing his hatred toward adults who are not able to remain in authority.

Because the once-abandoned child feels so insecure at his core, he constantly tries to push his primary parent's buttons to see if she is *indeed* strong enough for him to ultimately trust. The child has a constant need to feel and be reassured of an essential sense of safety. If the parent knows and understands this dynamic and can empathize with her child's insecurity, she can be objective and not take his provocative behavior personally. This compassionate stance is what a therapeutic parent must learn to take in order to accommodate her child's unyielding need to test and retest to assure he is safe.

Val needed Cassie to be stronger than she was so Val could feel safe and protected. When Val stated to her mother in a family therapy session, "Many of the feelings I feel for you are because you can't handle me. I hate this weakness in you. I'm disgusted at how you are unable to control me," she was genuinely feeling unsafe at her core. However, due to childhood imprinting, Cassie was not prepared for the task of staying strong while under attack by her child.

Of all the skills a therapeutic parent must acquire, being objective and empathic in the face of a child's chronic testing and hatred can be the most elusive. To learn this demanding skill, parents usually need the consistent guidance of a therapeutic parenting professional. Dealing with a child's core insecurity, which can feel terrifying for him, inevitably takes its toll on unsupported parents. The child's never-ending drive to take charge also drains the energy and personal resources he needs for his own proper development. He pushes hard to control when what he really needs is a parent strong enough to control and take care of him so he can feel secure enough to grow.

Another source of a child's hatred is his feeling of worthlessness, which he developed early on through lack of being truly valued and cared for. In being abandoned, the child learned that he was unworthy. If he experienced neglect, the child learned that voicing his basic needs elicited reactions of annoyance, anger, or disregard from his caregiver. He may even have been punished for expressing his needs—making them seem dangerous and wrong to him. Since it is a child's needs that define who he is as an infant, neglect leads the child to believe he is at least burdensome, and more so that he is loathsome.

Self-hatred, then, becomes an emotion that is not only one of the child's core feelings but also his definition of self—he is both full of hate and hateful all at once. Therefore hatred and shame permeate his whole being. The child may act on the hate he feels for himself by head banging, cutting himself, other forms of self-injury, or by having many "accidents." Most commonly, the child will act hateful toward others when he is feeling core shame, rejection, or failure.

When the child's self-hate and core shame become intolerable to contain, they overflow into his environment as he projects these feelings onto his whole world. To this child, his toys are like him—worthless and hateful—so he destroys them. He sees his pets and living things as like him—vulnerable and needy—they remind him of his own helplessness, which began when he was an abandoned infant.

A child who hurts or kills animals does so out of disgust for their vulnerability and then hates himself for it. He dismisses or pushes his loving family members away because they insist upon expressing love to him—which he is not able to receive because he sees himself as worthless at his shameful core.

Since the world is his mirror, the child sees himself in everything that is weak and in everyone who is bad. He feels vulnerable, worthless, small and weak, needy, full of shame, and unlovable. If the child recognizes any of these feelings in his primary parent, he will go after her emotionally, hoping to control her by taunting her and getting her to react, as did Val. The child is trying to rid himself of intolerable feelings of shame and self-hate by casting them onto his mother, which is relieving for him if even for a moment (Manfield, 1992, p. 58). Furthermore, controlling his parent gives the child a sense of power, which temporarily unburdens him of his shame and vulnerability.

A child can wield great power over his parent when the parent is unable to separate this child's negative projection of himself from her own self as was the case for Cassie. When the child expresses hatred toward his parent using specific insults that he knows will rattle her, the parent must remember that what may seem like personally tailored and directed abusive words are actually a reflection of how the child sees *himself*. The weakness Val saw in her mother mirrored Val's feelings of powerlessness, and she couldn't stand to be reminded of this feeling. So Val pushed Cassie away with verbal venom to feel powerful in the face of her own feelings of powerlessness.

These new concepts may initially seem impossible and confusing, and they are for many parents. Therapeutic parenting training takes time and parents must experience a major paradigm shift. What they once thought about parenting must radically change, and behaviors they thought of one way before must be redefined. Once a parent understands the new paradigm, translates the child's behaviors accurately, and rehearses new reactions to provocative behaviors with a trusted other, such as a close friend or a therapist, the parent may well begin to see the child healing.

You may be surprised to learn that when your child is projecting his self-hatred onto you, it is a prime opportunity for you to assist your child in healing his core shame. The key is for you to stay objective about the behavior. If you can manage to stay calm and detached in the face of your child's hatred, you are giving him the sense of safety he is pushing for, because he cannot knock you off balance. Stopping the gut-level reaction to your child's hatred, becoming objective, and finally proceeding as a therapeutic parent is a process to be mastered over time.

The first step is to remember that your child's expression of hatred is something other than what it appears to be—it is always a cry for help. The next step is to practice not reacting to your child's attempts to provoke you with his hatred. When your child expresses hatred toward you, pause before doing anything else. This step will help you reach a neutral emotional place before you attempt to meet your child's needs.

The final step is to provide a healing response. You begin this process by communicating empathy to your child for how awful he must feel inside. Voice your understanding and reflect to your child exactly what he is feeling to let him know you are with him and that you accept him just as he is—hatred and all. Once your child trusts that you understand and accept him despite the fact that he loathes himself, you have given him a stepping-stone toward healing.

24 Why Challenging Children Need the Therapeutic Parenting Approach

Frustrated parents of challenging children have found they need more tools than traditional parenting methods offer. Thus, they have created the demand for an alternative approach to parenting. As parents, Dan and Cassie were doing everything they knew how to do in dealing with the challenges of raising their children. Still, they were not able to handle many of their children's behaviors or meet some of their needs. Why did their traditional approach—the one parents have used for generations—prove insufficient to parent their children?

Children who have had difficult pasts don't always respond well to traditional parenting, which is often authoritarian. In fact, these challenging children may rebel against such an approach because they crave to be in control. These same children flounder as well with more lax parenting, because they need more structure and guidance than it offers. Most traditionally raised parents arrive at the point where they are out of parenting tools to deal with their hard-to-reach children, and they need more options.

The confounding behaviors of the challenging child demand that parents do something different. The physiological makeup of these children can prevent traditional approaches from having the expected effect. When the parent attempts to intervene in a traditional manner to correct a challenging child's behavior, that parent often will experience the child's opposition and failure to respond. Then the parent—inaccurately assuming the child is simply being willful—reacts negatively to the child's behavior. Inevitably, parental frustration leads to an escalation of the situation rather than a resolution. If parents of challenging children have an expectation that they are dealing with a child who can respond to common interventions, they can quickly become discouraged.

The challenging child engages at times in various out-of-control behaviors. A parent who demands that her child get control of himself may be setting that child up for failure. Often such a child is *physiologically incapable* of self-control. These children do not have the neurological structure that would allow them to choose self-control even if they wanted to. Their brains have not yet grown the capacity for self-regulation.

Another reason both traditional and lax parenting may not work is that the challenging child may be delayed developmentally in one or more areas. He may not yet be able to do the same things others his age can do physically, mentally, or emotionally. Alternatively, the child may be so advanced for his age that he cannot fit in with his peers.

The child who develops challenging behaviors may have an emotional or mental disorder or be handicapped in some other way. He may have suffered a trauma that negatively affects his ability to function. It is possible the child may have a genetic cognitive disorder that disrupts his ability to learn as others do. Such problems may render traditional parenting ineffective.

The hard-to-reach child does not know himself and gets confused at times at the interface between himself and the world. This child will not thrive when raised with a traditional parenting approach because it is necessary for him to have much more than limits and rules. He requires help interpreting his feelings, his motivations, and his needs.

It takes parental assistance for this child to understand his place in the world. The child must have a parent who can "read him" and help him to get to know himself. A parent who understands this child fully can lead him through the process of negotiating his world using his particular set of abilities.

The purpose of characterizing a child as challenging is not to blame the child or brand him in any way. Rather, it is a starting point for tailoring the parenting approach to suit the child's unique needs. Traditional parenting applies a more prefabricated, one-size-fits-all method to child rearing. This approach will bounce right off a child who is consistently challenging—it will not match his needs or his capacity to learn.

Trying to use traditional parenting with these children feels like trying to pound a square peg into a round hole. It is necessary for parents to have a parenting approach that is compatible with the individual child's available receptors so he is able to respond to the intervention.

For all of these reasons, professionals involved with helping parents negotiate the needs of abandoned, traumatized, and challenging children developed an alternative parenting approach called *therapeutic parenting*. Through this method, parents are able to meet the child's comprehensive needs more individualistically and fully. When parents use the therapeutic parenting approach, their power and efficacy in reaching their challenging child increase dramatically.

25 Keys to Therapeutic Parenting

Throughout this book, we refer to a method called *therapeutic parenting*. The word "therapeutic" is used to distinguish this particular type of parenting from more traditional approaches. Though many adoptive families need such specialized training, not all do. Some adopted children do very well with little to no specific intervention, and the use of traditional parenting techniques remains highly effective.

Using therapeutic parenting is necessary, however, for parents with challenging children. The essence of this approach consists of parents healing a child by providing him with remedial attention aimed at restoring his potential. Therapeutic parenting is a comprehensive method of working with children, whether they have abandonment issues, residual trauma, attachment disorder, identity problems, or disabilities. Typically, learning the therapeutic approach requires training and ongoing professional support.

Since success in therapeutic parenting relies on the establishment of a therapeutic relationship between parent and child, parents most easily learn this approach in a parallel manner—in their relationship with a trained therapist. In learning the method, most parents find it helpful to experience receiving the type of empathy they must learn to provide for their child. In addition, under the guidance of a professional, they learn how to *translate* their child's behaviors in order to meet his underlying needs.

Furthermore, because the deep healing needs of many adopted children often give rise to unmet emotional needs of their adoptive parents, the process of learning therapeutic parenting can become twofold. A therapist may actually employ the empathic healing approach in helping with the parent's issues while simultaneously teaching therapeutic parenting to the parent. As treatment proceeds, the parent's own healing is enhanced at the same time she is actively practicing therapeutic parenting with her child.

Cassie learned how to be a therapeutic parent *within* her relationship with me. Together, we created a space that felt accepting and safe to her, so Cassie could learn something entirely new. The paradigm shift between what Cassie's mother imprinted in her regarding what it was to be a mother and what Cassie had to learn to heal her children was profound. Consciously, Cassie had to *experience* the empathy she had not received maternally to be able to learn to be empathic herself.

Through a trained therapist's more experienced eyes, Cassie learned the new language of seeing beneath Val's behaviors, as well as how to translate them into her true needs. Cassie came to understand that what she had thought for 25 years was Val's "hatred" was actually her daughter's plea for ultimate security. Cassie's core beliefs about what it was to be a mother had to change, which was no small feat for a 60-year-old woman to achieve. The support and guidance of a specialized professional were vital for her success.

As an introduction to the method, here we will present a summary of the key elements of therapeutic parenting. Our intention is to orient you to the overarching approach, not to teach or train you in the particulars. It is important to remember that there is no substitute for working with a professional when learning to heal your child's wounded heart.

Where to Begin

Arrange for Assessments

At the outset, consider visiting an adoption counselor or a family therapist to assess the readiness of you and your family for adoption. After adopting, consider scheduling appointments for a comprehensive evaluation of your child, especially if you have specific concerns. Adoption agencies, school counselors, and other parents with challenging children who experienced early neglect are all good sources of referrals to specialists with the right expertise for your family's situation.

Consider Open Adoption and Its Options
Some adoptive parents have the choice to make their adoption "open," that is allow their child contact with members of his birth family. Carefully consider the options by talking with other parents who have chosen open and closed adoption. Read the current literature to find out the pros and cons of open adoption to get the information you need to make the right decision for you and your child.

Find Out About Your Child's History
As an adoptive parent, you need to acquire as much information as possible from the adoption agency about your child's history, including information about his birth family's health and history. This information will be important for the child, for you, and for any professionals with whom your family may interact in the present or in the future.

Surround Yourself With Support
You cannot raise a child, especially a challenging child, alone—you need support. Rally extended family members and find other parents with similar challenges with whom you can keep in touch regularly. Join a parent support group that meets regularly. Consider engaging the services of a family therapist who specializes in working with adoptive families.

Resolve Your Own Past Issues
To the task of parenting, each of us brings at least some old baggage from the past that may get in the way of the job at hand. There is also the possibility that as we proceed, the act of parenting a challenging child will bring up issues we never knew were there. Identify and work through any unfinished business you may have from childhood and your past with a professional, trusted others, or a support group.

Creating a Nurturing Atmosphere

Embrace the P.L.A.C.E. Attitude
World-renowned psychotherapist, consultant, and therapist trainer Daniel A. Hughes, PhD, who specializes in treating traumatized chil-

dren, has developed an acronym, P.L.A.C.E. (Playfulness, Loving attitude, Acceptance, Curiosity, and Empathy), to help parents remember
the comprehensive, compassionate attitude most effective in helping
their children heal.

Engage in Face-to-Face Interaction

One of the most important avenues through which your child learns
about himself, about his relationship with you, and about how to self-
regulate is through your gaze coupled with being cradled in your arms.
While you cradle your child, his brain and body receive your regulatory
signals, which pattern his brain for self-regulation. He learns that
through being in a relationship with you he gets his needs met. Your
child learns who he is from your responses to him.

Set Aside Daily Parent-Child Quiet Time

Your child will benefit greatly from spending quiet time with you on a
daily basis. Choose a time and a place that is free from distractions,
including interruptions by other family members, television, and
phones. Spend this special time with your child just sitting together
chatting, reading a book together, or rocking and listening to soothing
music. Make it a priority—you may find you look forward to this relax-
ing time as much as your child does!

Avoid Negativity

Shaming, shouting, overstimulation, and stress are some of the negatives you will want to actively avoid in your daily therapeutic parenting
work. These negatives can send your child into deep shame, into feelings of being overwhelmed, or can cause him to become out of control.
Therefore, avoiding them reduces the amount of time you'll spend
helping your child return to a more even-keeled place.

Make Relationship Repairs

Saying, "I'm sorry"—repairing a regrettable action—is an indispensable
aspect of human communication, one of the building blocks of a
strong bond. When you make a mistake, you model saying you're
sorry, which serves to teach your child that mistakes are forgivable—

not permanent marks of shame. You actually strengthen your relationship with your child each time you make a repair.

Helping Your Child Catch Up

Use Developmental Reparenting Techniques

The therapeutic parenting approach allows you to assist your child in catching up developmentally. On your own, or under a therapist's guidance, you can learn to interpret and respond to your child's *emotional/behavioral* age instead of his chronological age. Then according to your child's developmental needs, you choose from a variety of specific reparenting techniques to help him grow into his chronological age. For example, if you have a school-aged child who suffered infant neglect, you can help build foundational neuronal connections in his brain that support interpersonal relationships by pulling him into your lap to enjoy face-to face rocking sessions each day.

Employ Developmental Physical Therapy

A child who has only partially met physical developmental stages needs to go back and learn what he missed. For instance, if a child passed over the crawling stage because of being crib-bound at an orphanage, he may benefit from mastering this step in the present. Increasing sensorial integration and awareness may be an important aspect of your child's developmental catch-up as well. A child development specialist can assist in both assessment and creating a program for your unique child's needs.

Enjoy Movement, Music, and Play

Complete physical development also requires learning overall body coordination, linking of the senses, sequencing of movements, and building both brain and muscle memory. Parent-assisted, sometimes professionally prescribed and guided physical activity is essential for the once-neglected child's complete growth. A developmental professional can guide you in selecting from a variety of music, movement, and structured play activities aimed at helping your child reach his potential.

Taking Charge Gently

Work as a Parenting Team

The challenging child needs a solid united front as his home base so he can heal and grow. It is essential that you consistently work as a parental *team* in raising your child. Single adoptive parents find it is valuable to build a support network for their work as a therapeutic parent.

Set Clear Limits

All children need a solid sense of security. One of the most powerful ways you can instill security is through setting and maintaining clear, reasonable limits. If your child knows the boundaries and rules, and that you will reinforce them every time, it will reduce his need to constantly test you with challenging behaviors.

Choose Your Battles

Since no parent can make a child eat, sleep, carry out bodily functions, or learn on command, you must choose your battles wisely. Therapeutic parents can receive specialized training in the use of particular psychological techniques as necessary for steering their child in a healthy direction.

Employ the "S" Basics

Safety, security, sensitivity, simplicity, soothing, structure, supervision, and support are parenting essentials you will rely on daily in your work as a therapeutic parent.

Implement Logical Consequences Instead of Punishment

You may have come to the realization that a challenging child does not typically curtail his negative behaviors because of the threat of punishment or consequences. However, the use of *logical* consequences in therapeutic parenting—such as the child cleaning up a deliberate spill—is paired with the empathic healing talk as a response to undesirable behavior.

Learn and Use the Empathic Healing Talk

The empathic healing talk is a scripted parent-child interaction (see Appendix A) that therapeutic parents use to accomplish several goals.

Regular use of the talk establishes parents in the role of being the child's most reliable resource and safe harbor when he encounters difficulties.

Carefully crafted and interwoven with unconditional love, the empathic healing talk is a vehicle for you to translate your child's feelings and difficult behaviors into words that give voice to his underlying needs. Because the approach takes care not to elicit shame, you can talk directly with your child about his misbehavior in a way that provides him with an understanding of himself and his motives. Eventually, your child will learn to verbalize his needs rather than act them out with undesirable behaviors.

This approach, which takes time and confidence to master, is the *key* process of therapeutic parenting. Over time, the result of using the empathic healing talk is the creation of new neural pathways in the child's brain that allow him to have a conscience, socialize appropriately, and gain self-control.

Use Parental Detachment as Appropriate

Learn to match your child's present capacity for closeness so as not to overwhelm him. If possible, maintain a loving but somewhat detached distance from your child at first. In their excitement, new adoptive parents may struggle with this concept, but it is vital for a child who has been abandoned or traumatized to have space and not feel emotionally overwhelmed by well-intentioned parents.

Discovering Your Unique Child

Learn About Your Child's Temperament

Even birth children can have temperaments that differ from those of their parents. Observe your child to discern his temperamental type, and compare it with your own. You can find information on the various temperament types at your library or through an online search. It is important to identify the qualities of both your temperament type and your child's because temperamental differences can be the root of either harmony or dissonance in your relationship. Knowing the particulars will help you adjust your expectations and approach so your relationship with your child can be as harmonious as possible.

Listen Carefully to Your Child

Most children have a limited ability to express themselves verbally because they often don't have the necessary vocabulary or know exactly what they feel or need. Therefore, you need to take your child's attempts at communication seriously and work with him to figure out exactly what he needs.

Pay Attention to Your Child's Moods

Due to genetics, experiencing past trauma, or enduring chronic stress, some children display mood fluctuations that may need further attention. If you notice an enduring moodiness in your child either through his behaviors or via his verbal reports, you may want to seek a professional assessment.

Translate Your Child's Behavior

It is through behaviors that your child will most often express himself and his needs, even though he may not be aware of what he is "saying." Over time, you will learn what your child's every behavior means and how to respond to his needs accordingly.

Address Your Child's Identity Issues

From the very beginning, help your child come to terms with his identity. Prepare your child's school, church, and community as a whole for his integration. You also convey acceptance to your child when you acknowledge your child's uniqueness by helping him create his life story in a life book of his own.

Tell Your Child His Adoption Story

Begin right away telling your child his adoption story on a level that is appropriate and that he can understand. Tell it to him often, adding details as appropriate to his present stage of development. Some parents like to create an actual "my adoption" storybook with words and photos they can share with their child over and over. Being open with your child about his adoptive history conveys your acceptance of him.

Helping Your Child Succeed

Reinforce Desired Behavior

Use measured, specific praise of your child's desirable behaviors to positively shape his growth. Avoid using generalizations such as, "You're great!" when giving your child feedback, because a child with core shame will reject such a reflection and may act out negatively to prove that he is in fact not great. It works best if you describe and express your appreciation for your child's specific, positive behavior. For example, you might say, "I like the way you came right to dinner when I called."

Let Your Child Know What to Expect

Most of us like to know what's next, what's coming up, and what to expect. Children are no exception, especially those who have pasts that were difficult. Help your child succeed by letting him know what he will be doing each day, or each hour if a day's worth of plans is too much for him to think about all at once. Some children do best having a "5-minute warning" before shifting to a new activity as well.

Allow Your Child to Start Over Every Day

Help your child overcome his fear of failing and prevent him from feeling the shame of failure by making each day a new day. With your support, your child can let go of yesterday, and start over fresh each day.

Give Your Child Small, Attainable Goals

Children who are challenged due to difficulties in their pasts are often preoccupied and have trouble completing tasks. You can help your child focus and feel a sense of accomplishment if you divide a task into smaller steps. If your child needs to clean his room, for instance, you can help him break the job down into doable parts. First, he can pick up his shoes, and when he's done you congratulate him, and then he can pick up his blocks, and so on.

Instead of "Time Out," Use "Time In"

Because challenging children often have difficulty regulating themselves, they need you to stay close when they begin to get out of control. If you use "time out" by having your child go to his room, he may feel rejected and find it difficult to calm himself down. Using "time in" by keeping your child close to you or in your lap, gives him the message that you accept him while it simultaneously allows him to be soothed by your physical presence.

Be Careful How You Say "No" to Your Child

Children who struggle with shame tend to take it personally when they receive a "no" in response to something they are doing or wanting. Many of these children will hear a "no" as "You don't like me," or "You don't want me to be happy." When a child takes a "no" personally, he will often act out negatively in response. You can prevent this undesirable reaction in your child by saying "no" in a different way. For example, if your child wants a cookie right before dinner, you can say, "Okay, let's first eat dinner, and then you can have a cookie!"

Allow Your Child to Feel in Control

Children who have experienced abandonment or trauma have a great need to feel in control to feel safe. Whenever it is reasonable to do so, allow your child to have a choice. For example, either allow your child to choose his outfit for the day or give him a choice of two appropriate outfits so he can feel he has some control.

Limit Celebrations

Provide celebrations and gifts for your child that reflect the level of worthiness *he* feels is accurate for him. Literally asking your child how deserving he feels in the moment can be your guide to making the occasion or gift something that he will accept rather than reject. Tailor celebrations, gift giving, and compliments to match your child's ability to receive in the present.

Smoothing the Way for Your Child

Advocate for Your Child at School

Often, because of developmental delays, children who have rough starts struggle in one or more ways in school. Advocate for your child with his teachers, school counselor, principal, and staff to help him get his educational needs met. Try to get him the help he needs with schoolwork in the school setting so that it does not become your responsibility at home. Your child's "job" at home is to be with you and learn how to be in a give-and-take relationship with you.

Supervise Socialization

Since children facing challenges can be behind developmentally in some areas or across the spectrum, their socialization skills are potentially limited. Actively support and coach your child as he learns to interact appropriately with other children and adults. You may rehearse a desired behavior at home with your child before bringing him into a new social setting. Then use close parental supervision when your child is in the new setting until he masters the use of a new social skill.

Be Extra-Sensitive During Family Expansion

When bringing a new child into the family, be deliberately sensitive to the needs of your other child(ren). The addition of a child can be threatening and even traumatizing for a child who came first.

Being Kind to Yourself

Hold Onto Realistic Expectations

Establish realistic expectations for your child based on his current abilities and his *developmental* age while taking into consideration his past experience. Learn to fully accept and enjoy your child for who he is in the moment. Remember not to set the bar too high for yourself as well!

Accept Your Learning Curve

Learning therapeutic parenting can be challenging because the approach is not intuitive for most parents. Understanding the method takes time, as does learning the techniques. Allow yourself sufficient time to grow accustomed to your new role as a therapeutic parent. If you practice the various therapeutic parenting tools on a daily basis, they will become comfortable and a more natural part of your parenting repertoire.

Take Care of Yourself
Be proactive in setting aside time for yourself on a regular basis. Make time for yourself alone and with your spouse to relax, regroup, and rejuvenate. Make it a point to have some adult fun and relaxation every day.

✤

Although some of the interventions of therapeutic parenting may appear to be similar to those of more traditional parenting, there is a difference. It is the *degree* to which a parent engages in a particular parenting intervention that can distinguish the two approaches from one another.

For example, relative to his chronological age, a child with developmental delays requires much more intensive, one-on-one supervision throughout the day than does a child whose developmental and chronological ages are the same. As well, a therapeutic parent works more *intentionally* with her child due to his need for developmental catch-up.

The objectivity with which a therapeutic parent must approach her job, especially when her child is new in the family, is more akin to the parent being in a professional role with the child—as a teacher would be—than to being in a more intimate relationship. As her child's brain becomes patterned for interpersonal relationships, a therapeutic parent responds to her child's increased ability to be intimate and shifts in her role. The hard work of therapeutic parents is rewarded by the development of true bonds of attachment with their child.

26 Learning from the Richards' Experience

After the Richards' year in France, their return to the States brought with it a litany of difficult behaviors in their children that seemed unstoppable because no one fully grasped what was happening. Only Cassie had accepted the notion that adoption was at the root of the family problems. Without knowing it, she was right on top of what was causing the family strife, but she had no allies or support within the family.

> *For many families, adoption brings with it significant challenges that new research-based interventions can address successfully.*

The Richards' toolbox was nearly empty of the unique knowledge and approach they needed to effectively meet the challenges they were facing. It wasn't until years later that these parents finally learned what had gone on, sought precise help, and learned how to handle their children's special needs that had arisen from early trauma. This breakthrough came long after the family unraveling, which had taken place during the children's teen years.

When the family returned from France, Tony's depression deepened due to his not fitting in with peers in many ways—appearance, social skills, and intellectual ability. The coded message from Tony that he was suffering from depression got louder as he accelerated his stealing behavior. Stealing was Tony's attempt to escape the painful shame he felt as he continued to struggle with his identity. The rush of adrenaline Tony got from stealing may have temporarily lifted him out of his depressed physiological state as well.

Clinical depression is common in adopted children. Depression can arise from genetics or chronic, significant stress. Abandonment can be a depression-triggering stressor for many adoptees. Its effects can endure throughout their development into adulthood, and without intervention, depression may persist.

Tony was also entering that crucial time when his need for fathering was peaking. However, Dan was uncomfortable with the emotional needs of his son. Dan did not know how to give Tony what he needed because he had not experienced an emotionally close father-son relationship himself in his childhood.

Mr. Ulrich, Tony's counselor, was on track when he prescribed some special one-on-one time for Dan and Tony. The problem was that Dan did not know how to structure an activity that would end well for both father and son. By not knowing how to address Tony's critical attitude, Dan lost the opportunity to share an intimate, compassionate connection with his son. Ideally, Dan would have had a heart-to-heart talk with Tony, then would have scheduled another project to replace the failed first activity.

It is essential that fathers spend meaningful one-on-one time with their sons on a regular basis.

Cassie continued to battle with Val. Instead of being able to handle Val, Cassie's sense of failure at the task returned her time and again to feelings of low self-worth. Unfortunately, Cassie's toolbox was full of ineffective and even harmful tools that had accumulated during her childhood. She was obsessed about not repeating the harm she had endured herself as a child yet had no replacement tools to call upon. Nor did Cassie have the inner resources to prevent herself from continuing to lash back at Val.

Cassie's instinct to go to therapy was right on target, but she was not supported in doing so by her husband. Dan's dismissive style, his dominance in the marital relationship, and his fear that the inner workings of his family would be made public if they were in counseling sealed Cassie in helplessness and despair. She felt trapped.

Parents must address their own unresolved issues from childhood so they can be objective enough to see and meet their children's needs.

Above all else, children suffering from attachment disorder need to feel secure and will stop at nothing to make certain they are secure. Testing Cassie time and again with increasingly spiteful behaviors, Val persistently sought to meet her need for security. Counterproductively, the more Val pushed, the more Cassie moved away, both physically and emotionally, increasing Val's sense of insecurity.

Dan did not understand what was happening. He did not know that it was Val's abandonment that drove her to seek a mother whom she could never again "make" go away. Like many adopted children, Val subconsciously felt she must have done something wrong to make her own birth mother abandon her.

In being able to overpower her adoptive mother, Val's feeling that she really *was* bad became cemented in her psyche. Moreover, Val was sure, on some level, that her badness would eventually have the power to make Cassie abandon her, just as her birth mother had done. Therefore, she acted out incessantly. Meanwhile, Dan still could not entertain the notion that there was something devastatingly wrong in the family.

Mr. Ulrich, the therapist, did not understand either. Ulrich's "family adoption vote" misstep only added to the problem of Dan continuing to dismiss the notion that adoption issues were at the root of the family's problems. At the time, clinical knowledge about the effects and treatment of child trauma and attachment disorder was practically non-existent among professionals.

In the course of Cassie's initial search for information, only Mr. Oberg, the principal, truly understood adopted kids and intuited that Val was deeply insecure due to her abandonment. This was the first time Cassie could see that it was not her, personally, that was the core problem. For the first time ever, Cassie allowed herself the thought that abandonment had taken its toll on her daughter. Cassie's hopes and newfound perspective quickly disintegrated, however, as Dan summarily rejected the theory.

Struggling parents can get relief if they engage the services of knowledgeable professionals for guidance and support.

On top of this, Dan fell under Val's spell, unintentionally colluding in creating an even larger rift between Cassie and himself by allowing his daughter to spend evening time in his lap right in front of Cassie. Neither Dan nor Cassie understood the common phenomenon of the child with attachment disorder splitting his parents to increase his control as well as his distance from his mom.

Fears of abandonment can drive some children to try to seal their emotional safety by dividing and conquering their parents. In keeping distant from their mom with dad's unwitting help, these children can feel in control. They seek to assure themselves of never getting close to a mother figure again because they don't want to get hurt by the abandonment that they are sure is to come.

Parenting children with wounded hearts requires parents to stick together as a team to provide their children with the essential sense of security.

In addition, Val was jealous of the close relationship she observed between her parents. Dan and Cassie had the kind of relationship Val couldn't have and didn't know how to have. Val's jealously of their relationship played itself out during those evenings in Dan's lap and through her endless provocative behaviors.

However, as Val pushed and pushed, Dan eventually began to glimpse the problem. Even though Dan finally discontinued his evenings with Val, problems remained. No one knew what to do about the core situation because no one knew what it was really about.

A clue came through Val's admission in therapy about her inner state of unhappiness. The key to the puzzle was right there in sight for everyone to see. Finally feeling heard, Val felt some relief that someone understood her world. The sad thing was that although Val did know something was wrong with her, she felt as helpless as everyone else because she did not know what to do about it. Val wanted to be trustworthy but did not know how because trust requires that there be a relationship worth protecting and preserving.

Your children are always giving you behavioral clues as to what their feelings and needs are, so get whatever help you need to decipher them.

In an attempt to at least keep Val physically safe, her parents kept rules and levied consequences. However, for children suffering from attachment disorder, consequences do not matter because for them to work a child must be emotionally invested in the relationship with his parent. Whereas Tony was upset that his stealing had hurt his relationship with his mom, Val felt little remorse for her hate-filled behavior toward her mother. Cassie did not know where to turn for help because even her holdout belief that therapy could help had been eliminated by her experience with Mr. Ulrich.

The Richards' home atmosphere improved somewhat as the high school years started. Things were a bit better than in the past because Val was held within tight bounds. Although she was not aware of it, Val began to feel safer because she had definitive limits and controls that Dan had put in place.

Unfortunately, Cassie was still actively reacting to Val's rejection and was taking it personally, which compromised Val's fragile sense of security under her father's rules. Dan continued not to be fazed by Val's behavior, preferring to categorize it as that of a normal adolescent.

One clue that Val's behavior was not that of a normal teen came at holiday time when Val spoiled the family's enjoyment with her negative behaviors. Children who are abandoned early in life frequently cannot deal well with holidays or celebrations. This phenomenon arises because these children aren't able to handle the emotions and relationship demands that characterize these occasions. Feeling unworthy at the core makes accepting positive attention impossible for the once-abandoned child. The child lets the parents know this by acting out, which often serves to curtail family celebrations of any kind.

Parents trained in raising abandoned children frequently do not hold celebrations, or if they do, they downplay them significantly. This adjustment by parents allows the child to feel more at home and thus successful in handling life. Cassie did come to the conclusion that to expect holidays to be pleasant in the Richards' home was not a good use of her energy.

> *Staying attuned to your child's present sense of his own worth allows you to scale compliments and celebrations to his level of receptivity.*

At that point, without either parent being consciously aware of it, Cassie had stepped back as being the only active parent while Dan stepped forward to become more involved. Dan led in the implementation of new strategies that turned out to be quite effective. Even though they still did not fully understand why, Dan and Cassie's new approach began to pay off. Cassie focused on controlling her reactions to Val, which resulted in Val feeling safer to the point where she began to open up and confide in Cassie.

Dan and Cassie had figured out how to quell some of their daughter's more difficult behaviors when they followed through with consequences without allowing themselves to get riled up by her provocations. They also avoided overwhelming Val with positive attention she could not accept by camouflaging their delight when she behaved well.

Dan and Cassie purposely planted ideas that Val could think were her own so that she still felt in control. This enabled Val to feel safer and more able to focus on outward goals rather than being consumed by testing her parents to assure herself she was safe.

Dan and Cassie gave Val control over those aspects of her life that were safe to allow her to manage. They chose their battles and let Val live with the results of her decisions. Cassie stopped trying to please Val and let go of attempts to win her love. Inadvertently, and without specific training, Dan and Cassie had discovered some of the strategies that therapeutic parents of once-neglected children rely upon. At last, some of the mechanics were in place that allowed some household peace for a time.

> *Let go and give your child control over aspects of his life that are safe for him to manage while you remain in control in matters of life and death.*

Nevertheless, these newfound strategies left the deepest emotional needs of the children yet unmet. Without specialized training, Dan and Cassie could not possibly have known how to heal their children emotionally. Getting affirmation and feedback about the positive measures they were taking and having professional guidance in healing their children emotionally were the missing pieces for Dan and Cassie.

Tony was attached, but he was still insecure and unable to rely on any relationship other than the one with his mother. It was difficult for Tony to trust others deeply and to allow others to see inside him. His identity struggles left him with a depression that sadly went untreated.

Val was able to operate and manage life within the bounds that her parents had discovered worked for her. However, she remained unable to engage in an intimate relationship with anyone. Emotional healing remained the major area that the Richards' newfound strategies could not address.

In not having the understanding she needed, Cassie missed a prime opportunity to connect with her daughter around how difficult it was for Val to get close to her. At the time, Val's true emotional needs remained completely under Cassie's radar so she could not possibly see them, let alone meet them.

The same was true for Tony's need for connection with his father, which was unseen by Dan. What Tony ultimately needed was the emotional support and understanding that only an emotionally attuned father could give.

Cassie had started to go to individual therapy to learn how to detach herself from Val, while Val continued in her own therapy. Due to feelings of not belonging, Val had begun to fall into her own depression, which only added to the household gloom. Dr. Parks flatly told Cassie that there was absolutely nothing she could do to ease Val's pain. He told Cassie that Val craved coldness.

The truth was that Cassie could have eased Val's pain while easing her own as well. Coldness was the last thing that this teen suffering from attachment disorder needed. The problem was, however, that the family had entered a dead-end alley. At that point, no one—not even the professionals involved—knew what to do to bring about healing.

If you are experiencing an emotional disconnect from your child, find a family therapist you can trust to help you discover how to make that crucial connection.

Although Tony would not admit it even if he had been aware of it, Dr. Parks' support was crucial to his stability and well-being. To stay honest, Tony needed to know that he was accountable to an adult male who would listen to him with compassion. Tony had not found this at home, but it was clear that he had found it with Dr. Parks, because when he stopped seeing him for only one week, Tony reverted to stealing.

The success the Richards enjoyed during the beginning of their children's high school years was fragile. It was not built upon a strong knowledge base. The reasons that the strategies Dan and Cassie were using were successful eluded them. Knowing *why* structure, tight boundaries, child's choice, and nonemotional reactions worked would have been essential for Dan and Cassie to mold their strategies as things changed.

Look at your current parenting formula to discover exactly what tactics are working and why so you can continue those, then identify any problems that may remain so you can target these with new strategies.

Unfortunately, Dan retreated into his work, leaving Cassie alone to deal with the challenges their daughter presented. Without Dan's support, Cassie quickly lost her resolve to stay emotionally neutral. Cassie's backslide increased Val's sense of insecurity to the point where she began to even outdo her past behaviors. As Val pushed and pushed for that ultimate parental security, Cassie sank into a clinical depression that went untreated. The cumulative effects of her depression, anxiety, and stress brought Cassie to a life-threatening event—her first anaphylactic attack.

It took this incident to make Dan finally understand the seriousness of what was happening to Cassie. As did Cassie, Dan laid the responsibility for what was happening on their struggles with Val, who was in fact just an innocent child caught in the emotional disability of attachment disorder. The recipe for a cure would have started with the parents understanding that specific truth.

Healing Val required her parents to stand united and comfort Val in her epic internal conflict—needing to be close to them, yet not feeling safe doing so. Val needed steadfast parental strength to test and retest her fear that she might be abandoned again.

Surprisingly, it was Val who knew that this was what she needed, and she even was able to articulate it one day in Dr. Parks' office. In reference to Cassie, Val said, "Your problem is you're unstable as a person. Many of the feelings I feel for you are because you can't handle me. I hate this weakness in you. I'm disgusted at how you are unable to control me."

There it was—the core of the problem laid out for all to see—but no one could see it besides Val, who was not aware of the significance of her observation. Instead, Dr. Parks passed it by, unfortunately summing up the situation by pointing to only one aspect of the problem—that self-hatred was at the root of Val's behavior. The link between Val's need for security and her need to push Cassie hard to obtain it was not made.

Nevertheless, Dr. Parks did accurately describe how Cassie's past laid her open for taking Val's projection of self-hatred personally. He recommended that the bottom line be that Val should never be given the right to judge Cassie. Regrettably, Dr. Parks gave the family no instruction or skill training in how to accomplish this task. The suggestion was useless to the family without a specific plan that could have yielded the desired result. It was not until many years later that the Richards received the information and support they needed to be successful at not letting Val get to Cassie.

Staying committed to the process and seeking the information and support you need to parent effectively will eventually bring the success you desire.

Meanwhile, Cassie's depression deepened and her high anxiety kept her in a fight-or-flight mode. With Cassie in her broken state, Val continued to push her mother's limit. Cassie was consumed with just trying to stay alive and was deeply afraid that she would suffer a fatal anaphylactic attack. She did not have the biochemical balance, thus the presence of self, to put a limit on Val's behavior or to control her own reactions to her daughter.

Cassie and Val were now caught up in an emotional typhoon. The effect of Val's untreated attachment disorder on the family had become full blown. There was nothing or no one to stop the family's downhill trajectory at that point. The tragic dynamic now had a life of its own. All that was left was the struggle for survival without help yet on the horizon. The cause and cure for this dire situation were outside of anyone's understanding, including that of the therapists involved at that time.

            ❧

It was from her priest that Cassie first heard the lifesaving word *codependency*. What Cassie would find out in the weeks to come was that her codependency had started early in life as she tried to no avail to gain her mother's unconditional approval. Cassie was blind to this as she entered adulthood, then parenthood, with an unmet need for acceptance.

In continuing to live from her core need for approval, Cassie could not gain the objectivity she needed to parent her daughter. Meanwhile, a very unhappy little adopted girl with attachment disorder yearned deep down inside to feel secure as well. There simply was no safe place where mother and daughter could meet.

In agreeing to go to treatment, Cassie became the leader in her family's journey to healing. In earnest, Cassie began to look at herself and the effects of her childhood imprinting. Dan began to look at his contribution to the problems. Both parents worked diligently through a recovery that was grounded in the wisdom of the 12-step program. They did not give up their determination to figure out how to help their children.

Don't give up—capitalize on even your smallest success by repeating what has worked in the past, find new sources of help, talk to other parents in similar circumstances—hope can be just around the corner.

Years after Tony and Val had left home, the Richards' resolve to find out what had gone wrong in their home when their children were young paid off. They finally found the guidance they needed to understand the devastating effects of abandonment and neglect on their adoptive family.

Dan and Cassie Richards not only learned what they had needed to learn for so many years, they also directly applied their new knowledge to improving their relationships with their adult children. They practiced and mastered the therapeutic parenting skills they needed to begin to heal their children. Even as adults, their children responded in a deep way to Dan and Cassie's approach.

Today, the Richards continue to heal their family and their children one interaction at a time. The results are truly astounding. As soon as Dan and Cassie found the key, Val threw open the door of her heart and let them in. Tony, too, has begun to open his heart to his parents. Time will only improve relationships in the Richards family now that wounded hearts have finally begun to heal.

Frequently Asked Questions

Is there a "safe" age to adopt a child so that we can be sure our child will be free of attachment problems?

The answer to this question has to do with the child's past *experience* rather than his age: if a child who is free of genetic and gestational problems has received adequate care from a single primary caregiver from birth, his brain will grow the capacity for attachment; if there has been a gap in adequate care or multiple caregivers, his attachment capacity may be compromised.

Is attachment disorder curable—is there any hope that the child I adopted when he was 7 can become attached?

Since a child's brain remains somewhat "plastic" until he is in his 20s and attachment is a brain-based capacity, adoptive parents receiving specialized guidance can help their child to become attached through the therapeutic parenting approach.

We adopted our child 3 years ago when he was 10 months old and he still wakes screaming in the middle of the night several nights a month. Shouldn't he be over whatever it is that causes this by now?

Although having occasional nightmares is common for most children, persistent nightmares or night terrors may be an indication that a child who was adopted substantially after his birth may have suffered pread-optive trauma that remains unresolved, which parents can respond to in the moment of the child's distress by actively comforting him.

What if I cannot get any information about my adopted child's history?

The important thing is that parents understand their child's present *needs*, which can be determined via a thorough, professional assessment of a child's physical, emotional, cognitive, and behavioral development.

How do you manage the demands of a challenging child when you have other children in the home and need time to take care of yourself as well?

Parents of challenging children find it is possible to manage the needs of all by: (1) keeping the challenging child close by at all times and occupied—for example, he can play with Legos at the parent's feet while the parent helps another child with homework; and (2) scheduling a "relief parent" to take over for an hour or two on a regular basis.

I find myself getting easily frustrated with my adopted child whose nonstop behaviors seem to demand my constant attention. What should I do?

A child's behavior is the "language" he uses to express his needs, so when parents are able to translate and meet the core need he is expressing in the moment, his behaviors will settle down and his parents can relax.

My husband and I disagree about how to handle our adopted child's misbehaviors. What can we do?

Parents must first understand and agree upon the *meaning* of their child's behavior before they can address it, and it is this shared understanding of their child's *need* that can unite parents in handling the situation.

Should I allow my 3-year-old adopted child, who will not sleep through the night in his own room, to sleep with me?

Children who have abandonment or trauma histories are often developmentally behind their peers in ways that require parents to address their *presenting needs* rather than what their chronological age may dictate; therefore, a 3-year-old child may need the security of sleeping with his parent as he would if he were an infant.

Every time my child disobeys me, I get really agitated and have to hold myself back from yelling or hitting. What can I do?

Parents need to address what unfinished business from their own past a child's disobedience is triggering in them and causing their agitation, and then translate what the child is actually "saying" with his disobedience in order to effectively handle the behavior.

How do we handle our child's unusual or extreme behaviors such as sexualized behavior or aggression toward us?

Parents take a twofold approach to handling extreme behaviors in children: (1) setting specific, strict behavioral limits with the child and following through every time; and (2) getting professional help addressing the underlying cause of such significant behaviors.

How do we deal with our child's passive-aggression in its many forms?

Therapeutic parents determine what their child's behaviors mean and over time help him learn how to express these feelings and needs verbally instead of indirectly through behaviors.

Why does our adopted child act younger than he is?

Neglect and trauma can interrupt a child's development to the point where his behaviors reflect the brain structure more typical of a younger child. With therapeutic parenting, this delay can be remedied and the child can be brought up to or near his chronological age.

How do I deal with my child's noncompliant behavior?

Power struggles inevitably backfire, so therapeutic parents learn to choose their battles along the lines of preventing serious consequences for their child while allowing him those consequences that will naturally but safely teach him to choose behaviors that benefit him.

What should we do when our 12-year-old adopted child fights about doing any of the normal things he needs to do to be even minimally hygienic, such as taking a bath, toileting sanitarily, brushing his teeth and hair, and changing his clothes?

While parents cannot *make* a child do any of these self-care tasks, they can set their own standards and let the child choose. For example, the parents announce they are taking the family out to dinner and stipulate that those who are freshly bathed may go, and those who aren't may stay home with a sitter.

Is it typical that our adopted child seems to have no interest in interacting with others and, in fact, seems very uncomfortable, to the point of head banging, when others are around?

What is typical is that a child may not be as socially developed as his peers, and thus not ready to socialize at an expected level, but what is not typical is reacting to social pressures by head banging; so it is important to involve a professional in assessing what may be going on for a child with this behavior.

My parents think we are spoiling our adopted child because I spend so much time with him. Are they right?

It is difficult for those who are not familiar with the needs of the child to understand what attuned parents are doing; therefore, when others are open to learning, teaching them about your unique child and his needs can be helpful.

How do we explain our child's behaviors to our relatives in a manner that will encourage acceptance rather than further criticism?

Since a child's behaviors are actually evidence of his underlying needs, helping others understand what your child is "saying" can help them gain compassion for him as well as admiration for your expertise!

How do we work with a school system that doesn't seem to understand the needs of challenging children and relies on behavioral approaches that don't work rather than addressing our child's emotional needs and blames us, the parents, for his behavior?

Parents going it alone are often at a disadvantage when advocating for their child in school. Engaging the services of an outside professional who understands your child's needs when interfacing with school personnel can strengthen your message and credibility.

My adopted child's pediatrician believes that kids are kids and that I should just follow standard parenting practices. Is she right?

Because preadoptive trauma and neglect can delay an adopted child's development, traditional parenting methods when used alone may not meet his needs comprehensively. Therapeutic parenting may need to be employed to ensure complete development.

How do we locate a therapist who is competent at working with the challenges we are facing with our adopted child?

Referrals may be available locally through adoption agencies, schools, parenting organizations, other parents, or online: www.danielahughes .homestead.com (ask Dr. Hughes for a referral to therapists he has trained in your area), www.attach.org, or www.attachment.org.

Using the Empathic Healing Talk to Strengthen the Bond with Your Child

The empathic healing talk is a scripted parent-child interaction designed to allow parents to process their child's difficult behaviors with him. The talk is a powerful component of the therapeutic parenting toolbox, and is carefully crafted to help the child learn about himself without inducing shame. The empathic healing talk utilizes the five elements of P.L.A.C.E. (see chapter 25) and aims to both teach and heal a child gradually with each interaction.

As in the baby talk used with infants, therapeutic parents are careful to use a positive and pleasing voice along with words and ideas the child can understand when interacting with him during an empathic healing talk. The talk is nonthreatening and playful in tone with parents gearing their message to the child's ability to hear it. As the child develops, parents adjust their way of engaging in the empathic talk to match their child's presenting age.

The following is an example of the empathic healing talk that is based on an incident that occurred with Val in the Richards family. It was written by Cassie during her therapy with me as she was learning to parent therapeutically. Her evident grasp of conveying empathy touched me deeply and brought tears to my eyes.

> That evening when Dad got home, Mom would sit Val on her lap, with Dad alongside, and Mom would say, "Val, have I told you yet today how much I love you?" (Val might shake her head, "no.")
>
> Mom would then continue, "Well, I do love you with all my heart. I want to tell you that right now, because we need to talk a bit about a mistake you made today. (Val might be feeling some anxiety and would shift on Mom's lap.) We're going to talk about how you picked Sally's tulips today and try to figure some things out about that. Okay?" (Val might shrug.)

"My guess is that you might be thinking you're a bad girl because we are talking about this. But I want you to know I do not think you're a bad girl at all, even when you do something wrong on purpose. Do you know that? (Val might look down and shake her head, "no," a little bit.) No matter what you do, Val, I love you with all my heart and nothing can change that."

"You know what? Daddy loves you too, no matter what. I'd like you to tell him now about the tulips so you can see this for yourself." (Val might steal a quick glance at Dad, then look down again.)

"I picked some of Sally's tulips," Val might whisper. Mom might then hug her lightly and say, in a low-key tone, "Thank you, Val, for telling Daddy about the tulips. I know it was hard for you to tell Daddy that you did something wrong on purpose." (Val would nod, "yes.") Mom would turn to Dad and ask, "Do you still love Val, even though she made a mistake?" (Val would look at Dad.)

Dad might say, "Val, I want you to know that I still love you even though you picked Sally's tulips. Okay?" (Val might look unsure, then nod, "yes," slightly, and turn her head down again.)

Then Mom would say, "How 'bout if we try and figure what was up for you today when you picked those tulips? (Val might not react.) Would it be okay if I made some guesses and you let me know if one might be the right one?" (Val might shrug a bit again.)

"Okay. . . . Hmm . . . I wonder if you wanted to be mean to Sally today. (Val would shake her head, "no.") So that's not it. Hmm . . . I wonder if you wanted the tulips because they were so pretty, but you didn't want to ask Sally because she might have said no. (Val might hesitate, then barely nod, "yes.") Oh! Looks like I guessed right! . . . Wow. We're pretty good at this, aren't we?"

Mom might then say, "Let's see what we just figured out about you today. (Mom would pull up Val's first finger, as in 'This little piggy went to market.') First, we found out how much Mom and Dad love you all the time no matter what you do. (Mom lifts Val's second finger.) Then we found out sometimes you like to do things you know are wrong because you really, really want something, and even when that happens, Dad and Mom love you with all their heart anyway, right? (Mom lifts Val's third finger.) We learned that when you pick somebody's tulips without permission, they get mad, and we need to go buy new tulips and say you are sorry. (Mom lifts Val's fourth finger.) Last, we learned that Mom and Dad can always help you figure out what happened, right?" (Val would nod, "yes.")

"Wow, Val! Thanks for doing this hard work with us today. We are growing to trust one another a little more each time we work through a problem. You are a brave girl to do this with us!"

"Can we each give you a hug, honey, and then you can go play?" (Mom and Dad in turn give Val a little hug before she hops down to go and play.)

The following breaks the talk down into its parts so you can see a "formula" you can follow when you use the empathic healing talk with your own child.

The Structure of the Empathic Healing Talk

1) Tell your child what you are going to talk about and why:

That evening when Dad got home, Mom would sit Val on her lap, with Dad alongside, and Mom would say, "Val, have I told you yet today how much I love you?" (Val might shake her head, "no.")

Mom would then continue, "Well, I do love you with all my heart. I want to tell you that right now, because we need to talk a bit about a mistake you made today. (Val might be feeling some anxiety and would shift on mom's lap.) We're going to talk about how you picked Sally's tulips today and try to figure some things out about that. Okay?" (Val might shrug.)

2) Give your child feedback about what he might be feeling/thinking right now:

"My guess is that you might be thinking you're a bad girl because we are talking about this."

3) Reassure your child that no matter what, you are there for him:

"But I want you to know I do not think you're a bad girl at all, even when you do something wrong on purpose. Do you know that? (Val might look down and shake her head, "no," a little bit.) No matter what you do, Val, I love you with all my heart and nothing can change that."

"You know what? Daddy loves you too, no matter what. I'd like you to tell him now about the tulips so you can see this for yourself." (Val might steal a quick glance at Dad, then look down again.)

"I picked some of Sally's tulips," Val might whisper. Mom might then hug her lightly and say, in a low-key tone, "Thank you, Val, for telling Daddy about the tulips. I know it was hard for you to tell Daddy that you did something wrong on purpose." (Val would nod, "yes.") Mom would turn to Dad and ask, "Do you still love Val, even though she made a mistake?" (Val would look at Dad.)

Dad might say, "Val, I want you to know that I still love you even though you picked Sally's tulips. Okay?" (Val might look unsure, then nod, "yes," slightly, and turn her head down again.)

4) Explore some guesses about the reason/need underlying your child's behavior:

Then Mom would say, "How 'bout if we try and figure what was up for you today when you picked those tulips? (Val might not react.) Would it be okay if I made some guesses and you let me know if one might be the right one?" (Val might shrug a bit again.) "Okay. . . Hmm . . . I wonder if you wanted to be mean to Sally today. (Val would shake her head, "no.") So that's not it. Hmm . . . I wonder if you wanted the tulips because they were so pretty, but you didn't want to ask Sally because she might have said no. (Val might hesitate, then barely nod, "yes.") Oh! Looks like I guessed right! . . . Wow. We're pretty good at this, aren't we?"

5) Summarize what you've discovered with your child:

Mom might then say, "Let's see what we just figured out about you today. (Mom would pull up Val's first finger, as in 'This little piggy went to market.') First, we found out how much Mom and Dad love you all the time no matter what you do. (Mom lifts Val's second finger.) Then we found out sometimes you like to do things you know are wrong because you really, really want something, and even when that happens, Dad and Mom love you with all their heart anyway, right? (Mom lifts Val's third finger.) We learned that when you pick somebody's tulips without permission, they get mad, and we need to go buy new tulips and say you are sorry."

6) Make a commitment that you will continue to help your child learn about himself:

(Mom lifts Val's fourth finger.) Last, we learned that Mom and Dad can always help you figure out what happened, right?" (Val would nod, "yes.")

7) Express appreciation for your child's efforts, which have increased the trust between you:

"Wow, Val! Thanks for doing this hard work with us today. We are growing to trust one another a little more each time we work through a problem. You are a brave girl to do this with us! Can we each give you a hug, honey, and then you can go play?" (Mom and Dad in turn give Val a little hug before she hops down to go and play.)

You can actually write out your own script and refer to it as you practice doing empathic healing talks with your child. As long as you are using eye contact with your child as you speak to him, you can refer to your script as often as necessary to keep you on track. The following is a blank form, which you can copy as many times as you wish to write out what you'd like to say in your talk with your child. Parents find that writing out what they'd like to say helps them to sort out their thoughts and allows them to remain calm and objective. The more you practice, the closer you and your child will become!

Create Your Own Empathic Healing Talk

1) Tell your child what you are going to talk about and why:

_____

2) Give your child feedback about what he might be feeling/thinking right now:

_____

3) Reassure your child that no matter what, you are there for him:

_____

4) Explore some guesses about the reason/need underlying your child's behavior:

_____

5) Summarize what you've discovered with your child:

_____

6) Make a commitment that you will continue to help your child learn about himself:

_____

7) Express appreciation for your child's efforts, which have increased the trust between you:

My Perceptions of Myself as a Parent

Here is an opportunity for you to look more closely at the "ingredients" you bring to your parenting from your past experiences. This is not a test, but rather a way for you to get clear on areas of strength and those that may need improvement. The more honest you are, the better picture you will have of your ability in the present to handle parenting challenging children. Likewise, honesty will give you a more accurate accounting of the aspects of your parenting you may decide to work on to better meet the demands of the job.

Parenting Skills Self-Assessment

(Focus on *your* abilities, not whether your child is receptive to the interaction.)

None of the time	Some of the time	Half of the time	Most of the time	All of the time
1	2	3	4	5

I'm able to set and keep realistic expectations	1 2 3 4 5
I'm able to make and keep a commitment	1 2 3 4 5
I had effective, appropriate parenting in childhood	1 2 3 4 5
I had shaming-free parenting in my childhood	1 2 3 4 5
I'm able to maintain appropriate boundaries	1 2 3 4 5
I'm able to maintain objectivity	1 2 3 4 5
I'm able to nurture	1 2 3 4 5
I'm able to look at myself objectively	1 2 3 4 5
I'm able to create and maintain routine and structure	1 2 3 4 5

I'm able to maintain a parent-in-charge hierarchy	1 2 3 4 5
I'm able to convey modest self-assurance	1 2 3 4 5
I'm able to maintain self-control under stress	1 2 3 4 5
I'm able to maintain self-control most of the time	1 2 3 4 5
*I'm able to maintain a sense of humor	1 2 3 4 5
*I'm comfortable with giving physical affection	1 2 3 4 5
*I'm comfortable receiving physical affection	1 2 3 4 5
*I'm ready to comfort my child in his distress	1 2 3 4 5
*I'm able to be playful with my child	1 2 3 4 5
*I'm ready to listen to my child's thoughts/feelings	1 2 3 4 5
*I'm able to be calm and relaxed much of the time	1 2 3 4 5
*I'm patient with my child's mistakes	1 2 3 4 5
*I'm patient with my child's misbehaviors	1 2 3 4 5
*I'm patient with my child's anger and defiance	1 2 3 4 5
*I'm patient with my child's most difficult behaviors	1 2 3 4 5
*I'm comfortable expressing love for my child	1 2 3 4 5
*I'm able to show empathy for my child's distress	1 2 3 4 5
*I'm able to show empathy for my child's anger	1 2 3 4 5
*I'm able to set limits with empathy—not anger	1 2 3 4 5
*I'm able to give/follow through with consequences	1 2 3 4 5
*I'm able/willing to give my child much supervision	1 2 3 4 5
*I'm able/willing to give my child a lot of time	1 2 3 4 5
*I'm able to express anger quickly and to the point	1 2 3 4 5
*I'm able to quickly get over a conflict with my child	1 2 3 4 5
*I'm able to let my child experience consequences	1 2 3 4 5
*I'm able to accept the thoughts/feelings of my child	1 2 3 4 5
*I'm able to accept the behavior of my child	1 2 3 4 5
*I'm able to receive parenting support from others	1 2 3 4 5
*I'm able to acknowledge parenting failings/mistakes	1 2 3 4 5

*I'm able to ask for help from people I trust	1 2 3 4 5
*I'm able to let my child's problems be his own	1 2 3 4 5
*I'm able to cope with parenting criticism	1 2 3 4 5
*I'm able not to feel shame/rage over parenting failures	1 2 3 4 5
*I'm able to remain focused on the long-term goals	1 2 3 4 5

*Adapted from "Parenting Profile for Developing Attachment" by Daniel A. Hughes, PhD

Works Cited

Bowlby, J. (1980). *Attachment*. New York: Basic Books.

Bremner, J. (2005). *Does stress damage the brain?* New York: W.W. Norton.

Cooper, G., Hoffman, K., & Powell, B. "Understanding Attachment: Current Research and Treatment" (150-hour intensive professional training held in Missoula, MT by Marycliff Institute, Spokane, WA, 2002–2003).

Goldman, M. (1997). *Kleptomania: The compulsion to steal—what can be done?* Far Hills, NJ: New Horizon Press.

Hughes, D. (2007). *Attachment-focused family therapy*. New York: W.W. Norton.

Janus, L. (1997). *Enduring effects of pre-natal experience: Echoes from the womb*. Northvale, NJ: Jason Aronson.

Katherine, A. (1996). *Anatomy of a food addiction: The brain chemistry of overeating*. Carlsbad, CA: Gurze Books.

Kramer, P. (1997). *Listening to Prozac*. New York: Penguin Books.

Manfield, P. (1992). *Split object split self*. Northvale, NJ: Jason Aronson.

Marvin, R., Cooper, G., Hoffman, K., & Powell, B. (2002). The circle of security project: Attachment-based intervention with caregiver-preschool child dyads. *Attachment & Human Development*, 4, 107–124. (Available online).

Mellody, P. (1989). *Facing codependence: What it is, where it comes from, how it sabotages our lives*. New York: HarperCollins.

Erickson, M., & Egeland, B. (2002). Child neglect. In Myers, J., et al., (Eds.), *The APSAC handbook on child maltreatment* (pp. 3–20). Thousand Oaks, CA: Sage Publications.

Ogden, P., Minton, K., & Pain, C. (2006). *Trauma and the body: A sensorimotor approach to psychotherapy*. New York: W.W. Norton.

Perry, B., & Szalavitz, M. (2006). *The boy who was raised as a dog and other stories from a child psychiatrist's notebook*. New York: Basic Books.

Schore, A. (1994). *Affect regulation and the origin of the self: The neurobiology of emotional development*. Hillsdale, NJ: Erlbaum.

Siegel, D., & Hartzell, M. (2003). *Parenting from the inside out*. New York: Penguin Putnam.

Silverstein, D. & Kaplan, S. (1982). Seven core issues in adoption. Retrieved on February 12, 2008 from http://library.adoption.com/parenting-and-families/lifelong-issues-in-adoption/article/256/1.html

Suggested Reading

Archer, C. (2006). *First steps in parenting the child who hurts: Tiddlers and toddlers* (2nd edition). Philadelphia, PA: Jessica Kingsley Publishers.

_____. (2006). *Next steps in parenting the child who hurts: Tykes and teens*. Philadelphia, PA: Jessica Kingsley Publishers.

Archer, C., & Gordon, C. (2006). *New families, old scripts: A guide to the language of trauma and attachment in adoptive families*. Philadelphia, PA: Jessica Kingsley Publishers.

Becker-Weidman, A., & Shell, D. (Eds.) (2005). *Creating capacity for attachment*. Oklahoma City, OK: Barnes 'N' Wood.

Bowlby, J. (1980). *Attachment*. New York: Basic Books.

Bremner, J. (2005). *Does stress damage the brain?* New York: W.W. Norton.

Champnella, C. (2004). *The waiting child: How the faith and love of one orphan saved the life of another*. New York: St. Martin's Press.

Cline, F. (2001). *Uncontrollable kids: From heartbreak to hope*. New York: W.W. Norton.

Cline, F., & Fay, J. (2006). *Parenting with love and logic: Teaching children responsibility*. Colorado Springs, CO: Piñon Press.

Dorris, M. (1989). *The broken cord*. New York: Harper Perennial.

Eldridge, S. (1999). *Twenty things adopted kids wish their adoptive parents knew*. New York: Random House.

Eshleman, L. (2003). *Becoming a family: Promoting healthy attachments with your adopted child*. Lanham, MD: Taylor Trade Publishing.

Faber, A, & Mazlish, E. (2002). *How to talk so kids listen & listen so kids will talk*. New York: HarperCollins.

Fahlberg, V. (1991). *A child's journey through placement*. Indianapolis, IN: Perspectives Press.

Federici, R. (2003). *Help for the hopeless child: A guide for families*. Alexandria, VA: Dr. Ronald S. Federici and Associates.

Foli, K., Thompson, J. (2004). *Post adoption blues: Overcoming the unforeseen challenges of adoption.* Emmaus, PA: Rodale Press.

Goldman, M. (1997). *Kleptomania: The compulsion to steal—what can be done?* Far Hills, NJ: New Horizon Press.

Goleman, D. (1995). *Emotional intelligence: Why it matters more than IQ.* New York: Bantam.

Gray, D. (2002). *Attaching in adoption: Practical tools for today's parent.* Indianapolis, IN: Perspectives Press.

_____. (2002). *Nurturing adoptions: Creating resilience after neglect and trauma.* Indianapolis, IN: Perspectives Press.

Greene, R. (2005). *The explosive child.* New York: HarperCollins.

Greenspan, S., & Salmon, J. (1995). *The challenging child: Understanding, raising, and enjoying the five "difficult" types of children.* Cambridge, MA: Da Capo Press.

Hayden, T. (1992). *Ghost girl.* New York: HarperCollins.

_____. (2002). *One child.* New York: HarperCollins.

Hughes, D. (2006). *Building the bonds of attachment: Awakening love in deeply troubled children* (2nd edition). Northvale, NJ: Jason Aronson.

_____. (2007). *Attachment-focused family therapy.* New York: W.W. Norton.

Janus, L. (1997). *Enduring effects of pre-natal experience: Echoes from the womb.* Northvale, NJ: Jason Aronson.

Jernberg, A., & Booth, P. (1999). *Theraplay: Helping parents and children build better relationships through attachment-based play* (2nd edition). San Francisco: Jossey-Bass.

Karen, R. (1994). *Becoming attached: Unfolding the mysteries of the infant mother bond and its impact on later life.* New York: Warner Books.

Karr-Morse, R., & Wiley, M. (1997). *Ghosts from the nursery: Tracing the roots of violence.* New York: The Atlantic Monthly Press.

Katherine, A. (1996). *Anatomy of a food addiction: The brain chemistry of overeating.* Carlsbad, CA: Gurze Books.

Keck, G., & Kupecky, R. (1995). *Adopting the hurt child: Hope for families with special needs.* Colorado Springs, CO: Piñon Press.

_____. (1995). *Parenting the hurt child: Helping adoptive families heal and grow.* Colorado Springs, CO: Piñon Press.

Klaus, M., & Kennell, J. (1996). *Maternal infant bonding.* St. Louis, MO: C.V. Mosby.

Klaus, M., Klaus, P., & Kennell, J. (1995). *Bonding: Building the foundations of secure attachment and independence.* Reading, MA: Addison-Wesley.

Kleinfeld, J., & Wescott, S. (1993). *Fantastic Antoine succeeds: Experiences in educating children with fetal alcohol syndrome.* Fairbanks, AK: University of Alaska Press.

Kohn, A. (2005). *Unconditional parenting: Moving from rewards and punishments to love and reason.* New York: Atria Books.

Kramer, P. (1997). *Listening to Prozac.* New York: Penguin Books.

Levy, T., & Orlans, M. (1998). *Attachment, trauma and healing: Understanding and treating attachment disorder in children and families.* Washington, DC: CWLA Press.

Lynn, G. (2000). *Survival strategies for parenting children with bipolar disorder.* Philadelphia, PA: Jessica Kingsley Publishers.

Marvin, R., Cooper, G., Hoffman, K., & Powell, B. (2002). The circle of security project: Attachment-based intervention with caregiver-preschool child dyads. *Attachment & Human Development, 4,* 107–124. (Available online).

Melina, L. (1998). *Raising adopted children.* New York: HarperCollins.

Mellody, P. (1989). *Facing codependence: What it is, where it comes from, how it sabotages our lives.* New York: HarperCollins.

Miller, A. (1990). *For your own good.* New York: The Noonday Press.

Oaklander, V. (1988). *Windows to our children.* Highland, NY: The Gestalt Journal Press.

Pavao, J. (2005). *The family of adoption.* Boston, MA: Beacon Press Books.

Peck, M. (1983). *People of the lie.* New York: Simon & Shuster.

Pelzer, D. (1995). *A child called "It".* Deerfield Beach, FL: Health Communications.

Perry, B., & Szalavitz, M. (2006). *The boy who was raised as a dog and other stories from a child psychiatrist's notebook.* New York: Basic Books.

Siegel, D. (1999). *The developing mind: Toward a neurobiology of interpersonal experience.* New York: The Guilford Press.

Siegel, D., & Hartzell, M. (2003). *Parenting from the inside out.* New York: Tarcher/Putnam.

Stern, D. (1985). *The interpersonal world of the infant*. New York: Basic Books.

Van Gulden, H., & Bartels Rabb, L. (1993). *Real parents, real children: Parenting the adopted child*. New York: Crossroads Publishing.

Verrier, N. (1995). *The primal wound: Understanding the adopted child*. Baltimore, MD: Gateway Press.

Verny, T., & Weintraub, P. (2002). *Pre-parenting: Nurturing your child from conception*. New York: Simon & Schuster.

Weininger, O. (1992). *T.I.P.S.: Time-in parenting strategies*. Freud, S. Romanian Translation & Publication Fund, Inc.

Welch, M. (1988). *Holding time*. New York: Simon & Schuster.

Index

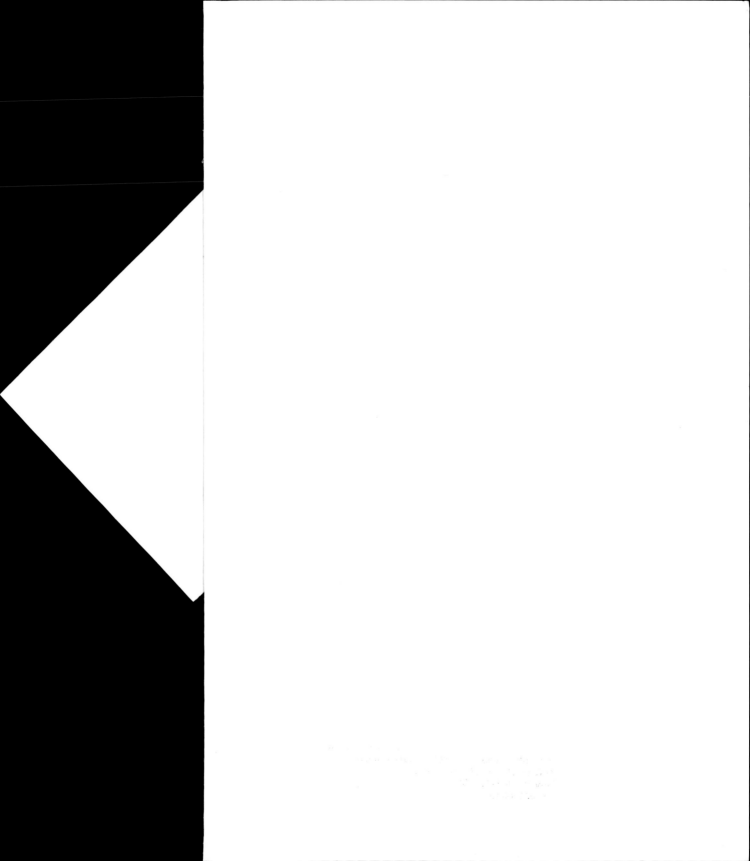

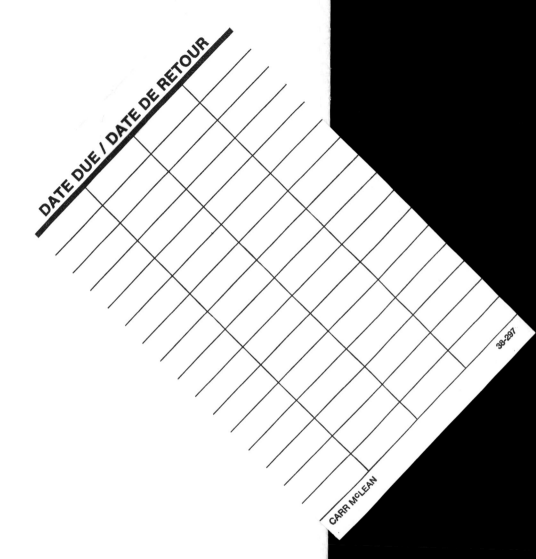

DATE DUE / DATE DE RETOUR

CARR McLEAN

38-297

Marion Powell Women's Health Information Centre
Women's College Ambulatory Care Centre
76 Grenville Street, Room 916
Toronto ON M5S 1B2
416-323-6045

Sept. 2/09